Lower-Intermediate Korean Grammar

Lower-Intermediate Korean Grammar
HowtoStudyKorean Unit 2

Seulgi Lee

Copyright © 2023 HowtoStudyKorean
All rights reserved.
ISBN: 9798851918971
Independently published

Table of Contents

Lesson 26: Using verbs to describe nouns: ~는 것 1
Lesson 27: Using ~던 and ~었/았던 to describe past tense 17
Lesson 28: Anomalies with ~는 것: Irregulars, 싶은 것, 있는 것 32
Lesson 29: Using ~기 and ~ㅁ/음 to make nouns 45
Lesson 30: 지 in sentences: 할지 모른다/한 지 1년 됐다 55
Lesson 31: Adding ~는 것 to 이다 73
Lesson 32: For the purpose of: ~려고/~러, To try to: ~아/어 보다 and 적 80
Lesson 33: The special noun of: 중 91
Lessons 26 – 33 Mini-Test 100

Lesson 34: Explanations of difficult words 104
Lesson 35: To be like, to seem like: ~ㄹ/을 것 같다 122
Lesson 36: To look like, to look (adj.): 보이다, ~아/어 보이다 132
Lesson 37: Because, therefore, so: ~아/어서 138
Lesson 38: Because, therefore, so: ~기 때문에 148
Lesson 39: Honorific ending ~(으)시, Honorific words: 드리다, 계시다, etc. 157
Lesson 40: The imperative mood: ~아/어, ~아/어라, ~(으)세요, ~(으)십시오 .. 165
Lesson 41: To do for somebody: ~아/어 주다 177
Lessons 34 – 41 Mini-Test 184

Lesson 42: When I do, when I did, whenever: ~ㄹ 때, ~했을 때 188
Lesson 43: If and when: ~ㄴ/는다면, ~(으)면 195
Lesson 44: Let's, Shall we: ~자, ~ㄹ래(요) 207
Lesson 45: I can, I can't: ~ㄹ 수 있다, ~ㄹ 수 없다 214
Lesson 46: I have to, I need to: ~아/어야 되다, ~ㄹ 필요가 있다 221
Lesson 47: Even though: ~지만 229
Lesson 48: Regardless of: ~아/어도 234
Lesson 49: May I, One doesn't need to: ~아/어도 되다, 안 ~아/어도 되다 240
Lesson 50: To have plans to, to be scheduled, to be ready to 246
Lessons 42 – 50 Mini-Test 254

Unit 2 Test 258

ABOUT THE AUTHOR 266

Lesson 26: Using verbs to describe nouns: ~는 것

Vocabulary

Nouns:
아줌마 = middle aged/older woman
물건 = thing, item, goods
복도 = hall, hallway
목적 = purpose, aim, goal
목적지 = destination
국가 = nation, country
동네 = neighborhood
학비 = tuition
무기 = weapon
정답 = right/correct answer
청소년 = youth
지역 = a certain area or region
경기 = match or game
점수 = grade, score
선수 = player (in sports)
목숨 = life
모기 = mosquito
허리 = waist
달 = moon
인사 = greeting
소금 = salt
담배 = tobacco, cigarettes
환자 = patients
옷걸이 = hanger
국제 = international
일반 = usual, normal, typical
사이 = space, gap
밖 = the outside of something

Verbs:
깎다 = to peel, cut, trim, shave
알아보다 = to recognize, to "try" to know
극복하다 = to overcome
맞추다 = to adjust, fix, set
합격하다 = to pass, to get accepted
결정하다 = to decide
이혼하다 = to get a divorce
물어보다 = to ask
피우다 = to smoke, to light a fire

불다 = to blow
계속하다 = to continue
다치다 = to injure, to hurt
답하다 = to answer, to respond

Adjectives:
틀리다 = to be incorrect
깨끗하다 = to be clean
남다 = to be remaining, to be left over
맑다 = to be clear, clean, pure

Adverbs and Other words:
무료 = free
영업 시간 = business hours

Introduction

Okay, it is time to kick it up a notch.

Most of what you learned in Unit 1 was taught simply to be a foundation to what you will learn here in Unit 2 (and later in Units 3, 4, 5 etc…). Of course, the content you learned in Unit 1 was very important (foundations are important) but here in Unit 2 it will be slightly different.

When learning Korean, you eventually reach a point where the only thing you are learning is other ways to end sentences. There are hundreds upon hundreds of different things that you can add to the end of sentences (to end them or to connect them to other sentences) to give a sentence a different meaning. I'm not going to lie: *most* of what you will learn from here on out (aside from vocabulary) will be these sentence enders/connectors.
Not today, though. Today you will learn *the* most important aspect (in my mind) of Korean grammar. It took me months to fully grasp this concept – but not because it is terribly difficult, but rather because I did not have good enough explanations when learning it. That is why I am here. I am going to break down this concept for you like crazy – spanning four lessons.

I am talking, of course, of ~는 것.

Understanding this concept will literally make your ability to create sentences increase dramatically. Let's get started.

This lesson is <u>long</u>. Very long. Please read the *entire* lesson to fully understand everything. If something is confusing, it will more than likely be resolved later in the lesson.

~는 것: Modifying Nouns with Verbs

Adjectives (in Korean and in English) get placed before nouns to describe them. You learned this a long time ago in Lesson 4. You learned that when you want to use an adjective to describe a noun, you must add ~ㄴ/은 to the stem of the adjective. For example:

예쁘다 = 예쁜
똑똑하다 = 똑똑한
젊다 = 젊은

To describe nouns in the following way:

Pretty girl: 예쁜 여자
Smart student: 똑똑한 학생
Young teacher: 젊은 선생님

Simple enough. But, what you don't know is that verbs can also describe nouns in this same way. It is the exact same premise with adjectives, but it is very difficult for English speakers to understand. This same thing (verbs describing nouns) is also done in English, but is done differently than in Korean. As you know, In English and Korean, when an adjective describes a noun, the adjective comes before the noun:

Pretty girl
Funny girl
Happy girl

However, In English, when a verb describes a noun, the verb comes after the noun:
The girl **who walks**
The student **who studies**
The teacher **who eats**

The word "who" was added in all three examples, but it doesn't necessarily need to be "who" in English. For example:
The girl **that walks**
The student **that studies**
The teacher **that eats**
In those three examples, "that" was added, and each example essentially has the same meaning as when "who" was written instead. You don't need to worry about if it should be "who/that" or whatever because you are not learning English – you are learning Korean. The point I am trying to get at here is that verbs can also describe nouns. In English, verbs are placed after the nouns to describe them.

The next sentence is the most important sentence of the entire lesson:
In Korean, verbs are placed before nouns to describe them – very similar to how it is done with adjectives.

How is this done? Like this:?

걷다 여자
공부하다 학생
먹다 선생님

Are those correct? Haha. No. Not by a long shot.

When you adjust adjectives to describe nouns, you know that you should add ~ㄴ/은 to the stem of the word.
When you adjust verbs to describe nouns, you must add ~는 to the stem of a verb:

걷다 = 걷는
공부하다 = 공부하는
먹다 = 먹는

These are all verbs that can now be placed before a noun to describe it:

걷는 여자 = the girl who walks
공부하는 학생 = the student who studies
먹는 선생님 = the teacher who eats

Now, I know what you are thinking. You are thinking "Okay, that is great, but when would I ever say 'the girl who walks' in a sentence?"
That is a good question. Really, you would never (or very rarely) say something like that in a sentence – but understanding that sentence is the foundation for understanding everything else about ~는 것.

Remember, in regular sentences (in English and Korean), it is very rare to just use the present tense conjugation. For example, are these natural?:
여자는 걷는다 = The girl walks
학생은 공부한다 = The student studies
선생님은 먹는다 = The teacher eats

Are those natural? Yes, they are natural, but who would ever just say "the girl walks."

Usually in everyday sentences, you would add more information or conjugate the sentence in other tense:

여자는 학교에 걸었어요 = The girl walked to school
여자는 학교에 걸을 거예요 = The girl will walk to school
여자는 빨리 걷는다 = The girl walks fast
etc…

You can use the same information to describe the noun (the girl):
The girl who walked to school
The girl who will walk to school
The girl who walks fast

Let's stick to the one in the present tense for now:
The girl walks: 여자는 걷는다
The girl who walks: 걷는 여자
The girl walks fast: 여자는 빨리 걷는다
The girl who walks fast: 빨리 걷는 여자

Okay, so what's the point? When would I ever want to say "The girl who walks fast"?

The thing is, now that you have made the noun "the girl who walks fast" (빨리 걷는 여자) you can now place that noun in sentences that:

- end in an adjective
- end in a verb
- end in 이다

You have been doing the exact same things with adjectives since Lesson 4.

예쁜 여자 = Pretty girl
- 예쁜 여자는 어려요 = The pretty girl is young
- 저는 예쁜 여자를 만났어요 = I met a pretty girl
- 저는 예쁜 여자예요 = I am a pretty girl

The three sentences above include a noun that is being described by an adjective.

빨리 걷는 여자 = The girl who walks fast
- 빨리 걷는 여자는 어려요 = The girl who walks fast is young
- 저는 빨리 걷는 여자를 만났어요 = I met a girl who walks fast
- 저는 빨리 걷는 여자예요 = I am a girl who walks fast

The three sentences above include a noun that is being described by a verb.

Those sentences may not be that common in either English or Korean, but that is the basis of this entire lesson. It is important to realize that entire clauses (including clauses that include complex grammatical principles within them) can be put before this ~는 것 form. These clauses can also include subjects within them. Typically, the subject within a clause that is used to describe an upcoming noun has the simple subject marker "~이/가" attached to it. Just like when a noun is being described by an adjective, once you have a noun that is being described by a verb (or by an entire clause), you can put it wherever you want in the sentence. Below are many more examples:

제가 만나고 있는 사람은 예뻐요 = The person I am meeting is pretty
제가 보고 있는 영화는 재미있어요 = The movie I am watching is funny
제가 먹고 있는 음식은 맛있어요 = The food I am eating is delicious
저는 제가 자주 가는 곳에 가고 있어요 = I am going to the place I often go to
친구는 제가 자주 가는 곳에 가고 있어요 = My friend is going to the place I often go

Actually, I feel like this is getting a little bit too complicated. I want to break this down one more time.

This sentence should be simple to you:

친구는 학교에 가고 있어요 = My friend is going to school

Simple enough. Subject – place – verb.

If you want to describe that school, you could do so with adjectives:
큰 학교 = big school
작은 학교 = small school
나쁜 학교 = bad school

… or verbs:
제가 자주 가는 학교 = The school I go to often

Then, it is simply a matter of putting those nouns into sentences:
친구는 큰 학교에 가고 있어요 = My friend is going to the big school
친구는 작은 학교에 가고 있어요 = My friend is going to the small school
친구는 나쁜 학교에 가고 있어요 = My friend is going to the bad school
친구는 제가 자주 가는 학교에 가고 있어요 = My friend is going to the school that I go to often

Incredibly complicated at first, incredibly simple once you get the hang of it. The only problem is that it is difficult for English speakers to get used to because we describe a noun with a verb after the noun.

Many more examples:
과학을 좋아하는 여자 = the/a girl that likes science
저는 과학을 좋아하는 여자들을 좋아해요 = I like girls that like science

제가 보고 있는 시험 = The exam I am writing
제가 보고 있는 시험은 어려워요 = The exam I am writing is difficult

제가 사귀고 있는 여자 = The girl who I am going out with
제가 사귀고 있는 여자는 미국에 갔어요 = The girl who I am going out with went to the US

엄마가 요리하는 음식 = The food that my mother cooks
엄마가 요리하는 음식은 항상 맛있어요 = The food that my mother cooks is always delicious

공부하지 않는 학생들 = students who do not study
공부하지 않는 학생들은 똑똑하지 않아요 = Students who do not study are not smart

제가 공원에 가는 날 = the day(s) I go to the park
저는 공원에 가는 날에 항상 행복해요 = I am always happy on the days I go to the park

이 동네에서 축구를 잘 하는 청소년들 = kids who are good at playing soccer in this neighborhood
이 동네에서 축구를 잘 하는 청소년들이 많아요 = There are a lot of kids who are good at playing soccer in this neighborhood

Actually, Korean people have the same problem with this concept when translating to English. If you meet a Korean person who can't speak English well, they will always say sentences like this in their 'Korean style.'

Instead of saying: "girls that like science," they say:
"like science girls'
Instead of saying "the exam I am writing," they say:
"I write exam"

Instead of saying "the girl I am going out with," they say:
"I go out with girl"

Instead of saying "the food my mother cooks," they say:
"my mother cooks food"

Anyways, enough of what Korean people say.

It is hard to translate the definition of this concept directly in English, but it sometimes translates to 'who,' 'when,' or 'that.' These words however don't need to be in the sentence in English, as you will see in the following examples.

Each of the following pairs of sentences have the same meaning in English:

My friend is going to the school I go to often
My friend is going to the school that I go to often

The exam I am writing is difficult
The exam that I am writing is difficult

The girl I am going out with went to the US
The girl who I am going out with went to the US
The girl that I am going out with went to the US

The food my mother cooks is always delicious
The food that my mother cooks is always delicious

Students that do not study are not smart
Students who do not study are not smart

I am always happy on the days I go to the park
I am always happy on the days that I go to the park
I am always happy on the days when I go to the park

"That" can be used in most situations. If the noun you are using is a person, "who" can be exchanged for "that." If the noun you are using is a time, "when" can be exchanged for "that."

I'm going to say this one more time. Read it a few times to make sure you understand it completely (it is complicated). The noun that you create by describing it with a verb can be placed anywhere that other nouns can be placed!

Let's describe one more noun and see where it can be placed:
내가 가르치는 학생들 = the students that I teach

- Placed as the subject of a sentence:
내가 가르치는 학생들은 수업을 듣고 싶지 않아 = The students that I teach don't want to come to class

- Before 이다:
그 사람은 내가 가르치는 학생이다 = That person is a student that I teach (I teach that student

- Placed in any clause within a sentence:
내가 가르치는 학생들이 수업에 오기 전에 나는 교실을 청소했어 = Before the students that I teach came to class, I cleaned the classroom

.. okay, I think you get it.

So far in this lesson you have learned how to describe nouns using verbs in the present tense:
The place I go
The food I eat
The student I teach

But what about the past tense?
The place I went
The food I ate
The student I taught

Or the future tense?
The place I will go
The food I will eat
The student I will teach

Let's talk about those now.

~는 것 Past Tense (~ㄴ/은 것)

You can also describe nouns with verbs in the past tense to make nouns like:

The place I went
The food I ate
The student I taught

To do this, instead of adding ~는 to the stem of a verb, you must add ~ㄴ/은. You must add ~은 to stems ending in a consonant (먹다 = 먹은), and ㄴ should be added directly to stems ending in a vowel (가다 = 간):

제가 간 곳 = The place I went
제가 먹은 음식 = The food I ate
제가 가르친 학생 = The student I taught

The general idea is the same as the present tense; the verb is simply conjugated into the past. More examples:

엄마가 요리한 음식은 너무 맛있어요 = The food my mom cooked is delicious
저는 엄마가 요리한 음식을 다 먹었어요 = I ate all the food my mom cooked
제가 어제 만난 사람은 저를 다시 만나고 싶어요 = The person I met yesterday wants to meet me again

남은 음식을 포장하고 싶어요 = I want to pack up the food that is left over
내가 회사에 가지 않은 날에 병원에 갔어 = On the day I didn't go to work, I went to the hospital
선생님은 학생들이 물어본 질문에 답했어요 = The teacher answered the question that the student asked
옛날에 담배를 많이 피운 환자가 많아요 = There are a lot of patients who smoked a lot a long time ago
내가 작년에 가르친 학생 한 명은 벌써 의사가 되었어 = One of the students I taught last year has already become a doctor

~는 것 Future Tense (~ㄹ/을 것)

You can also describe nouns with verbs in the future tense to make nouns like:

The place I will go
The food I will eat
The student I will teach

To do this, instead of adding ~는 to the stem of a verb, you must add ~ㄹ/을. You must add 을 to stems ending in a consonant (먹다 = 먹을) and ㄹ should be added directly to stems ending in a vowel (가다 = 갈).

For example:
내가 갈 곳 = The place I will go
내가 먹을 음식 = The food I will eat
내가 가르칠 학생 = The student I will teach

Many more examples:
제가 갈 곳은 제주도예요 = The place I will go is Jeju-do
저는 할 일이 있어요 = I have something/work to do
제가 받을 점수는 중요해요 = The score I will receive is important
저는 그 사람이 저에게 줄 선물을 받고 싶지 않아요 = I don't want to accept the gift that that person will give me

In Lesson 9, you learned how to create a future tense conjugation by attaching ~ㄹ/을 것이다 to words. For example, in Lesson 9, you saw this sentence:

저는 밥을 먹을 것이에요 = I will eat rice

If you look closely, the grammar being used in this type of sentence is the same as the grammar that I am presenting in this lesson. If you look at the two examples below:

저는 밥을 먹을 것이에요 = I will eat rice
제가 받을 점수는 중요해요 = The score I will receive is important

In both of the sentences above, the ~을 attached to the verb is performing the same function – in that it is describing the upcoming noun.

Remember, "것" is a noun, and in the first sentence above, "것" is being described by the word before it (먹다). For example, look how "것" is being described in the first example::

밥을 먹을 것 = A thing that will eat rice

In theory, the full sentence (저는 밥을 먹을 것이에요) could translate to "I am a thing that will eat rice." However, it would never be translated like that because when ~ㄹ/을 것이다 is used at the end of a sentence, it is usually done to create the future tense conjugation that would translate to "one will do…" This isn't imperative to your understanding, but it is good to recognize that ~ㄹ/을 has the same function in both of these types of sentences – which is describing the noun in-front of it.

There are many instances of a Korean grammatical principle having different English translations depending on the type of sentence it is used in. There might be one thing in Korean that represents many meanings in English, and there might be one thing in English that represents many meanings in Korean. Try to step out of the "English box" and understand that two vastly different languages will have very little similarities.
…Anyways…
…. All of this brings me to the last point of this lesson:

~는 것

The name for everything you learned in this lesson is "~는 것" (or ~ㄴ 것 for past tense and ~ㄹ 것 for future tense). So far, I have shown you many examples of other nouns in place of "것":

제가 먹는 음식 = The food I eat
제가 먹은 음식 = The food I ate
제가 먹을 음식 = The food I will eat
제가 가르치는 학생 = the student I teach
제가 가르친 학생 = the student I taught
제가 가르칠 학생 = the student I will teach
제가 가는 날에 = the day I go
제가 간 날에 = the day I went
제가 갈 날에 = the day I will go

Question:
So why is the grammar concept called "~는 것"?
Answer: (This answer is ridiculously important)
If you ever want to change a sentence (or any part of a sentence) into a noun, you must do so by adding ~는 것 to the clause. … which leads to the next question:

Question:
Why on earth would I want to change a sentence into a noun?

Answer:
Look at the following example:

You know this already:

저는 사과를 원해요 = I want apples

Very simple sentence. Subject – object – verb. But what if you wanted to say the following:

"I want my friend to bring apples."

The structure is actually identical in the two sentences:

I want apples
I want my friend to bring apples

In both cases, I will put the thing that you want in brackets:

I want (apples)
I want (my friend to bring apples)

In Korean:

저는 (apples)를 원해요
저는 (my friend to bring apples)를 원해요

The first one is easy, you already know:

저는 사과를 원해요

But the second one? How would I say this in Korean?:
저는 (my friend to bring apples)를 원하다

How can you say "my friend brings apples" in Korean?
친구는 사과를 가져와요 = My friend brings apples

But! You need to change that sentence to a noun. THIS is the situation when you will need to change clauses/sentences to nouns. Let's change that sentence into a noun:
친구가 사과를 가져오는 것

This is very hard to translate into English. 것 means "thing." The rest of it is an adjective describing that "thing." If I had to translate it, I would say "the thing of my friend bringing apples."... but, again, it cannot really be translated.

So, if we look at our sentences again:
I want (apples)
I want (my friend to bring apples)

Apples = 사과
My friend brings apples (noun form) = 친구가 사과를 가져오는 것

저는 (apples)를 원해요
저는 (my friend to bring apples)를 원해요

저는 (사과)를 원해요
저는 (친구가 사과를 가져오는 것)을 원해요

저는 사과를 원해요 = I want apples
저는 친구가 사과를 가져오는 것을 원해요 = I want my friend to bring apples

Wow, complicated.
Let's look at another example.

I like movies.
저는 영화를 좋아해요

Simple sentence. Subject – object – verb
But what if you wanted to say
"I like making movies," or
"I like watching movies"

Again, I will put the things that you like in brackets:

I like (movies)
I like (making movies)
I like (watching movies)

Movies: 영화
I make movies: 영화를 만들어요
I watch movies: 영화를 봐요

Into noun form?:
영화
영화를 만드는 것
영화를 보는 것

저는 (movies)를 좋아해요
저는 (making movies)를 좋아해요
저는 (watching movies)를 좋아해요

저는 (영화)를 좋아해요
저는 (영화를 만드는 것)을 좋아해요
저는 (영화를 보는 것)을 좋아해요

저는 영화를 좋아해요 = I like movies
저는 영화를 만드는 것을 좋아해요 = I like making movies
저는 영화를 보는 것을 좋아해요 = I like watching movies

I didn't realize this when I first learned this grammar concept. In almost every sentence you will ever say, you need to put this concept into use – whether you realize it or not.
Think about it, how often do you simply say "I want to eat food"? You usually make it more complex by saying:

나는 그 사람이 먹고 있는 것을 먹고 싶어 = I want to eat what that person is eating
나는 우리가 지난 번에 같이 먹은 것을 먹고 싶어 = I want to eat what we ate last time (together)
나는 엄마가 요리하는 것을 먹고 싶어 = I want to eat my mom's cooking

Etc…

Or, if you wanted to talk about what your dream is. Before this lesson, you could say this:
나의 꿈은 선생님이다 …

… but that translates to "My dream is teacher"…. Is that natural? My dream is teacher? Instead, it would sound more natural if you said:

나의 꿈은 선생님이 되는 것이다 = My dream is becoming a teacher
Below are many more examples of a verb (with a clause before it) describing a noun being used in sentences. The following sentences specifically use the vocabulary that is introduced at the beginning of this lesson. In addition, these sentences are slightly more complex than the simple sentences I have used to describe the ~는 것 concept up until this point.

소금을 많이 먹는 것은 건강에 안 좋아요 = It is not healthy to eat a lot of salt
담배를 피우는 것은 건강에 나빠요 = It is unhealthy to smoke cigarettes
저의 목적은 그 시험을 합격하는 것이에요 = My goal is to pass that exam
이 문제를 극복하는 것이 힘들 거예요 = It will be difficult to overcome this problem
모자를 쓴 학생을 알아보는 것이 어려워요 = It is difficult to recognize students wearing hats
네가 지금 말하는 것이 틀려 = (the thing that) What you are saying now is incorrect
친구가 머리를 깎은 것을 알아보지 못했어요 = I couldn't recognize that my friend cut his hair
복도에서 달리는 것은 위험해요 = It is dangerous to run in the hallway
우리 학교의 목적은 국제고등학교가 되는 것이다 = Our school's goal is becoming an international school
병원에서 넘어져서 팔을 다친 아줌마가 약을 무료로 받았어요 = The older lady who fell in the hospital and broke her arm received free medicine

----

Just one more quick note specifically about translating from English to Korean or vice-versa. Translations are often ambiguous from English to Korean, so you don't need to worry about this too much.

15

When you use ~는 것 to describe an upcoming noun, the translation is often "who," "that," or "where." For example:

걷는 여자
= The girl **who** walks
= The girl **that** walks

내가 간 곳
= The place **where** I went
= The place **that** I went

This type of translation is also appropriate when describing a "thing." For example:

내가 먹는 것은 밥이야 = The thing **that** I (am) eat(ing) is rice
내가 가장 원하는 것은 차야 = The thing **that** I want most is a car

However, when using ~는 것 to change a clause into a noun so that you can do something with that noun in a sentence, the translation of "to" or "~ing" is usually more appropriate. For example:

저는 친구가 사과를 가져오는 것을 원해요
= I want my friend **to** bring apples

나의 꿈은 선생님이 되는 것이다
= My dream is becom**ing** a teacher
= My dream is **to** become a teacher

저는 영화를 보는 것을 좋아해요
= I like watch**ing** movies
= I like **to** watch movies

In terms of Korean grammar, the purpose of ~는 것 in all of these types of sentences (i.e. whether it is being used to describe a noun or used to turn a clause into a noun) is the same. However, in English these look like entirely different sentences. Again, translations are often confusing and ambiguous. You don't necessarily need to worry about the different types of English translations. What is more important is that you understand the Korean grammar presented here.

That's it for this lesson, but in the next 3 – 4 lessons I will be going deeper and deeper into the ~는 것 grammar concept. This first lesson should give you a good first step.

Lesson 27: Using ~던 and ~었/았던 to describe past tense

Vocabulary

Nouns:
이유 = reason
방법 = way, method
예술 = art, the arts
예술가 = artist
내용 = contents
종업원 = employee, server, worker
기술 = technology, skill
공책 = notebook
달력 = calendar
주스 = juice
우체국 = post office
대사관 = embassy
휴지 = toilet paper
햄버거 = hamburger
비누 = soap
숟가락 = spoon
간호사 = nurse
약국 = pharmacy
사회 = community, society
충격 = shock, impact
법 = law
시민 = citizen
땀 = sweat
보험 = insurance
차이 = difference
손님 = guest, visitor
승객 = passenger
대통령 = president (of country)
회원 = member
오렌지 = an orange

Verbs:
담다 = to put something in/on/onto/into
서명하다 = to sign
그리다 = to draw
밝히다 = to lighten something, to reveal
발음하다 = to pronounce
포기하다 = to give up
지나다 = for something to pass by

실패하다 = to fail
근무하다 = to be employed
환승하다 = to transfer on a bus, subway
멈추다 = to stop
담기다 = to be put in/on/onto/into

Adjectives:
외롭다 = to be lonely
소중하다 = to be significant, precious

Adverbs and Other words:
따로 = separately, privately
영원히 = forever
한때 = once, at one time

Introduction

In the previous lesson, you learned how ~는 것 can:

– turn clauses/sentences into nouns to make sentences like this:
저는 친구가 사과를 가져오는 것을 원해요 = I want my friend to bring apples

– use verbs to describe nouns to make sentences like this:
저는 과학을 좋아하는 여자들을 좋아해요 = I like girls who like Science

Now, let's build on what you learned and apply the ~는 것 principle in other ways.

Describe Past Tense with ~던 and ~았/었던

Before I even begin this lesson, I want to point out that I will be describing things that most Korean people can't distinguish. When learning about subtle differences in a foreign language, it is often difficult to fully grasp because native speakers of that language can intuitively feel the difference, but not express it. I will do my best to describe this feeling, but keep in mind that most Korean people would probably have difficulty expressing what I will attempt to describe in this lesson.

For a long time now, you have been able to describe upcoming nouns with adjectives. For example:

예쁜 여자 = pretty girl
똑똑한 학생 = smart student
나쁜 선생님 = bad teacher

In the previous lesson, you learned to describe upcoming nouns with *verbs*. For example, in the present tense:

영어를 공부하는 학생 = the student **that/who** studies English
한국어를 가르치는 선생님 = the teacher **that/who** teaches Korean

… the future tense:

영어를 공부할 학생 = the student **that/who** will study English
한국어를 가르칠 선생님 = the teacher **that/who** will teach Korean

… and the past tense:

영어를 공부한 학생 = the student **that/who** studied English
한국어를 가르친 선생님 = the teacher **that/who** taught Korean

As you learned in the previous lesson (and as you can see in the two example sentences immediately above), you can attach ~ㄴ/은 to the stem of a verb to describe an upcoming noun in the past tense.

In addition to ~ㄴ/은, there are other ways that you can describe upcoming nouns in the past tense. The two additional ways to describe an upcoming noun in the past tense include the grammatical principle ~더~. Notice that there is a "~" both before and after the syllable "더." I include ~ both before and after to "더" to indicate that not only is ~더~ attached to things, but things are also attached to it.

~더~ is a fairly advanced grammatical principle and has multiple applications. I discuss ~더~ and introduce the various ways that it can be used in the later lessons of Unit 5; where I introduce ~던가 (Lesson 117), ~더라 (Lesson 118) and ~더니 (Lesson 120). For now, I will concentrate on the nuance that ~더~ adds by showing you how it can be used to describe an upcoming noun.

When you see ~더~ used as part of a grammatical principle, it signifies that the speaker is recalling/remembering some fact from the past that was experienced. ~더~ can be attached to the stem of a verb, and ~ㄴ/은 (the same ~ㄴ/은 that describes upcoming nouns in the past tense as learned in the previous lesson) can be attached to ~더~.

Simply put, one use is: Verb stem + ~더~ + ~ㄴ/은

What comes out is Verb stem + ~던 – and this can be used to describe an upcoming noun in the past tense. For example:

내가 입던 옷

Now, the difficult part of this lesson is trying to understand the difference between the following:

I'm not going to make full sentences yet because I'm still in the process of explaining the subtle difference between various ways to describe a noun in the past tense. Once we get all the grammar under our belt, I'll start making real sentences.

1) 내가 입은 옷 = The clothes I wore
2) 내가 입던 옷 = The clothes I wore

Despite their similar (/identical) translations, there is a difference between the two constructions above.

First of all, remember that the function of ~더~ is to indicate that the speaker is recalling/remembering some fact that was experienced. In the second example, the speaker is explicitly expressing that this thought is coming from memory – something that the person remembers doing or experiencing.

The first example is just a simple fact, and this additional "memory" feeling isn't present. This doesn't mean that the first example above isn't being "recalled/remembered," it just isn't being explicitly expressed.

I realize that this sounds ambiguous. I've talked about this with Korean people for years. When I try to get Korean people to explain the image they have in their brain when hearing ~더~ (and specifically ~던 compared to ~ㄴ/은) they move their hands in a way that shows that something is popping or exploding out of their head.

In theory, you could translate the usage of ~던 in a sentence differently. For example, you could say:

내가 입던 옷 = The clothes I recall wearing

However, I would never translate that sentence this way. The "recalling" feeling of ~더~ in these cases is very subtle – more of a feeling – and unless the context indicates otherwise, the focus is most likely on the clothes than on the recollection.

In addition to having this "memory from experience" feeling, the use of ~던 in the construction above indicates that an action occurred repeatedly in the past. I specifically chose the construction "내가 입던 옷" because it is an excellent example to describe this usage. The clothes that are being described are clothes that the speaker wore on multiple occasions (this makes sense, because they are clothes).

When you say "내가 입은 옷," again, you are just stating a simple fact, and there is no additional information regarding "memory" or if you wore the clothes once, or many times. All that is being stated is that - at some time in the past, you wore those clothes – and no additional information is given. ~ㄴ/은 is a very simply way to express that you wore these clothes in the past.

So, now we know that adding ~던 gives the meaning of personal experience/memory and that the action occurred repeatedly. Knowing this, look at the following examples and think about which one would be correct:

1) 내가 입던 옷
2) 내가 사던 옷

In the first example, the act of "wearing" an article of clothing can happen repeatedly over time. Therefore, this construction is possible. In the second example, the act of "buying" an article of clothing does not happen repeatedly. Once you buy one piece of clothing, you don't buy it again. Therefore, this construction would be unacceptable (or very uncommon).

The difference between the two constructions above illustrates this "repeated" meaning of ~던. There, I attached ~던 to two different verbs to illustrate this difference. Below, I have used the same verb, but this time have attached ~던 to the first one, and ~ㄴ/은 to the second one. Look at the following examples and think about which one would be correct:

1) 내가 태어난 도시
2) 내가 태어나던 도시

In the first example, ~ㄴ/은 indicates a simple past-tense fact, and there is no additional meaning attached unless implied within the sentence. Here, the speaker is describing the city as "the city that I was born in."

In the second example, the act of "being born" cannot happen repeatedly. Therefore, I can't imagine a situation where this would be appropriate.

I realize that I just keep piling on the meanings hidden behind ~던, but there is another subtlety that you should be aware of. When ~던 is used, we know that the speaker is recalling something from memory, and that the action occurred repeatedly in the past. It is also possible that this "repeated" action is still reoccurring into the present (or whatever current time is being described in the sentence). Unless otherwise specified in other parts of the sentence, this repeated action hasn't been stopped and is still re-occurring.

Let's look at our classic "clothes" example and outline this specifically:

내가 입은 옷
The speaker is describing the clothes that he wore. There is no deep/hidden/subtle meaning to it. All we know is that at some point in the past, he wore the clothes. Did he wear it often/repeatedly? Did he wear it once? Does he still wear it? Has he stopped wearing it? The answer to all of these questions is ambiguous – and rightfully so. A lot of the time in conversation you don't need to specifically describe the noun you are talking about. Simply saying "the clothes I wore" can be sufficient. In this English sentence ("the clothes I wore") is equally ambiguous to the sentence above.

내가 입던 옷

The speaker is describing the clothes that he recalls/remembers wearing (as is the function of ~더~). The clothes being described were worn repeatedly in the past, and are likely still presently being worn – not necessarily at this moment, but "these days" (or at whatever time is being described in the sentence). There is no specific information about whether he stopped wearing the clothes – and unless otherwise stated, he probably still wears the clothes from time to time.

With the constructions I have shown so far, there is no additional context given. In real situations with full sentences, you will most likely have additional information that will allow you to distinguish the sentence better. For example, I can put the construction above into a sentence:

내가 지금까지 입던 옷을 내일 버릴 거야 = Tomorrow, I am going to throw out the clothes that I have been wearing until now

The use of ~던 in the sentence can tell us the following:

- You have a recollection of wearing the clothes
- You wore the clothes repeatedly in the past
- The clothes haven't "stopped" being worn – and they are still being worn "until now." Of course, you won't be wearing them after today because you'll be throwing them out.

Here are many more examples:

내가 읽던 책은 재미없었어 = The book I was reading wasn't funny
이 빵은 내가 자주 먹던 빵이야 = This bread is bread that I ate often
제가 매일 마시던 주스를 샀어요 = I bought the juice that I drink everyday
여기가 내가 근무하던 곳이야 = This place (here) is the place that I worked

2015년에 쓰던 달력을 내일 버릴 거예요
= Tomorrow, I am going to throw out the calendar that I used to use in 2015

제가 자주 가던 약국이 오늘부터 문을 닫을 거예요
= The pharmacy that I had been going to often will close its doors from today

In the examples above, the object is being described by some action that "I" did. I mentioned earlier that one of the subtleties of ~던 is the feeling of "remembering/recalling." In the examples above, *of course* I am remembering them, because "I" am the person who performed the action. This subtle meaning of "remembering/recalling," although present, seems irrelevant. Nonetheless, you should remember that ~더~ contains this meaning.

In situations where the object is being described by some action that *another person* did, the subtleties of ~던 seem more apparent. For example, I could say these sentences:

이 빵은 슬기가 자주 먹던 빵이야 = This bread is bread that Seulgi eats often

이곳에 근무하던 우체국 직원이 삶을 영원히 포기했어요
= The worker/employee who used to work at this post-office gave up on his life forever

길을 밝히던 불이 꺼지고 나서 길이 어두워졌어요
= The street became dark after the light that used to brighten the street went out

방금 들어온 사람은 우리 가게에 자주 오던 손님이야
= The person who just came in is a customer who comes to the store often

I use the present tense "come" in the English translation above. You could argue than "came" or "used to come" would be more appropriate because we are describing the person as a customer who came in the past. However, because of the context of the sentence – they also "just came in" and are probably still there now – indicating that it could be used in the present tense. Again, it is difficult to translate these sentences in English. Pay more attention to the Korean sentence and use the English translation as a reference.

Because ~던 (through the usage of ~더~) indicates that one is "remembering/recalling" something, the bread is not only "bread that Seulgi eats often" but more specifically "bread that I specifically remember/recall/experienced Seulgi eating often."

Again, these types of translations are nonsense. I would never write a translation of these types of sentences to include "remember/recall/experienced." It's always better to just understand the subtle meanings that they can have and forget about English translations. I can't really think of a great translation for ~던. If you think about it, with all you know about ~던, how would you translate the following:

내가 입던 옷

Would you translate it to:

The clothes I wore
The clothes I used to wear
The clothes often wore

These sentences could all be possible in English to describe ~던 in this case, but in my mind don't accurately describe the subtleties that exist within ~던. To add to the confusion, there is another way to describe an upcoming noun that looks similar to ~던 and has a similar meaning. Let's talk about this next.

So far, you have seen how ~던 can be used to describe an upcoming noun and have compared it to ~ㄴ/은. For example:

내가 입은 옷 = The clothes I wore – (Simple description of the clothes in the past tense)
내가 입던 옷 = The clothes I wore – (Recalling/remembering the clothes that were worn repeatedly in the past and continued to the point in time being described)

It is also possible to add ~았/었~ between the verb stem and ~던. For example:

내가 입었던 옷 = The clothes I wore

Alright, now it's time to explain the difference between ~았/었던 and ~던 or ~ㄴ/은.

When ~았/었던 is added to a verb to describe an upcoming noun, the speaker is indicating that the action has completely finished and is not currently occurring. For example, if we go back to our tried and tested example:

내가 입었던 옷
The speaker is describing the clothes that he wore in the past. Because ~더~ is included within this, the speaker is describing the clothes that he recalls/remembers. The clothes being described were worn at some time in the past (this could be indicated elsewhere in the sentence), and are not pants that the speaker wears anymore.

The meaning and feeling of ~았/었던 is similar to the meaning and feeling of ~ㄴ/은. Most Korean people would tell you at first glance that they are the same. I will do my best to distinguish them for you.

As I mentioned before, when you say "내가 입은 옷," you are stating a simple fact, and there is no additional information regarding "memory" or if you wore the clothes once, or many times, or if you still wear those clothes these days too. All that is being stated is that - at some time in the past, you wore those clothes – and no additional information is given. ~ㄴ/은 is a very simple way to express that you wore these clothes in the past.

Saying "내가 입었던 옷" is similar, but the usage of ~더~ describes that the speaker is "remembering/recalling" this from memory/experience. Saying "내가 입었던 옷" is also specifically indicating that the action of "wearing the clothes" is finished and doesn't happen anymore. It is possible that ~ㄴ/은 can be used to express this, but its meaning is more broad and doesn't state this explicitly.

Korean people often incorrectly assume that the use of ~았/었던 indicates that *a lot* of time has passed since the last action. Many Korean people have described this to me, so it is hard to call it "incorrect" because if Korean people feel that way about their own language, than in a way, it is correct. However, the time interval from when the action stopped happening to the present time is irrelevant. For example, you could say:

오늘 아침에 입었던 바지

The use of ~았/었던 is not used to show that the pants were worn a long time ago (of course, "this morning" was not a long time ago). Rather, it is used to show that the pants were worn, and are currently not being worn anymore. If you were to say the sentence above, at some point since the morning, you would have had to change or take off the pants being described because the use of ~았/었던 indicates that you are no longer wearing them. Compare the construction above to the following:

오늘 아침에 입은 바지

Because the pants were worn (or put on) in the morning, it's likely that you are still wearing these pants. This sentence does not explicitly state if you have taken them off or if you are still wearing them.

Below are examples of ~았/었던 in use. Notice that it is difficult to translate the nuance of ~았/었던 to English. Using the past perfect "had" is a common way to express this feeling in English, but depending on the context this doesn't always need to be the case. When reading the sentences below, try not to pay attention to the English translations and try to remember the purpose of ~았/었던:

그 컴퓨터는 작년에 썼던 거예요
= That is the computer I had used last year

저는 애기가 썼던 휴지를 다 버렸어요
= I threw out all the tissue paper that the baby had used

한때 포기했던 시험을 다시 공부했어요
= I again studied for the exam that I once gave up on

우리가 지난 번에 먹었던 곳에서 먹고 싶어요
= I want to eat at the place that we ate at last time

대통령이 여기서 살았던 시민들에게 돈을 줬어요
= The president gave money to those who once lived here

우리가 지난 주에 배웠던 내용을 다시 공부할 거예요
= I will study the contents that we had learned last week again

작년에 사업에 실패했던 남자가 새로운 기술을 발견했어요
= The man who had failed at (starting his own) business last year discovered a new technology

한때 저의 손님이었던 사람이 이제는 유명한 예술가가 되었다
= The person who had been my customer at one time has now become a famous artist

고장으로 계속 멈추는 버스를 탔던 승객들이 다른 버스를 탔어요
= The passengers who had been riding the bus that kept stopping because it is/was broken got on another bus

Let's organize everything that has been presented so far:

~ㄴ/은: Attached to a verb to describe a noun where the action occurred sometime in the past. There is no additional meaning given to it. All we know is that at some point in the past, the action happened.

~던: Attached to a verb to describe a noun where the action is recalled to have occurred repeatedly in the past, and is continually repeating to the present (or to the time described in the sentence).

~았/었던: Attached to a verb to describe a noun where the action is recalled to have occurred in the past, but has finished occurring and currently does not occur.

I don't like distinguishing these grammatical principles based on their English translations. Given the number of possible situations that could come up, there is no perfect way to accurately translate any of them. However, the examples below show common translations for each of these grammatical principles in use:

내가 입은 바지 = the pants I wore
내가 입던 바지 = the pants I used to wear (I find this translation particularly insufficient)
내가 입었던 바지 = the pants I had worn

I think you might be comfortable with this now. Unfortunately, we need to discuss how ~던 and ~았/었던 can be added to adjectives.

As you know, adding ~ㄴ/은 to an adjective allows you to describe a noun. For example:

예쁜 여자 = (a) pretty girl

Although "예쁜" is indicating that the girl is currently pretty, we can infer that she also was pretty in the past. Most of the time, if a noun is described a certain way by an adjective in the present, the same could be true of that noun in the past.

Earlier in the lesson you learned about adding ~았/었던 to verbs. ~았/었던 can also be added to adjectives, and it has a similar function as when used with verbs. When used with a verb, the speaker is indicating that the action happened in the past, but has since finished and does not occur anymore.

If you attach ~았/었던 to an adjective to describe a noun, you are indicating that the noun *was* that way in the past, but is no longer that way anymore. For example, think about how unfortunate of a situation this would be:

예뻤던 여자

This would indicate that this girl *was (or "had been")* pretty. However her being "pretty" has finished and she is no longer pretty anymore. The use of ~더~ also carries this "remembering/recalling" from experience subtlety. As you know, I hate translating these types of constructions; but if I were to translate the construction above:

예뻤던 여자 = The girl who I recall being pretty, but is not pretty anymore

Up until now, I have been able to describe the subtle difference in nuance between ~ㄴ/은, ~던 and ~았/었던 when added to verbs.

I have also been able to describe the subtle difference in nuance between ~ㄴ/은 and ~았/었던 when added to adjectives.

Adding ~던 to an adjective is possible but is *very* confusing.

I had a lengthy discussion with a Korean grammar teacher recently. After writing everything you see above (i.e. this whole lesson until now) I discussed every point with her to hear her opinion about my observations. We discussed the differences between ~ㄴ/은, ~던 and ~았/었던 when added to verbs. We then talked about ~ㄴ/은 and ~았/었던 when added to adjectives.

All of this led me to this question:

"If ~던 is added to verbs to indicate that one 'remembers/recalls' an action occurring repeatedly in the past and continuing to the present, how can this meaning be transferred to adjectives?"

I figured this would not make sense, but I showed her this construction:

예쁘던 여자

She said that this would not be used. She then said that it would be incorrect to add "~던" directly to adjectives because an adjective can't "occur" repeatedly in the past. Puzzled, I looked at her and said "absolutely, ~던 can be added to adjectives." She challenged me and said "okay, come up with a situation where ~던 can be added to an adjective."

Remember, this conversation happened between a Korean person who, as her profession, teaches Korean language to Korean high school students and a dude from Canada.

The example is a little bit above your level, but I started singing the song "나에게 넌" in front of her:

소중했던 우리 푸르던 날을 기억하며
우~~후회없이 그림처럼 남아주기를
나에게 넌 내 외롭던 지난 시간을

Notice that ~던 is added directly to two adjectives in the short lyrics above. It is attached to 푸르다 in the first line and to 외롭다 in the third line. The first word, 소중하다 has ~았/었던 attached.

After she heard my amazing singing, she realized she was wrong. She then thought about it more and said that adding ~던 to an adjective has the same meaning as when adding ~았/었던, but the latter would be much more common.

I figured that explanation was nonsense. There is no way that ~았/었던 and ~던 could have identical meaning. The only reason why I'm sharing this story with you is so you can realize that even Korean people, including those you would call "experts" in their own language, have a hard time distinguishing these things.

I've spent a lot of time reflecting on ~던 being attached to adjectives and how I can present it to you. It's not that simple because when used separated from a sentence just shown with one noun, it often sounds very unnatural. For example:

예쁜 여자 = the pretty girl
예뻤던 여자 = the girl who I recall being pretty, but is not pretty anymore
예쁘던 여자 – Grammatically this is correct, but Korean people would tell you that this would never be said

However, there are cases where the adjective and noun being used could make it appropriate. For example:

시끄러운 교실 = the noisy classroom

시끄러웠던 교실 = the classroom that I recall being noisy, but is not noisy anymore

시끄럽던 교실 – This construction is possible. Although the "repeated" function of ~던 can't really be applied, the function of indicating that something occurs to the present tense can be applied. If you said "시끄럽던 교실" to a Korean person, they would assume that the classroom was loud up until the present, but it *just* stopped being loud. If we compare this to "시끄러웠던 교실," Korean people would say that the classroom was loud further in the past, and there is a gap between when it stopped being loud until the present.

This could explain why the construction "예쁘던 여자" would be unnatural. It's not really possible for you to recognize that a girl was pretty in the past, and notice that this continues all the way until present and for her to all of a sudden not be pretty anymore. However, it could be possible (however unfortunate) for a girl to have been pretty in the past, and for some time to pass, and then (presumably during that time period) for the girl to stop being pretty.

Because of this, it seems that it is more appropriate to use some adjectives and nouns with ~던, but it wouldn't be appropriate with others. For example:

Again, please don't pay too much attention to the English translations:

조용하던 길 = The street that I recall being quiet until now
따뜻하던 날씨 = The weather that I recall being warm until now
맑던 하늘 = The sky that I recall being clear until now

For example:

맑던 하늘이 갑자기 어두워졌어요
= The sky that I recall being clear until now suddenly became dark

따뜻하던 날씨가 비가 오고 나서 추워졌어요
= The weather that I remember being warm until now got cold after it rained

조용하던 길이 사람들이 집에서 나오기 시작하고 나서 시끄러워졌어요
= The street that I recall being quiet until now got loud after people started coming out of their houses

----

There is something that I want to discuss in the midst of all of this confusion. In most cases – in both English or in Korean (or in any language, I guess), these subtle differences don't need to be distinguished. For example, if I said:

"The clear sky became dark"

Was the sky clear until the present and then became dark?
Was the sky clear sometime in the past and then became dark sometime in the past?
Was the sky clear sometime in the past and then became dark in the present?
Was the sky clear every day (habitually) before becoming dark?
Will the sky become clear again after becoming dark?

The answer to all of these questions – and any other questions you can think of - is irrelevant. As learners of Korean, we often find ourselves overthinking things and getting worked up over the meaning of something away from context. In reality, context will usually explain everything for you.

For example, look at the ambiguous way that I describe "the sky" (하늘) in the following example:

맑? 하늘이 갑자기 어두워졌어요

Regardless of what replaces the "?" in the example above, the context from the rest of the sentence would be able to clarify the meaning and result of the sentence for you. Much like how the English sentences below, in effect, have the same result:

The sky that was clear all of a sudden became dark
The sky that had been clear all of a sudden became dark
The sky that used to be clear all of a sudden became dark
The sky that is habitually clear all of a sudden became dark
The sky that I recall being clear all of a sudden became dark

----

That's as far as I'm going to go. As I said at the beginning of this lesson – the difference between ~던 and ~았/었던 (compared with other grammatical principles that you learned in the previous lesson) is very confusing. If you have reached this point and think to yourself "I am still a little bit unclear of the difference" – Congratulations! You're just like a typical Korean person.

As I have discussed, Korean people – including those who you would consider "experts" in their own language – can't describe the difference precisely. I hope that you have enjoyed my discussion about these, and I hope that you are able to distinguish them a little bit.

Above all, I hope that this lesson hasn't completely turned you off of Korean forever!

Lesson 28: Anomalies with ~는 것: Irregulars, 싶은 것, 있는 것

Vocabulary

Nouns:
어른 = adult
어린이 = child, children
공주 = princess
영향 = influence
글 = some sort of writing
문학 = literature
지방 = district, local area
이웃사람 = neighbor
환경 = environment
농장 = farm
부분 = part, section
광고 = advertisement
농구 = basketball
배구 = volleyball
지구 = earth
방귀 = fart
고개 = head
방향 = direction
해외 = abroad, overseas
자체 = itself, its own
시대 = times, period
주의 = caution

Verbs:
연구하다 = to research
집중하다 = to concentrate
나누다 = to divide
이용하다 = to use
등록하다 = to register
메다 = to carry on one's shoulder
세우다 = to stand/line something up
움직이다 = to move
정리하다 = to arrange
취소하다 = to cancel
지키다 = to protect, to defend
놓치다 = to miss (a train/buss/opportunity)

Adjectives:
적다 = to be few

강하다 = to be strong
불편하다 = to be uncomfortable
충분하다 = to be enough, to be sufficient
졸리다 = to be sleepy
솔직하다 = to be honest/frank
정확하다 = to be exact
친하다 = to be familiar with, to be close with
급하다 = to be urgent

Adverbs and Other words:
결국 = eventually
내내 = throughout a time
드디어 = finally, at last
그냥 = only, just
약간 = slightly/a little bit
철저히 = thoroughly

Introduction

In this lesson, you will learn a lot of weird things about ~는 것 that don't really make sense. Here, you will learn thing that are counter-intuitive, but still very important to know about this principle. For example, you will learn about irregular conjugations, saying "my favorite thing" and other small things that you wouldn't expect. Let's get started.

Irregulars with ~는 것
Present Tense

In Lesson 7, you learned that irregular words change as a result of adding different additions. In Lesson 21, you learned the change that results to a stem when a solid ㄴ is added. Specifically, you learned that the addition of ~니 or ~나 does not cause a change to any irregular except the ㄹ irregular. We see the same phenomenon when adding ~는 to a verb because this also falls into the category of a solid ㄴ.

Here is a table showing how ~는 것 is added to the stem of a verb from each irregular. Notice that the ㄹ irregular is the only case where the stem changes as a result of ~는 것.

Present Tense Addition of ~는 것		
Irregular	Word	Application
ㅅ	짓다	짓는 것
ㄷ	걷다	걷는 것
ㅂ	돕다	돕는 것
ㅡ	잠그다	잠그는 것
르	부르다	부르는 것
ㄹ	열다	여는 것

Here are some example sentences:
저는 친구가 문을 여는 것을 봤어요 = I saw my friend opening the door
마음에 드는 부분이 있나요? = Do you have a part/section that you like?
저는 아는 것만 하고 싶어요 = I only want to do things that I know
옆에 사는 이웃사람이 너무 시끄러워요 = The neighbor who lives next to me is too loud
우리가 사는 지역이 조금 위험해요 = The area we live in is a little bit dangerous
농장에서 사는 게 싫어요 = I don't like living on a farm
옆 집에서 사는 사람과 친해지고 있어요 = I am getting close to the person who lives next door

Past and Future Tense

In Lesson 4, you learned how to attach ~ㄴ/은 to adjectives to describe an upcoming noun. In Lesson 7, you expanded on that knowledge and learned how to apply this to irregular adjectives.

~ㄴ/은 can also be added to verbs. We should take a minute to discuss how this addition causes irregular verbs to change. The principle is the same as when it is added to adjectives, but I feel it is important to bring up again nonetheless.

- The ㅅ irregular and ㄷ irregular follow similar principles. In each case, the stem of the word originally ends with a consonant. For example:
  짓다
  걷다

  Therefore, when we have to decide if we add ~ㄴ or ~은, we much choose ~은:
  짓은
  걷은

  However, each respective irregular rule indicates that the placement of a vowel immediately following the stem causes it to change. The above should be changed to:
  지은
  걸은

- When adding ~ㄴ/은 to a verb that ends in ㅂ, the same rule applies as if you were adding it to an adjective. The ㅂ changes to 우, and ㄴ is added to 우. For example:

  Adjectives:
  쉽다 + ~ㄴ/은 = 쉬운
  춥다 + ~ㄴ/은 = 추운

Verbs:
눕다 + ~ㄴ/은 = 누운
돕다 + ~ㄴ/은 = 도운

Remember that the ㅂ in 돕다 changes to 오 only when ~아/어 (or one of its derivatives) is added to it. When any other vowel is added, ㅂ changes to 우.

- When adding ~ㄴ/은 to a verb that ends in ㄹ, the same rule applies as if you were adding it to an adjective. The ㄹ is eliminated, and ㄴ is added to the remainder of the stem. For example:
Adjective:
길다 + ~ㄴ/은 = 긴

Verbs:
열다 + ~ㄴ/은 = 연
살다 + ~ㄴ/은 = 산

Here is a table showing how ~ㄴ/은 것 should be added to the stem of a verb from each respective irregular. Notice that this applies to the ㅅ, ㄷ, ㅂ and ㄹ irregulars:

Past Tense Addition of ~ㄴ/은 것		
Irregular	Verb	Application
ㅅ	짓다	지은 것
ㄷ	걷다	걸은 것
ㅂ	돕다	도운 것
ㅡ	잠그다	잠근 것
르	부르다	부른 것
ㄹ	열다	연 것

In Lesson 9, you learned how ~ㄹ/을 causes irregular words to change. The addition of ~ㄴ/은 results in the same change.

Now that you have a better idea of how versatile ~ㄹ/을 is, let's look at a table again to remind ourselves how the addition of ~ㄹ/을 causes verb stems to change. Notice again that this applies only to the ㅅ, ㄷ, ㅂ and ㄹ irregulars and is exactly the same as the table above except for that ~ㄹ/을 is used instead of ~ㄴ/은:

Future Tense Addition of ~ㄹ/을 것		
Irregular	Word	Application
ㅅ	짓다	지을 것
ㄷ	걷다	걸을 것
ㅂ	돕다	도울 것
ㅡ	잠그다	잠글 것
르	부르다	부를 것
ㄹ	열다	열 것

Here are some example sentences:

ㅅ irregular:
그 집을 지은 사람은 누구예요? = Who is the person that built that house?
저는 집을 지을 거예요 = I will build a house
Remember that the future tense conjugation of ~ㄹ/을 것이다 is actually just the future ~는 것.

ㄷ irregular:
그 사람은 서울에서 부산까지 걸은 첫 번째 사람이었다 = That person was the first person who walked from Seoul to Busan

ㅂ irregular
제가 도울 게 있나요? = Is there something I can help you with?
것이 is often contracted to 게 in speech.

ㄹ irregular:
그는 문을 열 사람이에요 = He is the person who will open the doors
… I'm not sure when you would say that sentence, but it's difficult to think up of a sentence where I can apply this irregular and make it sound natural. This irregular is often applied when conjugating to the future tense by adding 'ㄹ/을 것이다' to the end of a sentence:

저는 내일 시장에서 사과를 팔 거예요 = I will sell apples at the market tomorrow
그 광고를 만든 사람이 진짜 잘 만들었어요 = The person who made this advertisement did a really good job

My Favorite Thing: 가장 좋아하는 것

Saying "My favorite..." is one of the first things that people want to learn whenever learning a new language. In Korean, the grammar within this sentence is a little bit difficult (you only just learned it), so that is why you are just learning about it now.

There is no word in Korean for "favorite." Instead, they use a combination of 좋아하다 (to like) and "제일/가장" (which you learned in Lesson 19). You have known how to use 제일/가장 with 좋아하다 for a long time now. Here are some simple sentences:

저는 우리 학교를 좋아해요 = I like our school
저는 우리 학교를 가장 좋아해요 = I like our school most

But you haven't yet learned how to specifically say "My favorite ____ is…"

Let's look at adjectives first. These should all be easy to you:

가장 큰 것 = the biggest thing
가장 작은 것 = the smallest thing
가장 어려운 것 = the most difficult thing

However, in those sentences, only adjectives are describing the noun. Now that you have learned how to describe nouns with verbs, you can now say:

내가 가장 좋아하는 것 = the thing that I like most (which is also – my favorite thing)

Notice that it is *not* "나의 가장 좋아하는 것." Really, you are not saying "my favorite thing" – you are saying "the thing that I like most." So even though in English we say "my," in Korean you shouldn't use 나의/저의 in place of 내가/제가 in these sentences.

You could take 가장 out to simply mean "the thing that I like"

내가 좋아하는 것 = the thing that I like

Or change the subject:

저의 친구가 가장 좋아하는 것 = The thing that my friend likes most

Now that you have created the noun of "the thing that I like most" you can place it in sentences:

제가 가장 좋아하는 것은 음식이에요 = My favorite thing is food
음식은 제가 가장 좋아하는 것이에요 = Food is my favorite thing

You can also replace "것" with any other noun:

제가 가장 좋아하는 음식은 김치예요 = My favorite food is kimchi
제가 가장 좋아하는 날은 금요일이에요 = My favorite day is Friday

As I said before, people often don't realize the power of the ~는 것 principle. Now that you can describe nouns with verbs, you can say much more complicated (and natural) sentences. Look at the following example:

내가 가장 좋아하는 것은 영화야 = My favorite thing is movies

This sentence is natural, but you could more precisely describe what you like if you used ~는 것. For example, you could say that your favorite thing is "watching movies" or "making movies." You learned in Lesson 26 how to make these nouns:

영화를 보는 것 = watching movies
영화를 만드는 것 = making movies

내가 가장 좋아하는 것은 영화를 보는 것이다 = My favorite thing is watching movies

The easiest mistake to make in that sentence is (incorrectly) not changing the latter part of the sentence to a noun. Many learners of Korean would just say the following:

내가 가장 좋아하는 것은 영화를 봐…

But that just translates to "My favorite thing watches movies." You need to say "My favorite thing **is** watch**ing** movies" which requires you to change the second clause of the sentence to a noun and then add 이다 (is).

친구는 선생님**이다** = My friend **is** a teacher
내가 가장 좋아하는 것은 영화를 보는 것**이다** = My favorite thing **is** watching movies

… heh, complicated. That's why I waited until this lesson to teach it to you.

If you specifically want to say that your "favorite thing *about* X is Y" you can attach "~에 있어서" to a noun in the sentence. ~에 있어서 typically translates to "when it comes to…" in English. For example:

한국에 있어서 내가 가장 좋아하는 것은 한식이야
= My favorite thing about Korea is Korean food
(or, "When it comes to Korea, my favorite thing is Korean food")

Not only can you do that, but now that you have learned about the ~는 것 principle, you can create more complex nouns throughout the sentence. For example, instead of saying the sentence above, you could say:

한국에서 사는 것에 있어서 내가 가장 좋아하는 것은 한식이야
= My favorite part about *living in* Korea is Korean food

한국에서 사는 것에 있어서 내가 가장 좋아하는 것은 한식을 매일 먹는 것이야
= My favorite part about *living in* Korea *is eating* Korean food *every day*

~는 with 싶다, 있다 and 없다

There are a few words that seem a lot like verbs but are actually adjectives.

In Lesson 17, you learned about 싶다 and how it can be used to say that one "wants" to do an action. For example:

저는 한국어를 배우고 싶어요 = I want to study Korean
저는 캐나다에 가고 싶어요 = I want to go to Canada

In that lesson, I told you that 싶다 is an adjective. As such, you must treat it as any other adjective when describing a noun. This means that if you want to describe nouns in the present tense using 싶다 you must add ~ㄴ/은:

예쁜 사람 = beautiful person
똑똑한 사람 = smart person
내가 만나고 싶은 사람 = the person (who/that) I want to meet

Below are many examples:

제가 가장 만나고 싶은 사람은 유재석이에요
= The person who I want to meet most is 유재석

배구를 하고 싶은 사람이 없어요
= There isn't anybody who wants to play volleyball

체육수업시간에 농구를 하고 싶은 사람이 있어요?
= Is there anybody who wants to play basketball during PE class?

이 수업을 등록하고 싶은 사람이 적어요
= There aren't many people who want to register for this class

이 수업을 등록하고 싶은 사람이 충분하지 않아요
= There aren't enough people who want to register for this class

먹고 싶은 것이 있어요? = Do you want something to eat?
(literally – do you have something that you want to eat?)

~았/었던, which you learned in the previous lesson, can be added to 싶다 to carry the meaning that it creates. Essentially, the speaker can indicate that there was something he/she "wanted" to do in the past but currently doesn't want to do anymore. For example:

그것은 제가 말하고 싶었던 것이었어요 = That was what I had wanted to say

In Lesson 5, you learned how to use 있다 to indicate that one "has" something. I explained that this usage of 있다 is an adjective. For example:

나는 펜이 있다 = I have a pen
나는 차가 있다 = I have a car

When using adjectives to describe nouns in the present tense, you know that you should add ~ㄴ/은 to the stem of the adjective. For example:

예쁜 사람 = beautiful person
똑똑한 사람 = smart person

Grammatically it *should* be correct to do this with 있다 as well:

펜이 있은 사람

But this is incorrect. Even though this usage of 있다 is an adjective, you must treat it as a verb when describing an upcoming noun. For example, the following is correct:

펜이 있는 사람

The same rule applies to 없다. For example:

펜이 없는 사람

Actually, when speaking to a large group of people (for example, a teacher speaking to a group of students), it is common to ask "is there anybody who has (or doesn't have) x?" by using this form without a predicating word. That is, it is common to say:

펜이 있는 사람!? = Does anybody have a pen? (Is there anybody who has a pen)?
펜이 없는 사람!? = Does anybody not have a pen? (Does everybody have a pen)?

This is why ~는 (instead of ~은) is added to words like "재미있다 or 재미없다" and "맛있다 or 맛없다" when describing an upcoming noun. The inclusion of "to have" or "to not have" with 있다 and 없다 requires them to describe upcoming nouns by using ~는 instead of ~은.

For example:

저는 재미있는 영화를 봤어요 = I watched a fun/funny movie
저는 맛있는 밥을 먹었어요 = I ate delicious rice/food

관심 translates to "interest" and is commonly used to indicate that one "is interested" (or not interested) in something. To indicate that one has (or does not have) interest in a topic, 있다 or 없다 can be used.

For example:
저는 과학에 관심이 없어요 = I am not interested in Science
저는 과학에 관심이 있어요 = I have interest in Science
(When saying that one is interested in something, it is also common to replace 있다 with 많다 to indicate that one is really interested in a topic)

We can attach ~는 to 있다 and 없다 here to describe somebody who is interested. For example:

과학에 관심이 있는 사람이 없었어요 = There was nobody who was/is interested in Science

When using 있다 to indicate that something is in the "state" of an action using ~아/어 있다 (introduced in Lesson 18) or to indicate that one is progressively doing something using ~고 있다 (also introduced in Lesson 18), 있다 is seen as a verb. Therefore, as a verb ~는 should be attached, but this technically isn't seen as "strange" because in this form it is a verb anyways. It is only "strange" when adding ~는 to 있다/없다 when it is an adjective.

Below are many examples of ~는 것 being used with 있다:

이렇게 앉아 있는 것이 불편해요 = It is uncomfortable to sit like this
열쇠를 가지고 있는 사람이 드디어 왔어요 = The person who has the key eventually came

수업에 집중하고 있는 학생이 없어요
= There aren't any students who are concentrating on the class

주문을 취소하고 있는 사람이 많아요
= There are a lot of people who are cancelling their order

정부가 그 병을 연구하고 있는 회사에게 돈을 줄 것이다
= The government will give money to the company researching that disease

~았/었던, which you learned in the previous lesson, can be added to 있다 to carry the meaning that it creates. Essentially, the speaker can indicate that something "was" in a place in the past, but is currently not in the place anymore. For example:

그곳에 있었던 사람들은 다 죽었다 = All the people that were there died
그 자리에 앉아 있었던 사람이 다른 데로 갔어요 = The person who had been sitting there went to another place

----

Only in a few grammatical principles is it appropriate to add ~은 to 있다 or 없다 to create 있은 or 없은. When a grammatical principle creates a meaning that specifies that an action was done in the past and we are looking at the time since that action, ~은 can be used. Two practical examples where you can see this is when adding ~ㄴ/은 후 to a word (Lesson 24) and adding ~ㄴ/은 지 to a word (Lesson 30)

Using 그 (and other smaller words) in ~는 것 sentences

One thing that I want to mention before this lesson ends is how to include words like 이/그/나의/저의 in 는 것 sentences. It's hard to describe what I mean without examples (it's not really a "concept" so I better show you some examples.)

In English, we could say:
The person who I met. That would be easy to translate to Korean:

내가 만난 사람

However, in English, we could also say something like "that person I met." Almost the same meaning, but not exactly the same. If you were to translate that directly, it would come out like this: 그 내가 만난 사람

But in Korean, they always place those small words that can go before nouns (이/그/저/나의/저의) immediately before nouns. So, instead of saying:

그 내가 만난 사람 you should say:
내가 만난 그 사람

It's hard to translate some of these sentences into Korean. Look at next example. You will probably be able to understand it completely, but translating it to English is very difficult:

선생님이 본 나의 영화

It would translate to something like "my movie that the teacher watched" but that sounds a little bit unnatural in English. When these sentences come up, you should realize that the noun being described (영화 – movie) is being described by two different things:

나의 영화 = **my** movie, and
선생님이 본 영화 = the movie **that the teacher watched**

Even though it is unnatural to say the full sentence in English (my movie that the teacher watched), you should be able to understand the meaning without needing to translate it directly.

Really, learning about the ~는 것 principle is *the* most confusing part about Korean grammar. After conquering it, there isn't much more to be all that confused about (the difficulty later on doesn't come from confusion – it just comes from the pain of memorization, haha). There are *still* 2 or 3 more lessons where we will be talking about ~는 것. Stay tuned, because they will be coming right after this.

Lesson 29: Using ~기 and ~ㅁ/음 to make nouns

Vocabulary

Nouns:
싸움 = a fight
기쁨 = happiness, gladness
도움 = help
걸음 = step
죽음 = death
느낌 = a feeling
행정 = administration
구역 = zone, area
보행자 = pedestrian
좌석 = seat
사전 = dictionary
언어 = language
국어 = the Korean language
노동자 = laborer
음악가 = musician
능력 = capabilities
자료 = data
제품 = products
사업 = business
감정 = emotion
쌀 = uncooked rice
방송 = broadcast
접시 = plate
역할 = role
정보 = information
모양 = shape
마을 = village/town
합법 = legal
불법 = illegal
효과 = effects
순간 = moment, second

Verbs:
확대하다 = to expand, to enlarge
검색하다 = to search for, to surf the internet
훔치다 = to steal
즐기다 = to enjoy oneself
변하다 = to have changed
붙이다 = to stick/stamp/label/attach

쳐다보다 = to stare
모이다 = to gather, to congregate
낳다 = to give birth
넘다 = to cross over, to climb over
주차하다 = to park a car
보호하다 = to protect
표현하다 = to express

Passive Verbs:
붙다 = to be stuck

Adverbs and Other words:
현대 = modern times
직접 = directly
스스로 = for oneself/by oneself

Introduction

In the past few lessons, you have learned a lot about adding ~는 (or ㄴ/은 for past tense and ㄹ/을 for future tense) to verb stems to turn them into descriptive words that can describe nouns. One more time, for example:

밥을 먹다 = to eat rice
밥을 먹는 사람 = the person who eats rice

빨리 가다 = to go fast
내가 빨리 가는 곳 = the place I am going to fast

A lot of times, the noun following the descriptive verb is 것, which allows an entire sentence to be turned into a noun:

나는 사과를 가져온다 = I bring apples – is a sentence
내가 사과를 가져오는 것 – is the same sentence as above, but in *noun* form. This noun can now be placed in other sentences just like other nouns:

나의 여자 친구는 내가 사과를 가져오는 것을 원했다 = My girlfriend wanted me to bring apples

So that's what you already know. What you don't know is that in addition to the ~는 것 principle, there are other ways that you can modify verbs to change them into nouns. We will look at this today.

Changing Verbs to Nouns ~기

Adding ~기 to the stem of a verb changes that verb into a noun. The noun can technically be used like any other noun:

가다 = to go
가기 = the noun form of "to go"

읽다 = to read
읽기 = the noun form of "to read"

먹다 = to eat
먹기 = the noun form of "to eat"

So… the million dollar question is, "what is the difference between '~는 것' and '~기'?" Well, first, notice exactly what ~는 것 is. Adding ~는 to a verb stem allows you to describe nouns (것, 사람, 음식, etc…). Adding ~기 to a verb stem does not allow you to describe anything. It just turns verbs into nouns.
But, turning verbs into nouns is *one* of the functions of ~는 것. Remember, there are two main functions of ~는 것:

1) To change verbs into things that can describe nouns:
밥을 먹고 있는 사람 = the person who is eating rice

2) To change a clause into a noun
사과를 가져오는 것 = the noun form of "to bring apples" – "bringing apples"

Adding ~기 is essentially the same as the *second* function described above. That is, you can use ~기 to turn a clause into nouns – but you cannot use ~기 to describe nouns. So this:

내가 사과를 가져오는 것 and 내가 사과를 가져오기 essentially have the same meaning, being "the noun form of "to bring apples."

Which means you can use ~기 in sentences like:

나의 여자 친구는 내가 사과를 가져오기를 원해 = My girlfriend wants me to bring apples

Technically you can say it that way, but I very rarely hear verbs turned into nouns using ~기 in that way. If you ask a Korean person, they will say that sentence sounds fine, but somebody like me who analyzes grammar will notice that it is not used as much as "나의

여자 친구는 내가 사과를 가져오는 것을 원해."

However, there are certain cases where using ~기 is more natural than using ~는 것. In later lessons, you will see ~기 used in various grammatical principles. For example:

~기 때문에 (Lesson 38)
~기도 하고 (Lesson 51)
~기 바라다 (Lesson 61)
~기로 하다 (Lesson 87)

Before you see ~기 being applied in those grammatical principles, I would like to introduce some simple, practical uses of ~기 that you can use right away.

~기 시작하다
When one "starts" an action, you can attach ~기 to the verb that starts to occur followed by 시작하다. For example:

가다 = to go
가기 시작하다 = to start to go

먹다 = to eat
먹기 시작하다 = to start to eat

These types of constructions can then be placed in sentences. For example:

나는 밥을 벌써 먹기 시작했어 = I already started to eat
다음 달에 한국어를 배우기 시작할 거야 = I will start learning Korean next month

어제부터 사람들이 거기서 모이기 시작했어요
= People started gathering there from yesterday

쌀을 물에 넣은 후에 쌀의 색깔이 변하기 시작했어요
= After I put the rice in the water, the color of the rice started to change

이상한 행동을 한 다음에 사람들이 저를 쳐다보기 시작했어요
= After acting strangely, people started staring at me

~기 싫다
It is also very common to put verbs before ~기 싫다 to indicate that you don't want to do something. Literally, this translates to "I don't like _____"

밥을 먹기 싫어 = I don't want to eat
가기 싫어 = I don't want to go
쌀을 씻기 싫어요 = I don't want to wash the rice

This form isn't commonly used with 좋다 (the opposite of 싫다). Instead, I guess it would be more common to say "밥을 먹고 싶다/가고 싶다."

Actual Words
There are also a handful of words where it is common to use the ~기 form as an actual word.

For example, if you are going for a run, I could use the word "달리기"
저는 달리기를 할 거예요 = I will go for a run

The word for skipping (jump-rope skipping) is the word 줄 (rope) combined with the word 넘다 (going over) with ~기:
저는 줄넘기를 못해요 = I'm bad at skipping

When writing a language test, there will often be many sections. For example, there might be a "writing" section, a "reading" section and a "listening" section:

Writing = 쓰기
Reading = 읽기
Listening = 듣기

Here's an example of these actually being used in a sentence:

Person 1: 시험은 어땠어?
Person 2: 쓰기랑 듣기는 너무 어려웠어. 하지만 읽기는 너무 쉬웠어.

Person 1: How was the exam?
Person 2: The writing and listening (parts) were really hard. But the reading (part) was really easy.

Making Lists
When making a list of things that you are going to do, it is also common to end the phrase by using ~기. This essentially makes the entire phrase a noun, which is similar to what we do in English. For example, if I made a to-do list, I could write:

커피를 만들기 = Make coffee
책상을 정리하기 = Organize my desk
방 청소하기 = Clean my room
쌀을 사기 = Buy rice
인터넷에 자료를 검색하기 = Look for data on the internet

Another example; if I made a list of goals for myself for the year, I could write:

매일매일을 즐기기 = Enjoy every day
집 청소를 매일 하기 = Clean the house every day
숙제를 매일 하기 = Do my homework every day
감정을 표현하기 = Show my emotions
책을 매일 읽기 = Read books every day
운동을 등록하기 = Register at a gym (to exercise)

Buttons
On a computer, if you wanted to "zoom" in on a picture, you would press the "zoom" button. In Korean, the verb "zoom" is "확대하다." On Korean computers, they usually don't put verbs on buttons on the screen – instead they put the noun form of the verb. For ~하다 verbs, the noun form is easy to find. The noun form of 확대하다 is 확대. Simple.

But, what is the noun form of 보다? (to see)

What about 열다? (to open)

If you wanted to see something on a Korean screen, or click on the "view" button at the top of every screen, you would have to press "보기."
If you wanted to open something, you could press the "열기" button.

Want to close something? Press "닫기."

Want to search? You might see a "찾기" button or "검색" – which is the noun form of 검색하다 also meaning "search/find."

Want to send an e-mail? You would have to press "보내기."

There are a lot of applications for ~기, they just might not seem apparent at the moment. As you learn more and more Korean grammar, you will see that there will be more applications where you can use ~기. In later lessons, you will see ~기 paired up with other grammatical priciples.

Up to now, the applications you should be aware of are:

1) Turning any verb into a noun: 사과를 가져오기, 달리기
2) Put before 시작하다: 먹기 시작했다
3) Put before 싫다: 먹기 싫어
4) Making Lists: 쌀을 사기
5) On buttons: 보내기

Before we go further, let's look at *another* way you can turn verbs (or adjectives) into nouns.

Changing Verbs/Adjectives to Nouns ~ㅁ/음

Adding ~ㅁ/음 to verbs or adjectives to turn them into nouns. ~ㅁ gets added to stems ending in a vowel, and ~음 gets added after stems that end in a consonant.
This form *can* be used to change entire sentences into noun forms, just like with ~는 것:

나는 네가 먹고 있는 것을 알았어 = I knew you were eating
나는 네가 먹고 있기를 알았어 – sounds wrong to a Korean person, but would look correct to a foreign learner of Korean
나는 네가 먹고 있음을 알았어 = I knew you were eating

Like I said earlier. You *can* use ㅁ/음 to turn entire sentences into nouns, but this is rarely done in speech. It is done much more commonly in books/poems (for whatever reason).

The main usage of ㅁ/음 is to turn single words (verbs or adjectives) into nouns, and not full sentences. Some of these you may have already come across:

싸우다 = to fight
싸움 = a fight

꾸다 = to dream
꿈 = a dream

아프다 = to be sore/sick
아픔 = pain

기쁘다 = to be happy/glad
기쁨 = happiness/gladness

돕다 = to help
도움 = help

죽다 = to die
죽음 = death

걷다 = to walk
걸음 = a step

느끼다 = to feel
느낌 = a feeling

Adding ㅁ/음 to verbs/adjectives is usually done to words that don't end in 하다. The reason for this is because there is already a very simple way to make a 하다 verb/adjective a noun – by removing the 하다 from the rest of the word (설명하다 = to explain – 설명 = an explanation).

These noun form words can then be added to sentences as usual:
나는 형이랑 싸움에서 이겼어 = I won in a fight with my brother
나는 아빠의 죽음을 잊지 않았어 = I didn't forget the death of my father

In Lesson 7, you learned how irregular words change as a result of adding different additions. This is the first time you have been introduced to adding ~ㅁ/음. Let's look at how irregulars change as a result of adding this grammatical principle.

- The ㅅ irregular, ㄷ irregular and ㅂ irregular all follow the same rules that were introduced in Lesson 7. The addition of the vowel causes a change (or elimination) of the last letter of the stem.

- The ㅡ and 르 irregular are not affected by this addition.

- Adding ~ㅁ/음 to a word that follows the ㄹ irregular brings about a change you are not familiar with. Normally, you would add ~ㅁ to the stem of a word ending in a vowel, and ~음 to the stem of a word ending in a consonant. For example:
싸우다 + ~ㅁ/음 = 싸움
죽다 + ~ㅁ/음 = 죽음

- However, when you add ~ㅁ/음 to a stem of a word that ends in ㄹ, ㅁ is added beside the ㄹ and a double consonant is created. Korean people often don't even know this rule.

  In fact, this is how some common nouns are created in Korean. The verb 살다 means "to live." The addition of ㅁ to the stem of the verb creates the noun "삶," meaning "life" or "living."

- Adding ~ㅁ/음 causes a change to ㅎ irregular words. The ㅎ is removed, and ~ㅁ is added to the stem. For example:
그렇다 + ~ㅁ/음 = 그럼

Below is a table showing the changes that result from adding ~ㅁ/음 to a word.

Irregular	Word	+ ~ㅁ/음
ㅅ Irregular	짓다 (to build)	지음
ㄷ Irregular	걷다 (to walk)	걸음
ㅂ Irregular	쉽다 (to be easy)	쉬움
ㅂ Irregular	돕다 (to help)	도움
ㅡ Irregular	잠그다 (to lock)	잠금
르 Irregular	다르다 (to be different)	다름
ㄹ Irregular	살다 (to live)	삶
ㅎ Irregular	그렇다 (to be like that)	그럼

Notice that I also included the word 돕다. As you learned in Lesson 7 – ㅂ changes to 오 when ~아/어 (or any derivative) is added in 돕다. When any other vowel is added (for example, ~음), ㅂ changes to 우 as you can see above.

You will see these same changes to irregulars anytime you add something that begins in ~ㅁ/음. For example:
~ㅁ/음에도 (Lesson 74)

In Lesson 23, you learned about the word 그렇다. ~ㅁ/음 is commonly added to this word when somebody asks a question and you just say "yeah, of course." This is basically the same as saying "yes," but it would be more like "Yes, it is like that." For example:

운동을 매일 해요? = Do you exercise every day?
그럼요 = Yes (it is like that)

차를 스스로 주차했어요? = Did you park the car by yourself?
그럼요 = Yes (it is like that)
Notice that you can add "요" to make the response formal. In informal situations, this can be removed.

This is one of the usages of 그럼. 그럼 actually has other usages, but these are actually a contraction of a grammatical principles that you haven't learned yet, so I will not introduce you to these here.

Lesson 30: 지 in sentences: 할지 모른다/한 지 1년 됐다

Vocabulary

Nouns:
택배 = delivery
가격 = price
용돈 = allowance
아르바이트 = part-time job
빛 = a light
시인 = poet
주제 = subject
그룹 = group
요금 = fare, price
위치 = position, location
해안 = the coast
가정 = family
재료 = materials, ingredients
자유 = freedom
책임 = responsibility
입구 = entrance, way in
출구 = exit, way out
출입 = enter and exit
수술 = surgery, operation
훈련 = training
비상 = emergency
계단 = steps, stairs, staircase
전통 = tradition, culture, heritage
호선 = a subway line
기간 = a period of time
구체적 = detailed, specific

Verbs:
꺼내다 = to take out, to remove something
전하다 = to convey, to deliver
정하다 = to set
줄이다 = to reduce, to decrease
데려오다 = to bring a person (coming)
데려가다 = to bring a person (going)
막다 = to obstruct, to block
허락하다 = to allow, to permit
버리다 = to throw away
잊어버리다 = to forget
벌다 = to earn

기르다 = to raise (a child, pet), to cultivate
조심하다 = to act carefully
관리하다 = to manage, to administer
치료하다 = to treat, to cure
헤어지다 = to break up with a person
줄다 = to be reduced, to be decreased
깨지다 = to be broken, cracked, smashed

Adjectives:
쌀쌀하다 = to be chilly
밝다 = to be bright
목마르다 = to be thirsty

Introduction

Up to now, you have learned a lot (probably too much!) about using ~는 것 (or one of its derivatives) with a clause to describe an upcoming noun. For example:

내가 가고 있는 곳 = the place I am going
내가 만난 사람 = the person I met
내가 먹을 음식 = the food I will eat

In this lesson, you will learn about adding ~는지 to indicate that the preceding clause is a guess or something uncertain. Let's get started.

A Clause of Uncertainty: ~는지

I didn't know what title to give to "~는지," but I came up with the "clause of uncertainty" which I feel describes it well. By placing ~는지 at the end of a clause, you can indicate that the clause is some sort of guess, question or uncertainty.

A common situation where there is uncertainty is when there is a question word in a sentence.
For example: 저는 친구가 어디 가는 것을 몰라요

If we break that sentence down into more simple pieces, we get:
저는 (---) 몰라요 = I don't know (----)

What don't you know? You don't know the noun within the brackets:
저는 (친구가 어디 가는 것을) 몰라요

So the sentence reads:
저는 친구가 어디 가는 것을 몰라요 = I don't know where my friend is going

However, because "친구가 어디 가는 것" is uncertain, ~는지 should be added to the clause instead of ~는 것. For example:

저는 친구가 어디 가는지 몰라요 = I don't know where my friend is going

It is also worth pointing out here that the future tense ~겠다 is commonly added to 모르다 in these types of sentences. When 모르다 is used like this (as "모르겠다"), it does not have a future tense meaning. Rather, it is just a common (and slightly more polite) way to say that one "does not know something." Therefore, it would be more common to see the sentence above written/spoken as:

저는 친구가 어디 가는지 모르겠어요 = I don't know where my friend is going

You will continue to see "모르겠다" used instead of a present tense conjugation of 모르다 in the rest of this lesson and throughout your Korean studies.

By default, if a clause contains a question word (누구, 뭐, 언제, 어디, 왜, etc...) ~는지 is usually added due to the uncertainty that it contains. For example:

엄마가 **누구**랑 먹는지 모르겠어요 = I don't know **who** mom is eating with
엄마가 **뭐** 먹는지 모르겠어요= I don't know **what** mom is eating
엄마가 **어디**서 먹는지 모르겠어요 = I don't know **where** mom is eating
엄마가 **왜** 먹는지 모르겠어요= I don't know **why** mom is eating

However, a question word does not need to be included in order to use ~는지. All that is needed is that there is uncertainty in the sentence. When there is no question word in a sentence that includes "~는지" the English word "if" is usually used. For example:

엄마가 지금 먹고 있는지 모르겠어요 = I don't know **if** mom is eating now

Below are more examples. Also notice that the final word of the sentence does not need to be "모르다." Any verb or adjective that makes sense along with the preceding uncertain clause can be used. For example:

그 사람을 왜 데려오는지 물어봤어요
= I asked him why he is bringing that person

비상출입구가 어디 있는지 찾았어요
= We found where the emergency exit is

해안까지 어떻게 가는지 물어봤어요
= I asked how to get to the beach/coast

엄마가 무슨 재료를 쓰고 있는지 모르겠어요
= I don't know what ingredients mom is using

정부가 외국인 선생님 예산을 왜 줄이는지 모르겠어요
= I don't know why the government is decreasing the budget for foreign teachers

학생들은 선생님들이 돈을 얼마나 버는지 몰라요
= Students don't know how much money teachers earn

저는 그 학생이 어느 대학교를 다니는지 기억(이) 안 나요
= I don't remember which university that student attends

Past tense:
The same concept can be used to indicate a guess, question or uncertainty in the past tense. In order to express this, ~았/었 should be added to the verb at the end of the uncertain clause, followed by ~는지. For example:

저는 엄마가 왜 먹었는지 모르겠어요 = I don't know why mom ate
저는 엄마가 뭐 먹었는지 모르겠어요 = I don't know what mom ate
저는 엄마가 언제 먹었는지 모르겠어요 = I don't know when mom ate
저는 엄마가 어디서 먹었는지 모르겠어요 = I don't know where mom ate
저는 엄마가 밥을 먹었는지 모르겠어요 = I don't know if mom ate

The form above (using ~았/었는지) is officially correct in Korean. However, in speech, it is very common to hear ~ㄴ/은지 being used instead. For example:

저는 엄마가 왜 먹은지 모르겠어요 = I don't know **why** mom ate
저는 엄마가 뭐 먹은지 모르겠어요 = I don't know **what** mom ate
저는 엄마가 언제 먹은지 모르겠어요 = I don't know **when** mom ate
저는 엄마가 어디서 먹은지 모르겠어요 = I don't know **where** mom ate
저는 엄마가 밥을 먹은지 모르겠어요 = I don't know **if** mom ate

There really isn't any difference between the two sets of sentences, especially in speech. Both sets of sentences sound natural to a Korean speaker. However, the correct grammatical form is to use ~았/었는지, and the use of ~ㄴ/은지 is more used in spoken Korean.

Other examples:
그 셔츠를 언제 버렸는지 기억이 안 나요 = I don't remember when I threw away that shirt
열쇠를 어디 두었는지 잊어버렸어요 = I forget where I put my keys
우리가 이것을 언제 정했는지 모르겠어요 = I don't know when we set it
그가 저에게 무슨 말을 전했는지 기억이 안 나요 = I don't remember what that person told me (conveyed to me)

Future tense:
The same concept can be used to indicate a guess, question or uncertainty in the future tense. In order to express this, ~ㄹ/을 should be added to the verb at the end of the uncertain clause, followed by ~지. For example:

택배가 언제 올지 모르겠어요 = I don't know when the delivery will come
용돈을 얼마나 줄지 모르겠어요 = I don't know how much allowance I should give
오후에 비가 올지 모르겠어요 = I don't know if it will rain in the afternoon
수술을 받을지 확실하지 않아요 = It is not certain if I will get surgery
내일 공원에 갈지 모르겠어요 = I don't know if I will go to the park tomorrow
내일 영화를 볼지 모르겠어요 = I don't know if I will see a movie tomorrow

When the uncertain clause doesn't have a question word in it, it is common to use the word "might" in the English translation. For example

오후에 비가 올지 모르겠어요 = It might rain in the afternoon tomorrow
수술을 받을지 모르겠어요 = I might get surgery
내일 공원에 갈지 모르겠어요 = I might go to the park tomorrow
내일 영화를 볼지 모르겠어요 = I might see a movie tomorrow

English speakers are often confused about how the same Korean sentence can seemingly translate to different things in English. My answer is: They don't translate to different things. The Korean usage of "~ㄹ/을 지 몰라요" just indicates that something may or may not happen. Both translations above ("I don't know if" and "might...") indicate that something may or may not happen. Remember that sometimes it is difficult to translate a Korean sentence perfectly into English. As such, I always suggest that you understand the general meaning of the *Korean* sentence, and try to focus less on the given English translations. The nuance of using "~ㄹ/을지 몰라요" can translate to many things in English, all which (as a result of being a completely different language) cannot perfectly describe this nuance.

Using ~는지 with Adjectives

It is also possible to attach ~는지 to an uncertain clause that is predicated by an adjective. However, instead of adding ~는지, ~ㄴ/은지 should be added. Notice that the difference in ~는지 and ~ㄴ/은지 is the same as the difference when attaching ~는 or ~ㄴ/은 to verbs and adjectives to describe an upcoming noun. For example:

먹는 것
가는 것

행복한 것
밝은 것

Below are some examples of ~ㄴ/은지 being used with adjectives:

제가 준 것이 괜찮은지 모르겠어요 = I don't know if the thing that I gave is good
이 빛이 충분히 밝은지 모르겠어요 = I don't know if this light is bright enough
제가 구한 아르바이트가 좋은지 모르겠어요 = I don't know if the job I found is good
제가 가져온 자료가 충분한지 모르겠어요 = I don't know if I brought enough materials
제가 강아지를 기르고 싶은지 모르겠어요 = I don't know if I want to raise a puppy
그 책이 얼마나 긴지 모르겠어요 = I don't know how long that book is

To use this form with adjectives in the past or future tenses, you can add the same thing as with verbs. For example:

그 시대가 그렇게 길었는지 깨닫지 못했어요 = I didn't realize that era was so long
그 일이 힘들지 모르겠어요 = I don't know if that work will be difficult
내일 날씨가 쌀쌀할지 모르겠어요 = I don't know if tomorrow's weather will be chilly

If… or not…

In all of the above examples, only one situation is indicated in the sentence. It is possible to indicate more than one situation by using more than one verb or adjective connected to ~는지 in the sentence. The simplest way to do this is to include the opposite situation, followed by ~는지. For example:

내일 영화를 볼지 안 볼지 모르겠어요 = I don't know if I will see a movie tomorrow or not
수술을 받을지 안 받을지 확실하지 않아요 = It is not certain if I will get surgery or not
그가 제 말을 들었는지 안 들었는지 모르겠어요 = I don't know if he was listening to me or not
저는 엄마가 밥을 먹었는지 안 먹었는지 모르겠어요 = I don't know if mom ate or not
제가 구한 아르바이트가 좋은지 안 좋은지 모르겠어요 = I don't know if the job I found is good or not

When you are dealing with non-하다 verbs (like 먹다), you need to write out the verb again to indicate "I don't know if mom ate **or not**." However, when dealing with 하다 verbs, the sentence can usually be shortened by eliminating the word before ~하다 when you say the verb the second time.

For example, instead of saying:
저는 엄마가 공부했는지 안 공부했는지 모르겠어요

You could just say:
저는 엄마가 공부했는지 안 했는지 모르겠어요 = I don't know if mom studied or not

Remember that Korean people love shortening their sentences, and taking out the redundant "공부" the second time around is more natural in Korean.

In all of the above examples, two possibilities are listed, and the speaker is indicating that he/she doesn't know which one will happen amongst the two. The examples above simply use the positive and negative outcomes of the same situation. It is also possible to list two (or more) outcomes that are unrelated to each other. For example:

내일 공원에 갈지 영화를 볼지 모르겠어요
= I don't know if I will see a movie or go to the park tomorrow

제가 구한 아르바이트가 좋은지 나쁜지 모르겠어요
= I don't know if the (part-time) job I found is good or bad

수술을 받을지 그냥 약으로 치료할지 확실하지 않아요
= It is not certain if I will get surgery or just treat it with medicine

You can also use "~지" to form a question. For example, if you are asking somebody if they know how to do something. The most common word that finishes the sentence would be "알다." For example, you can say:

서울에 어떻게 가는지 알아요? = Do you know how to get to Seoul?
그 단어를 어떻게 발음하는지 알아요? = Do you know how to pronounce that word?
그 학생이 책을 왜 버렸는지 알아요? = Do you know why that student threw out his book?
물을 어떻게 막는지 알아요? = Do you know how to block the water?

I call clauses with ~지 "clauses of uncertainty", but that is just a name I gave it because it describes it well in most situations. There are times when "지" represents something certain. For example, the answers to those questions would be:

서울에 어떻게 가는지 알아요 = I know how to get to Seoul
그 단어를 어떻게 발음하는지 알아요 = I know how to pronounce that word
그 학생이 책을 왜 버렸는지 알아요 = I know why that student threw out his book

In those examples, "지" technically doesn't represent something uncertain.... so why do we use "지?" In these cases, the use of the question word in the sentence makes it more natural to use "지" as the noun instead of "것." Also note that there is another way to say that one "knows how to do something" (which is more based on ability than knowing something). This other way is discussed in Lesson 85.

Attaching ~도 to ~지

It is common to find ~도 attached to ~지. Adding ~도 to ~지 can have two meanings:

1) To have the "too" or "also" or "either" meaning that ~도 usually has. For example:

저는 밥도 먹었어요 = I ate rice **too**
저도 밥을 먹었어요 = I **also** ate rice
저는 밥도 안 먹었어요 = I didn't eat rice **either**

This first meaning of ~도 will be discussed in a later lesson (Lesson 107). This usage is more about the use of ~도 and not really related to the usage of ~지. I will just show you one example sentence so you can understand what I mean:

문을 열지도 몰라요 = You don't **even** know how to open the door

Let's focus on the more ambiguous meaning of ~도, which will be talked about in #2:

2) To have very little meaning or purpose in a sentence. Look at the two sentences below:

내일 비가 올지 모르겠어요 = It might rain tomorrow
내일 비가 올지도 모르겠어요 = It might rain tomorrow

Assuming ~도 isn't being added to have the meaning described in #1 above (which is possible), the use of ~도 does not really change the sentence. Same goes for these two sentences:

내일 공원에 갈지 모르겠어요 = I might go to the park tomorrow
내일 공원에 갈지도 모르겠어요 = I might go to the park tomorrow

For seven years, I've been curious about the specific nuance that ~도 adds to these types of sentences (again, assuming that ~도 is not the ~도 from #1 above). All of my research, all of my studying, and all of my exposure to the language has lead me to believe that they are essentially the same. I've always thought to myself – "they can't be *exactly* the same… the ~도 must have some purpose… right?"

Recently, I had discussions with many people to try to better understand this nuance. I want to show you conversations I had with two people because I think it will not only help you understand how subtle this difference is, but it will also show you that even Korean people don't really know what the difference is.

My first conversation was with a Korean person who is a fluent English speaker. Below is how our conversation went.

Me: Explain the difference in nuance that you feel between these two sentences:
내일 비가 올지 모르겠어요 = It might rain tomorrow
내일 비가 올지도 모르겠어요 = It might rain tomorrow

Her: The use of ~도 makes it seem like you don't know if it will happen *or not*. It's possible that it will happen, but it is also possible that it won't happen.

Me: But isn't that sort of implied in the first sentence as well?

Her: Technically yes, but it's just two different ways to say the same meaning. It would be like saying "I don't know if it will rain tomorrow or not" and "It might rain tomorrow."

Me: I feel like that first sentence that you just said would be better written as
"내일 비가 올지 안 올지 모르겠어요."

Her: Ah, yes. I feel like these two sentences mean exactly the same thing:
내일 비가 올지도 모르겠어요
내일 비가 올지 안 올지 모르겠어요.
I feel like the use of ~도 adds that extra nuance that something might happen or not.

After speaking with that person, I discussed this problem with a teacher who teaches Korean grammar to Korean high school students. I can only assume that her understanding of Korean grammar is excellent, although sometimes it is hard for somebody to understand the grammar of their own language. Either way, she cannot speak English and our entire conversation was in Korean. This is how it went:

Me: Explain the difference in nuance that you feel between these three sentences:
내일 비가 올지 모르겠어요
내일 비가 올지도 모르겠어요
내일 비가 올지 안 올지 모르겠어요

Her: The first two sentences are identical. In the third one, you are indicating the two possibilities of "it might rain" or "it might not rain."

Me: I just talked with another Korean person, and she said that the use of "~도" in the second sentence sort of implies those two possibilities as well. She said that the second and third sentences had the same meaning. What do you think about that?

Her: I don't feel that way when I hear it. I feel the first two are the same, and the third one is listing more possibilities.

So here I had two Korean people – one with excellent English and the other with a lot of Korean grammar knowledge, and they gave me opposing answers. My conclusion from this and all of my studying, researching and exposure to the language is:

~ㄹ/을지 모르다 and
~ㄹ/을지도 모르다

Have the same, or effectively the same meaning.

Let me take a minute to explain when you would use ~도 in this case.

~도 is added to uncertain clauses that are conjugated in the future tense to express one's uncertainty of if something will happen in the future (or not). You will typically not see ~도 added to an uncertain clause in the past or present tense *unless* it is being used to have the meaning as discussed in #1 above.

~도 is not added to uncertain clauses where there is a question word in the clause. For example, it would be unnatural to say something like this:
비가 언제 올지도 모르겠어요
This "rule" leads me to believe that the purpose of ~도 is somewhat closer to having the "if or not" meaning as it was described by the English speaking Korean person in our conversation. Just like how adding "or not" would be unnatural to add to the following English sentence, it would be unnatural to add "~도" to its Korean translation:
비가 언제 올지~~도~~ 모르겠어요 = I don't know when it will rain ~~or not~~

Again, this usage is not the usage of ~도 from #1 above. In that usage, ~도 can be added to ~는지, ~았/었는지 or ~ㄹ/을지 to have the meaning that ~도 usually possesses when it is added to nouns. It can also be added to uncertain clauses that have question words. I will discuss this meaning in a future lesson.

Wow. All of that work to understand one syllable.
We're not done yet. That syllable (지) has another meaning… one that is easier to dissect.

I have been doing X for Y – 지

Up to this point, this lesson has explained the meaning of ~는지 as a grammatical principle that is attached to its previous clause. For example:

저는 친구가 어디 가는지 모르겠어요 = I don't know where my friend is going

When ~는지 is added to 가다, notice that there is no space between 가다, ~는 or 지. In this usage, ~지 is not a noun but instead just a part of a larger grammatical principle that can be attached to verbs or adjectives.

지 has another meaning that is completely unrelated to the meaning of ~지 that was described earlier in this lesson. I would like to talk about this other meaning in this lesson as well.

In this other meaning, you will see ~지 used after a verb with ~ㄴ/은 attached to the verb. *Notice that ~ㄴ/은 is the same addition that is added to verbs in the past tense of ~는 것*

For example, you will see:

사귀다 + ㄴ/은 지 = 사귄 지
먹다 + ㄴ/은 지 먹은 지

I want to take a moment to explain what you are seeing here.

Remember that ~ㄴ/은 (just like ~는 in the present tense and ~ㄹ/을 in the future tense) is added to verbs when they will describe an upcoming *noun*. For example:

우리가 먹은 밥 = The food we ate
우리가 먹는 밥 = The food we eat
우리가 먹을 밥 = The food we will eat

In this same respect, 지 is also a *noun*. However, this is the type of noun that I like to call a "pseudo-noun." These are nouns that can be described by a verb (using ~는 것) or by an adjective (just like any other noun), but they can't be used on their own.

You will eventually learn more of these nouns in your Korean studies. Below are some of the pseudo-nouns that you will come across shortly:

적 in ~ㄴ/은 적이 없다 | Introduced in Lesson 32
(For example: 그것을 한 적이 없어요 = I haven't done that)

수 in ~ㄹ/을 수 있다 | Introduced in Lesson 45
(For example: 그것을 할 수 있어요 = I can do that)

줄 in ~ㄹ/을 줄 알다 | Introduced in Lesson 85
(For example: 그것을 할 줄 알아요 = I know how to do that)

Let me explain the situation where you can use the pseudo-noun "지."

Again, when placed after a verb with ~ㄴ/은 attached:

사귄 지
먹은 지

… and when followed by an indication of time:

사귄 지 6 개월
먹은 지 5 분

… and then followed by 되다 conjugated to the past tense:

사귄 지 6 개월 됐다
먹은 지 5 분 됐다

Remember, 지 is officially a noun. Nouns have meaning. The meaning of "지" is the representation of the period of time that has passed since the action took place until the present. To English speakers, it is hard to imagine that a noun represents a figurative period of time like this.

Let's put this construction into a sentence and look at how this could be translated.

여자 친구랑 사귄 지 6 개월 됐어

Possible translations for this could be:
= I have been going out with my girlfriend for six months
= It has been six months since I started/have been going out with my girlfriend

Let's look at another example – specifically one that illustrates the importance of context when understanding these sentences:

밥을 먹은 지 5 분 됐다

Imagine you are eating, and your friend walks into the room and witnesses you eating. If your friend asks "how long have you been eating?" you could respond with:

밥을 먹은 지 5 분 됐다
= I have been eating for five minutes
= It has been five minutes since I started/have been eating

However, imagine you are *not* eating, and your friend walks into the room and witnesses you *not* eating. If your friend asks "how long has it been since you last ate? (How long has it been since you have not been eating?)" you could respond with the same sentence used above. Remember, "지" represents the time period from when the action took place until the present. It's possible that the action is still occurring, but it's also possible that the action has stopped. In the context where the action has stopped, and where one wants to indicate how long it has been since something last occurred; the Korean sentence can be the same as the context where the action is continuing. The Korean sentence may be the same, but the English translation would be different because of this context. For example, in response to your friend asking "how long has it been since you last ate?" you could respond:

밥을 먹은 지 5 분 됐다
= I haven't eaten for five minutes
= It has been five minutes since I last ate

That's the explanation for 지. Before I get into some deeper discussion, let's look at some examples to get you familiar with these types of sentences.

In the example sentences below, the translations are assuming that the action is still occurring, and thus, the speaker is referring to how long it has been since the action started.

한국에서 산 지 25 년 됐어요
= I have been living in Korea for 25 years
= It has been 25 years since I started living in Korea

강아지를 기른 지 10 년 됐어요
= I have been raising a dog for 10 years
= It has been 10 years since I started raising a dog

그 그룹이 훈련을 받은 지 다섯 시간 됐어요
= That group has been receiving training for 5 hours
= It has been 5 hours since that group started receiving training

이 아르바이트를 한 지 2 주일 됐어요
= I've had this part-time job for 2 weeks
= It has been 2 weeks since I started this part-time job

한국에 온 지 2 년 됐어요
= I have been in Korea for 2 years
= It has been 2 years since I came to Korea

Let's discuss some things. I already discussed the idea that "지" in the sentence "밥을 먹은 지 5 분 됐다" can be used to refer to the amount of time that has passed (to the present) since one started eating, or since one finished eating. You would have to rely on context to know specifically which translation would work best.

This possibility of two meanings can only be applied to certain verbs. For example:

밥을 먹은 지 5 분 됐다

This can be used to mean:

= I have been eating for five minutes (in the case that you are currently eating), or
= It has been five minutes since I last ate (in the case that you are currently not eating)

However, let's go back to the first sentence we created using 지:

여자 친구랑 사귄 지 6 개월 됐어

As you have seen, this sentence can be used to have the following meaning:

= It has been six months since I started/have been going out with my girlfriend

For the translation above to work, you would have to still be going out with your girlfriend. However, if you are currently *not* going out with your girlfriend, you would not be able to use this sentence. That is, the sentence above could not translate to "It has been six months since I was going out with my girlfriend." In order to create that sentence, you would have to use the opposite verb, for example:

여자 친구랑 헤어진 지 6 개월 됐어 = It has been six months since I broke up with my girlfriend

Likewise, look at the following sentence with the translations provided:

이제 결혼한 지 1 년 됐어요
= I have been married for one year
= It has been a year since I got married

The sentence above would be used if you are currently married, but *not* if you are not currently married.

In trying to understand which verbs can hold this dual meaning – my brain keeps trying to tell me that it is related to whether or not the verb is able to repeat or continue itself. For example, when you eat, the act of eating is not one instant, and the action continues to progress.

When you exercise, the act of exercising is not one instant, and the action continues to progress. If you are exercising hard and look very sweaty, your friend might ask you "how long has it been since you started exercising?" In response, you could say:

운동한 지 한 시간 됐어요
= I have been exercising for one hour
= It has been one hour since I started exercising

However, if you just came home and threw your exercise bag on the couch, your friend might ask you "how long has it been since you last exercised (or stopped exercising)?" In response, you could again say:

운동한 지 한 시간 됐어요
= I haven't exercised in an hour
= It has been an hour since I stopped exercising

—

When you shower the act of showering is not one instant, and the action continues to progress. If you are in the shower, your friend might ask you "how long it has been since you started showering?" In response, you could say:

샤워한 지 10 분 됐어요
= I have been showering for 10 minutes
= It has been 10 minutes since I started showering

However, if your friend gets a whiff of your armpit and finds it to be very stinky, your friend might ask you "how long has it been since you last showered?" In response, you could again say:

샤워한 지 10 분 됐어요
= I haven't showered in 10 minutes
= It has been 10 minutes since I stopped showering

—

However, some words don't continue to progress. For example, 결혼하다 refers to the act of getting married, not the state of being married. It doesn't start or stop – it just happens. As such, if I were to say:

이제 결혼한 지 1 년 됐어요

You would have to still be married to say that sentence. You never "started" getting married. You never "stopped" getting married. You just got married, and "지" represents the time from that point until the present.

This can also be applied to the word "오다," which you already saw in an example sentence earlier:

한국에 온 지 2 년 됐어요
= I have been in Korea for 2 years
= It has been 2 years since I came to Korea

In this case, 오다 refers to the (completed) action of arriving in Korea. It doesn't start, and it doesn't finish. It just happens, and "지" represents the time from that point to the present. Thus, you would have to still be in Korea to say that sentence.

Another example would be the word "졸업하다" (to graduate):

고등학교를 졸업한 지 1 년 됐어요
= I graduated one year ago
= It has been a year since I graduated

You would have had to have graduated to say that sentence. You never "started" graduating. You never "stopped" graduating. You just graduated, and "지" represents the time from that point until the present.

The good news is – it is never this complicated in real conversations. The only reason why this is getting so complicated is because the sentences I'm providing don't have any context. In everyday conversations, it is much easier to pick up the meaning using other information. In addition, it is also possible to specifically indicate that it has been a certain amount of time since an action finished. In order to do this, you can describe "지" with a negative sentence. For example:

우리가 안 만난 지 2 주일 됐어요 = We haven't met in 2 weeks
밥을 안 먹은 지 아홉 시간 됐어요 = I haven't eaten in nine hours
용돈을 안 받은 지 1 년 됐어요 = I haven't received (an) allowance in a year

―

지 refers to the period of time from when an action occurs until the present. You cannot use 지 to refer to a time that completed some other time in the past. If you want to indicate the period of time that an action occurred in the past, you can use sentences like this:

저는 두 시간 동안 먹었어요 = I ate for two hours

English speakers will quickly point out that "I ate for two hours" and "I had eaten for two hours" do not have exactly the same meanings. Korean people usually don't distinguish between these two meanings in their sentences and instead rely on context to make the specific meaning clear.

You can also use this same type of sentence to ask questions about how long one has been doing something by using 얼마나 or words like 오래. For example:

한국어를 공부한 지 얼마나 되었어요? = How long have you been studying Korean?
운동한 지 오래 됐어? = Have you been exercising for a long time?

It is common to use the construction "얼마 안 되다" to indicate that you haven't been doing something for very long. For example

제가 한국에서 산 지 얼마 안 됐어요 = I haven't been living in Korea for very long
제가 우리 학교에서 일한 지 얼마 안 됐어요 = I haven't been working at our school for very long

You also saw in Lesson 28 that this is one of the acceptable times where ~은 can be added to 있다. For example:

여기에 있은 지 얼마나 되었어요? = How long have you been here for?

That's it for this lesson!

Lesson 31: Adding ~는 것 to 이다

Vocabulary

Nouns:
미소 = smile
배달 = delivery
반지 = ring
입술 = lips
미술 = art
목걸이 = necklace
귀걸이 = earrings
수영복 = bathing suit
간식 = snacks
목표 = goal
숲 = forest
주머니 = pocket
칠판 = blackboard, chalkboard
딸기 = strawberry
상추 = lettuce
공사 = construction
교시 = class, period
종교 = religion
시청 = city hall
동갑 = the same age
긍정적 = positive
부정적 = negative

Verbs:
어울리다 = to get along with
알리다 = to tell, to inform
아끼다 = to cherish, to save
남기다 = to leave something
면도하다 = to shave
빌리다 = to borrow, to lend
샤워하다 = to shower
덮다 = to cover
없어지다 = to disappear
따라가다 = to follow
따라오다 = to be followed
지나가다 = to go and pass by
키우다 = to raise, to train, to develop
참다 = to hold back, to endure
선택하다 = to choose

깨닫다 = to realize
쓰이다 = to be written on

Adjectives:
부럽다 = to be envious

Adverbs and Other Words:
식 = a certain way/method
아까 = earlier
꽉 = tightly

Introduction

I keep saying this, but you have learned a *lot* about using the ~는 것 principle. Don't think that you're out of the woods yet – because there is still a lot to know. In this lesson, you will learn how to use ~는 것 with 이다. Let's get started.

Using ~는 것 with 이다

You've learned a lot about how to add ~는 것 to any verb (and technically adjectives as well by using ~ㄴ/은 것), but you have yet to learn about how to add it to 이다.

You are probably asking yourself: When would I ever want to add ~는 것 to 이다?

(I just want to point out that this is actually the same thing as adding ~ㄴ to "~적이다" words, which you learned in Lesson 16.)

Let's remember what ~는 것 does:

If you want to just say a noun, you can just say a noun. For example:
Person = 사람

If you want to describe that noun, you can use adjectives:
똑똑한 사람 = smart person

Or verbs:
먹고 있는 사람 = the person who is eating

But… now think about this for a second… what if you want to describe a noun with a *noun*? Look at the difference (or similarities) between the three following sentences:

똑똑한 사람 = the smart person (or – person who is smart)
먹고 있는 사람 = the person who is eating
_____ = the person who is a teacher

How would you do that? Remember that 이다 is conjugated as an adjective. Using the ~는 것 principle with 이다 is really no different than adding ~ㄴ/은 to an adjective to describe an upcoming noun. Because 이다 is conjugated as an adjective, the following would not be correct:

선생님이는 남자…

Instead, 이다 gets conjugated as ~인. For example:

[직업이] 선생님인 사람들은 인기가 많아요 = People who[se jobs] are teachers are popular
(It sounds slightly more natural to say "직업이 선생님인 사람들" in this case instead of just "선생님인 사람들." Remember here that the entire clause before "~인" is describing the upcoming noun. In this case, the clause is "직업이 선생님이다" which would unnaturally translate to something like "the job is a teacher". However, when put in the place of describing an upcoming noun, it can translate to "직업이 선생님인 사람들 = people whose jobs are teachers". At any rate, try not to worry about the use of "직업" (as I realize it might be difficult) in that sentence and focus more on the big picture of what adding "~ㄴ" to 이다 accomplishes.

The thing is, as you can see with my big blurb above, this may not be as simple as it should be. Most of the time, there would be a better way - using another word or something to accomplish the same sentence. For example, in the sentence above "직업이 선생님인 사람들은 인기가 많아요", is the meaning not exactly the same (in English) if we just say "Teachers are popular"? For example:

선생님들은 인기가 많아요 = Teachers are popular

Here, we are accomplishing the same thing but don't need to use 이다 as a descriptor in the sentence.

Another great example would be if you wanted to say something like:

"Students who are girls wear skirts"

That would translate to something like:

여자인 학생들은 치마를 입는다

But, that sentence sounds ridiculous (in both English and Korean). In Korean, it would sound much better if you just used the word "여학생", which literally means "female students." For example:

여학생들은 치마를 입는다 = female students wear skirts
(I would much rather say "female students <u>must</u> wear skirts," but you haven't learned how to do that yet, and I try not to use examples that use a concept you haven't learned)

Despite this, there will be some times where you will find the need for using ~는 것 with 이다. Some times this happens when you come across a noun that has the feeling of an adjective. For example, the word "부자" literally means "rich person." In English, if we wanted to say "that person is rich," the word "rich" acts as an adjective. However, in Korean, they would say:

그 사람은 부자야 = That person is (a) rich (person)

Here, 부자 acts as a noun, and the whole sentence is predicated by 이다. In this case, you might find it useful to use 이다 + ~ㄴ to describe an upcoming noun. For example:

내 친구는 부자인 아버지를 자랑했어 = My friend boasted about/was showing off his rich father

Another example using the word "불법" which, as a noun, translates to "illegal":

슬기는 불법인 일을 하고 있어요 = Seulgi is doing something illegal

It is also common to see this form attached to somebody's job title to describe their name. Sort of like saying "He is Rob, the CEO of Samsung". For example:

Titanic 배우인 Leonardo Dicaprio는 잘생겼어요 = Leonardo Dicaprio, who is an actor in Titanic is handsome

At this point, you might be saying "all of this sounds really complicated and I can't even really understand when I would use this form." I agree with you, this looks complicated. The thing is, the foundation of many other (more complicated) grammatical principles have ~는 것 incorporated within them. These grammatical principles, in addition to being able to attach to verbs and adjectives, are able to attach to 이다 as well.

Here are some other sentences using other grammatical principles that you have <u>not</u> learned yet. I'm including these just so you can see that attaching ~ㄴ to 이다 is important to your Korean studies as you progress:

그 사람은 가난한 사람인 것처럼 행동했어요 = That person acted like a poor person
(처럼 is introduced in Lesson 67)

그는 축구선수인 만큼 달리기를 잘해요 = He runs as well as a soccer athlete/player
(만큼 is introduced in Lesson 72)

그 사람이 너의 아버지인 줄 몰랐어요 = I didn't know that person is your father
(줄 is introduced in Lesson 85)

In each case above, ~ㄴ is attached to 이다 to form "인". You can see in each example that "인" is used to describe an upcoming noun. There are many more examples of how 이다 can be used to describe an upcoming noun like this, but I don't need to include them all here, as you will learn about them as they become important.

~는지 is also added to 이다 in this same way. Again, because 이다 acts as an adjective ~ㄴ/은 should be added to it (이다 + ㄴ/은지 will always be ~인지). For example:

그 사람이 선생님인지 모르겠어요 = I don't know if that person is a teacher
그 사람이 선생님인지 아닌지 모르겠어요 = I don't know if that person is a teacher or not
우리가 동갑인지 몰랐어요 = I didn't know that we were the same age
이것이 저의 엄마의 목걸인지 어떻게 알아요? = How do you know that this is my mother's necklace?

Often times 이다 is attached to a question word to predicate a sentence. In this same sense, you will often see ~인지 attached to question words.

For example:

Note that the pairs of sentences below are not dialogues. I organized them this way to show you the similar format that you can see between using ~인지 and using 이다 to predicate a sentence.

비상출구가 어디예요? = Where is the emergency exit?
비상출구가 어디인지 모르겠어요 = I don't know where the emergency exit is

지금 몇 시예요? = What time is it now?
지금 몇 시인지 모르겠어요 = I don't know what time it is now

당신의 목표가 뭐예요? = What is your goal?
저의 목표가 무엇인지 알아요? = Do you know what my goal is?

이 일의 관리자가 누구예요? = Who is the manager of this job?
이 일의 관리자가 누구인지 알아요? = Do you know who the manager of this job is?

가격이 얼마예요? = How much is this?
가격이 얼마인지 모르겠어요 = I don't know how much the price is

It is also possible, as it is with attaching ~는 것 to a verb or ~ㄴ/은 것 to an adjective, to turn an entire clause into a noun, and then predicate the sentence using a verb. Just like how you learned how to write this sentence in Lesson 26:

I am only including the brackets below to show you that we are still using the same basic sentences of subject - object - verb.

저는 (사과)를 원해요 = I want apples
저는 (친구가 사과를 가져오는 것)을 원해요 = I want my friend to bring apples

You can do the same thing but with 이다 here:
내가 (열쇠를 안 가져온 것)을 깨달았어 = I realized that I didn't bring my keys
내 (행동은 실수인 것)을 깨달았어 = I realized that my actions (what I did) is/was a mistake

Lesson 32: For the purpose of: ~려고/~러, To try to: ~아/어 보다 and 적

Vocabulary

Nouns:
기적 = miracle
차량 = vehicle
관객 = audience
치과 = dentistry
공연 = performance, show, concert
업무 = administrative work
탈의실 = change room
표 = ticket
표 = graph, table
간장 = soy sauce
고생 = some sort of hard time or hardship
휴대폰 = cell phone
뜻 = meaning
세일 = sale
이력서 = resume, curriculum vitae
비서 = secretary
연예인 = celebrity
행사 = event, function
일자리 = job position
평일 = a weekday

Verbs:
명령하다 = to order, to command
빼다 = to pull out, to extract
지원하다 = to apply for
신다 = to put on shoes or socks
신기다 = to put shoes or socks on somebody
따르다 = to pour
채우다 = to fill
비우다 = to empty
끊다 = to cut off, to quit something
살리다 = to save (a life)
썰다 = to chop, to slice
예매하다 = to purchase in advance
판단하다 = to judge
해결하다 = to solve, to resolve
구하다 = to search for a worker or job
통제하다 = to control
연락하다 = to contact

예약하다 = to reserve
평가하다 = to evaluate
갈아입다 = to change clothes
끊기다 = to be cut off
막히다 = to be congested

Adjectives:
약하다 = to be weak
자세하다 = to be detailed
취하다 = to be drunk
심심하다 = to be bored

Introduction

In this lesson, you will learn about how to use ~려고 and ~러 in sentences to have the meaning of "for the purpose of/in order to." You will also learn how to add ~어/아 보다 to verbs to have the meaning of "attempt/try to," which is often used with the noun '적'.

With the intention of doing…: ~(으)려고

Adding ~(으)려고 to the stem of the verb gives it the meaning of "with the intention of" or "in order to." ~려고 gets added to stems ending in a vowel and ~으려고 gets added to stems ending in a consonant. For example:

밖에 나가려고… With the intention of going outside/in order to go outside…
그 사람을 살리려고… With the intention of saving that person/in order to save that person

The constructions we have created above are not full sentences – they are just clauses that we can put into sentences. We can create full sentences by adding a clause to the end of them.

For example:
밖에 일찍 나가려고 숙제를 빨리 했어요
= I did my homework fast in order to go out early

저는 신발을 신으려고 잠깐 앉았어요
= I sat down for a minute in order to put on my shoe

The translation of "to", "so that", or "with the intention" are also usually appropriate, as they all describe the same thing. For example:

밖에 일찍 나가려고 숙제를 빨리 했어요
= I did my homework fast so that I could go out early

밖에 일찍 나가려고 숙제를 빨리 했어요
= I did my homework fast to go out early

밖에 일찍 나가려고 숙제를 빨리 했어요
= I did my homework fast with the intention of going out early

Here are many more examples:
저는 그 사람을 살리려고 경찰관을 불렀어요
= I called the police officer in order to save that person

그 문제를 해결하려고 우리는 잠깐 만났어요
= In order to solve that problem, we met for a little bit

그 뜻을 이해하려고 책을 두 번 읽었어요
= In order to understand that meaning, I read the book twice

이렇게 많은 내용을 학생들에게 가르치려고 고생을 많이 했어요
= I worked hard/suffered in order to teach that much content to the students

저는 일을 구하려고 그 회사에 이력서를 냈어요
= I submitted my resume to that company with the intention of getting a job

저는 그 일에 지원하려고 그 회사에 이력서를 냈어요
= I submitted my resume to that company with the intention of applying for that job

학생들을 평가하려고 내일 시험을 볼 거예요
= In order to evaluate the students, they will do an exam tomorrow

You can specifically use ~(으)려고 at the *end* of a sentence when the remainder of that sentence can be assumed. When used like this, it typically indicates what the speaker is just about to do. It is usually used in response to a question. For example:

마트에 갔어요? = Have you gone to the store?/Did you go to the store?
아니요~ 지금 가려고요 = No, but I'm going right now/I'm just about to go
일을 다 했어? = Have you finished the work/Did you finish the work?
지금 하려고 = I'm doing it right now/I'm just about to do it/finish it

Notice that these constructions look like incomplete sentences because ~(으)려고 is usually used between clauses (as you can see in the examples provided earlier in the lesson), and not to end a sentence. However, the language has evolved to allow the above constructions to be correct. Also notice that you can add the honorific "요" to "(으)려고" when used at the end of a sentence to make the sentence more formal.

You will learn many other grammatical principles throughout your Korean studies that typically connect two clauses, but can be used at the end of a sentence like this if the context allows for it. In most of these cases, it is acceptable to attach "요" to make it polite, even though it is not an actual conjugated word.

The clauses that you can add after ~(으)려고 are, for all intents and purposes, endless as long as the situation makes sense. However, one verb that is very commonly used after ~(으)려고 is "노력하다", which means "to put effort into". We will talk about this after our discussion of irregulars.

In Lesson 7, you learned how irregular words change as a result of adding different additions. This is the first time you have been introduced to adding ~(으)려고. Let's look at how irregulars change as a result of adding this grammatical principle.

- The ㅅ irregular, ㄷ irregular and ㅂ irregular all follow the same rules that were introduced in Lesson 7. The addition of the vowel causes a change (or elimination) of the last letter of the stem.

- The ㅡ and 르 irregular are not affected by this addition. The final letter in both types of stems is a vowel, so ~려고 is added instead of ~으려고.

- The purpose of adding ~으려고 to a stem that ends in a consonant, and ~려고 to a stem that ends in a vowel is to make pronunciation easier. For example, it would be difficult to pronounce 받다 (to receive) if ~려고 were attached to it. Therefore, instead of being "받려고" the correct form is "받으려고." However, grammatical principles that start with ㄹ can be added directly to stems that end in ㄹ – and the optional vowel is not used. Therefore, when adding ~(으)려고 to a stem that ends in ㄹ, ~려고 is added directly to the stem. For example:
썰다 + ~(으)려고 = 썰려고

- Adding ~(으)려고 causes a change to ㅎ irregular words. The ㅎ is removed, and ~려고 is added to the stem. Anytime you have the option of adding ~(으) as part of a grammatical addition, the ㅎ will be removed from the stem and the grammatical addition without "으" will be added to the remainder of the stem. For example:
그렇다 + ~(으)려고 = 그러려고

Below is a table showing the changes that result from adding ~(으)려고 to a word.

Irregular	Word	+ ~(으)려고
ㅅ Irregular	짓다 (to build)	지으려고
ㄷ Irregular	걷다 (to walk)	걸으려고
ㅂ Irregular	돕다 (to help)	도우려고
ㅡ Irregular	잠그다 (to lock)	잠그려고
르 Irregular	자르다 (to cut)	자르려고
ㄹ Irregular	살다 (to live)	살려고
ㅎ Irregular	그렇다 (to be like that)	그러려고

You will see these same changes to irregulars anytime you add something that begins in ~(으)ㄹ…. For example:
~(으)라고 (Lesson 54)
~(으)려면 (Lesson 96)

<u>To try to: ~려고 노력하다</u>

If you want to say "I try to ___" you can use the verb 노력하다 after ~(으)려고. For example:

그 친구를 매 주말 만나려고 노력해요 = I try to meet that friend every weekend
한국어를 배우려고 노력하고 있어요 = I am trying to learn Korean

노력하다 itself means to try/put effort into something. So literally, the sentences means

"In order to meet that friend every weekend, I try", and
"In order to learn Korean, I am trying"

But neither of those sentences in English are natural. It is more natural to just say "I try…"

You could also add this to a long line of other words. It's hard to explain, and you would never really need to say something like this, but understanding it will help you with grammar (a little bit). When I first started learning things like this, I always asked how I would say "I think I want to start to try to learn Korean." Perfect sentence, but nobody would ever really say anything that ridiculous. You know everything in that sentence except "I think," so with what you learned today, you should know how to say "I want to start to try to learn Korean:"

한국어를 배운다 = I learn Korean
한국어를 배우려고 노력한다 = I try to learn Korean
한국어를 배우려고 노력하기 시작한다 = I start to try to learn Korean
한국어를 배우려고 노력하기 시작하고 싶다 = I want to start to try to learn Korean

... Heh, like I said – saying something that complex is unnecessary, but understanding it is always good grammar practice.

To Come/Go to... ~(으)러

The clause connector ~(으)러 is very similar to ~(으)려고, but is specifically used when one is "going to" or "coming from" a place in order to do something. To distinguish it from the sentences earlier, these two would not be appropriate:

밖에 일찍 나가러 숙제를 빨리 했어요 = I did my homework fast in order to go out early
저는 신발을 신으러 잠깐 앉았어요 = I sat down for a minute in order to put on my shoe

Instead, ~(으)러 should be used when one is *going to* or *coming from* a place in order to do something. This usually means that the predicating verb of the whole sentence should be either 가다 or 오다, but other variations of those verbs are also acceptable (for example: 내려가다, to go down; 내려오다, to come down; 들어가다, to go in; 들어오다, to come in). Here are some examples:

친구를 만나러 왔어 = I came (here) to meet my friend
공부하러 학교에 가고 있어 = I'm going to school to study
표를 예매하러 극장에 가고 있어요 = I am going to the theater to buy the tickets (in advance)
그 연예인을 보러 행사에 갔어요 = I went to the event to see that celebrity
일자리에 지원하러 왔어요 = I came to apply for that job
옷을 갈아입으러 탈의실에 갔어요 = He went to the change-room to change his clothes
저는 영화를 보러 나가고 싶어요 = I want to go out to see a movie

As you saw before, you cannot use ~(으)러 instead of ~(으)려고.
That is, while this sentence is okay:

밖에 일찍 나가려고 숙제를 빨리 했어요

The following sentence is not correct because it does not use 가다, 오다, or a similar "come/go" verb:
밖에 일찍 나가러 숙제를 빨리 했어요

However, the opposite *can* be done. That is, ~(으)려고 can be used instead of ~(으)러. For example, all of the sentences below are okay:

표를 예매하려고 극장에 가고 있어요
그 연예인을 보려고 행사에 갔어요
일자리에 지원하려고 왔어요
옷을 갈아입으려고 탈의실에 갔어요
심심해서 저는 영화를 보려고 나가고 싶어요

In Lesson 13, you learned about adding ~을/를 위해 to nouns to mean "for." For example:

나는 나의 여자 친구를 위해(서) 꽃을 샀어 = I bought flowers for my girlfriend

You can also use "위해" to say that you do something "for (the purpose of)" a verb. To do this, you attach ~기 위해 to a verb, just like you did with ~(으)러 or ~(으)려고. For example:

친구를 만나기 위해 여기로 왔어 = I came here to meet a friend
친구를 만나러 여기로 왔어 = I came here to meet a friend
친구를 만나려고 여기로 왔어 = I came here to meet a friend

공부하기 위해 학교에 가고 있어 = I'm going to school to study
공부하러 학교에 가고 있어 = I'm going to school to study
공부하려고 학교에 가고 있어 = I'm going to school to study

It is important to notice that in all of these cases the tense is indicated in the final clause of the sentence. That is – no indication of tense is to be made before ~기 위해/~(으)러/~(으)려고. For example, notice how the tense is indicated in the final clause of the following sentences:

친구를 만나러 학교에 갔어요 = I went to school to meet a friend
친구를 만나러 학교에 가고 있어요 = I am going to school to meet a friend
친구를 만나러 학교에 갈 거예요 = I will go to school to meet a friend

공연을 보러 행사에 갔어요 = I went to the event to see the performance
공연을 보러 행사에 가고 있어요 = I am going to the event to see the performance
공연을 보러 행사에 갈 거예요 = I will go to the event to see the performance

Before we finish this lesson, let's look at another grammatical principle that is often translated similarly to the ones above.

<u>To attempt/to try: ~아/어 보다</u>

Adding ~아/어 보다 to the stem of a verb gives it the meaning of "to attempt/try." The translations to English are very similar – if not identical to ~(으)려고/~(으)러/~기 위해 but the meanings are very different. Notice the similarities in the English translations of the following sentences:

나는 밥을 먹으려고 노력했다 = I tried to eat rice
나는 밥을 먹어 봤다 = I tried to eat (the) rice

I would like to describe the meaning of ~아/어 보다 by distinguishing it from the use of "try" in the translation of ~(으)려고/(으)러/기 위해.

나는 밥을 먹으려고 노력했다
Means that you *tried* to eat rice in the sense that you put effort into eating. A less ambiguous (but less natural) translation would be "I put effort into eating the rice."

나는 밥을 먹어 봤어
Means that you tried rice, similar to the meaning that you "tried something out." This meaning is not related to the effort of eating the rice, but instead the experience of the "test" or "trial" or "attempt" of trying the rice. Another good way to translate that sentence would be to say "I gave the rice a try."

It is a little bit confusing at first because the best translations of both sentences above is to use "try," which can be very ambiguous. In my examples below, I prefer to use the simple translation of "try" when using "~아/어 보다" because it is usually the most natural way to express that meaning. When reading the English translations below, keep in mind that the usage of "try" is not related to effort, but instead related to a "trial/test/attempt." Let's look at some examples:

엄마가 요리한 음식을 먹어 봤어? = Did you try the food mom cooked?
결혼하기 위해 남자들을 만나 봤어 = In order to get married, I tried meeting a lot of men
그 신발을 신어 봤어요 = I tried on the shoes
옛날 친구를 연락해 봤어요 = I tried contacting an old friend
그 셔츠를 탈의실에서 입어 봤어요 = I tried on that shirt in the change room
비상출구를 찾아 볼 거예요 = I will look for the emergency exit
그 업무를 처음으로 해 봤어요 = I tried that work for the first time
그 회사에 지원해 볼 거예요 = I am going to try to apply to that company
이력서를 회사에서 일하는 비서에게 줘 봤어요 = I tried giving my resume to the secretary who works at that office

One of the most common usages of ~아/어 보다 is when you are telling somebody to do something. In essence, telling somebody to "try/attempt" something. I have yet to teach you about the imperative mood (this will be discussed in Lesson 40), so you won't understand these example sentences completely. Regardless, examine the following example sentences to try to understand how ~아/어 보다 is being used.

그것을 확인해 봐!! = Check that! (Try checking that!)
이것을 먹어 봐! = Eat this! (Try eating this!)
여기 와 보세요 = Come here (Try coming here)
지금 앉아 봐 = Sit down (Try sitting down)
문을 열어 봐 = Open the door (Try opening the door)
먼저 가 봐 = Go first (Try going first)
이거를 봐 봐 = Look at this (Try looking at this)
이것을 드셔 보세요 = Eat this (Try eating this)
이 차를 마셔 보세요 = Drink this tea (Try drinking this tea)

Another common usage of the ~아/어 보다 grammatical form is used in conjunction with the pseudo-noun 적, which we will talk about next.

The noun of experience: 적

In Lesson 30, you learned about the pseudo-noun '지.' For example:

밥을 먹은 지 5 분 됐다 = I have been eating for 5 minutes

In that lesson, you learned that 지 is one of a handful of nouns that have no meaning when used on their own. However, when used in connection with a describing verb or adjective, they have a special meaning.

"적" is another one of these nouns which cannot be used on its own. However, if you add ~ㄴ/은 to a verb stem and place 적 after ~ㄴ/은, "적" has the meaning of "experience." Notice that ~ㄴ/은 is the same addition that is added to verbs when the past-tense form of ~는 것 is added.

So, let's go through this step by step. First, you need a verb: 먹다
- Add ~ㄴ/은 to the verb stem. ~은 gets added to words ending in a consonant, ~ㄴ gets added directly to words ending in a vowel: So we get: 먹은
- Add 적: 먹은 적

If I were to say:
김치를 먹은 적

It would mean "the experience of eating kimchi." Remember that '적' is a noun that means 'experience' when used this way.

But, you can't end sentences with nouns, so you need to finish the sentence with 있다 or 없다 to mean "to have the experience of eating kimchi" or "to not have the experience of eating kimchi."

For example:
김치를 먹은 적이 없어요 = I don't have the experience of eating kimchi…
… which is translated naturally to "I have never eaten kimchi"

Here are many more examples:

거기에 간 적이 없어요 = I have never gone/been there/I haven't been there
그 여자를 만난 적이 없어요 = I have never met that girl/I haven't met that girl
연예인을 만난 적이 없어요 = I have never met anybody famous
이런 업무를 한 적이 없어요 = I have never done this type of work before

이런 공연을 평일에 본 적이 없어요 = I have never seen a performance like this on a weekday
그 영화를 본 적이 있어요? = Have you seen that movie?

Because 적 refers to an experience, it is common to attach ~아/어 보다 to the preceding verb to indicate that the particular experience was "tried/attempted."

거기에 가 본 적이 없어요 = I have never been there (tried going there)
그 여자를 만나 본 적이 없어요 = I have never met that girl (tried meeting her)
저는 치과에 가 본 적이 없어요 = I have never (tried going to) been to the dentist
이력서를 만들어 본 적이 없어요 = I have never tried making a resume before
그 영화를 봐 본 적이 있어요? = Have you tried seeing that that movie?

Notice that even in the final example, the word 보다 (to see/watch) is not the same as the 보다 in the ~아/어 보다 grammatical principle. Therefore, it is not unnatural to say 보다 twice in a row.

Lesson 33: The special noun of: 중

Vocabulary

Nouns:
장면 = movie scene
냄비 = pot, pan
모습 = one's figure, appearance
수표 = cheque
자 = ruler
지우개 = eraser
지리 = geography
태극기 = the Korean flag
국기 = flag
가구 = furniture
미팅 = a kind of group blind date
강의 = lecture
전원 = electricity, power
프린터 = printer
집값 = price of houses
변명 = excuse
규칙 = rule, regulation
주름 = wrinkle
마늘 = garlic
교환학생 = exchange student
상가 = a building with a bunch of stores in it
계약 = contract
웃음 = laughter, smile
학기 = semester
외모 = a person's outside appearance
제한 = limit, restriction
무제한 = something without limit
현금 = cash
물고기 = fish
오랫동안 = for a long time
그중 = of those things
감정적 = emotional

Verbs:
상담하다 = to consult
높이다 = to heighten, to increase
올리다 = to raise, to lift, to increase
편집하다 = to edit
촬영하다 = to film

보관하다 = to store
복구하다 = to restore, recover
보증하다 = to guarantee

Adjectives:
민감하다 = to be sensitive
상하다 = to be hurt, to be damaged
옳다 = to be right, to be proper, to be correct

Adverbs and Other Words:
원래 = originally
짜리 = the one worth…
일부러 = on purpose

Introduction

In this lesson, you will learn how to use 중 in Korean. By itself, it has a meaning of "middle" but it is never really used on its own. Combined with other words or grammatical principles, this one word can have a lot of meanings – most of them similar to the meaning "middle." The Chinese (Hanja) character for this word is one of the easiest to know and recognize, as it is one of the few characters where the character actually represents the meaning of the word: 中 (the strike down the "middle"). Let's look at how we can use 중 in Korean.

Present Progressive: ~는 중

중 is a noun, which means it can replace 것 in the ~는 것 principle. When this is done, it gives the sentence the meaning of "I am …ing… (I am in the middle of)." For example:

나는 먹는 중
나는 공부하는 중

Notice however, that 중 is a noun – and you can't just end a sentence with a noun like that. Therefore, if you want to make those sentences perfect, you need to conjugate the noun using 이다. For example:

나는 먹는 중이야 = I am eating
나는 공부하는 중이야 = I am studying

Notice that these sentences would have the same meaning if ~고 있다 (which you learned in Lesson 18) was used instead. For example:

나는 먹고 있어 = I am eating
나는 공부하고 있어 = I am studying

Below are many more examples:

우리는 그 감정적인 장면을 촬영하는 중이에요 = We are filming that emotional scene now
아저씨가 프린터를 복구하는 중이에요 = The man is restoring the printer
제 모습을 거울에서 보는 중이에요 = I'm looking at myself (my appearance) in the mirror
오빠가 미팅을 하는 중이에요 = My brother is on a "meeting" (a group blind date)
저는 그 동영상을 지금 편집하는 중이에요 = I am editing that video now
제 삶에서 옳은 길을 찾는 중이에요 = I'm looking for the right path in my life
제가 아주 중요한 규칙을 설명하는 중이에요 = I am explaining a very important rule

Sometimes you will see "중" being used immediately after the noun form of a verb without the use of ~는 것. The nouns used in these situations are usually ~하다 nouns (that is, verbs that we can remove ~하다 from to form nouns). For example:

나는 공부 중이야 = I am studying
저는 생각 중이에요 = I am thinking

Many more examples:

그 상가가 지금 공사 중이에요 = That building is under construction
모든 선생님들은 회의 중이에요 = All the teachers are in a meeting
그 선생님은 강의 중이에요 = That teacher is giving a lecture
의사가 환자랑 상담 중이에요 = The doctor is having a consultation with a patient
저는 가구를 다 보관 중이에요 = I'm storing all of my furniture

It is common to see this usage of "중" on signs that inform people what is happening in a certain place.

For example, outside of a construction site, you might see a sign that says:
공사 중 = Under construction

Outside of a classroom in a University, you might see a sign that says:
강의 중 = Class in progress, or
수업 중 = Class in progress

Outside of a doctor's office or some other business office where people need "consulting" you might see a sign that says:
상담 중 = Consultation in progress

Outside of an office meeting room, you might see a sign that says:
회의 중 = Meeting in progress

Outside a set for a TV show or movie, you might see a sign that says:
촬영 중 = Filming in progress

Before you learn more about how to use 중, let's first look at how you can use ~는 동안.

While … : ~는 동안

You learned in Lesson 11 that you can place 동안 after a unit of time to describe the duration of that time. The usual translation for that usage is "for." For example:

저는 10분 동안 걸었어요 = I walked for 10 minutes
저는 30분 동안 공부했어요 = I studied for 30 minutes

You can also place 동안 as the noun in ~는 것, similar to how you use 중 in this situation. When used like this, the second action occurs "during" the duration of the first action. This usually translates to "while …" For example:

저는 집에 가는 동안 친구랑 얘기했어요 = I talked with a friend while I walked home

You typically won't see verbs that happen instantly (and don't continue) used before ~는 동안. For example, when you study, that action continues for a long time, and other actions could happen "while" you are studying. However, you wouldn't usually see something like:

내가 일어나는 동안… = While I was standing up…

The action of "standing up" occurs almost instantly and it is rare for other actions to occur while "standing up" occurs. Below are many more examples:

저는 수학을 공부하는 동안 연필과 자와 지우개를 다 썼어요
= I used a pencil, eraser and a ruler while I was studying

아줌마가 말을 하는 동안 저는 그 아줌마의 주름을 쳐다봤어요
= I was staring at the older lady's wrinkles while she was talking

종업원이 보증 기간에 대해 설명을 하는 동안 저는 그 종업원의 말을 듣고 있지 않았어요
= I wasn't listening when the worker was explaining about the warranty period
핸드폰에 전원이 꺼져 있는 동안 전화를 받지 못했어요
= While (the power on) my phone was turned off, I couldn't answer my phone

그 남자의 모습을 보는 동안 웃음을 참지 못했어요
= While looking at that man's appearance I couldn't keep from laughing

내가 밥을 먹는 동안 열쇠를 잊어버린 것을 깨달았어
= While I was eating I realized that I forgot my keys

영화를 보는 동안 다른 사람들이 너무 시끄러웠어요
= While I was watching the movie, the other people were really loud

Pretty simple grammatical principle that can be used in a lot of applications. Now that you know that, let's move on to learn more about 중.

Of/Among…:중에

In this usage, 중 is placed after a list of two or more things. For example:

밥과 빵 중에

It could also be placed after one noun that *represents* two or more nouns. For example:

나의 남동생 세 명 중에…
나의 친구들 중에…

Placing 중에 after some representation of two or more things, you can create the meaning of "of (those things)" or "among/between (those things)." For example:

밥과 빵 중에 = Between rice and bread…
나의 남동생 세 명 중에… = Among/of my three younger brothers
나의 친구들 중에… = Among/of my friends

Notice the meaning of these constructions. The examples above are not complete, but you can fill in the latter part of the sentences as you please. The latter part of the sentence usually describes something about *one* of those things. For example:

밥과 빵 중에 밥이 더 맛있어요
= Between rice and bread, rice is more delicious

나의 남동생 세 명 중에 그는 가장 똑똑해
= Of all my younger brothers, he is the smartest

나의 친구들 중에 나는 슬기를 가장 좋아해
= Of all my friends, I like Seulgi the most

It is slightly easier to grasp the meaning of this concept if you remember the meaning of "중" is "middle." Essentially, by making these sentences, you are saying "in the middle of all my friends." Heh, not sure if that helps you, but it helped me understand it.

Many more examples:

수업 중에 지리 수업을 제일 좋아해요 = Of all classes, I like Geography the most
남자와 여자 중에 여자들이 감정에 더 민감해요 = Between boys and girls, girls are more sensitive
이 두 계약 중에 이 계약이 나아요 = Between these two contracts, this one is better
모든 프린터 중에 이것이 제일 싸요 = Among all the printers, this one is the cheapest
우리 중에 누가 제일 잘생겼어요? = Who is the most handsome among us?

부산과 서울 중에 어디 가고 싶어요? = Where do you want to go between Seoul and Busan?
제가 받은 요청 중에 그 요청이 제일 이상해요 = Of all the requests that I've received, that one is the strangest

(Notice in the first example that the noun "수업" is singular. When followed by "중에," it can be assumed that you are talking about more than one thing because "중에" always refers to more than one thing.)

The structure of sentences where "중에" is placed after a simple noun (as shown in the examples above) is very easy. However, "중에" can also be placed after nouns that have been created through the use of ~는 것. For example:

모든 영화 중에.. would mean "of all the movies…"

But if you wanted to specifically say "of all the movies (that) I have seen," you need to use the ~는 것 principle to describe 영화. For example:

내가 본 영화 = The movie I saw/The movies I have seen
내가 본 영화 중에… of all the movies I have seen

With people, as was described earlier, you use a simple noun, like this:

나의 친구들 중에 = Of all my friends…

You could also use the ~는 것 principle to express "Of all my friends (that) I have…" In these cases, you shouldn't use 있다 to talk about people – because you can't really "possess" friends. When you want to express "Of all my friends (that) I have…" you should use 만나다 to change the meaning to "Of all the friends (that) I have met…"

내가 있는 친구들 중에 – incorrect
내가 만난 친구들 중에 = Of all the friends I have met (of all the friends I have)
내가 만난 친구들 중에 너는 내가 가장 좋아하는 친구야
= Of all of my friends (that I have met), you are my favorite

When talking about places you have gone, or things you have eaten or tried, ~아/어 보다 (which you learned about in Lesson 32) is usually attached to the verb before 중에.

For example:

내가 먹어 본 음식 중에… = Of all the food I have eaten…
내가 가 본 곳 중에… = Of all the places I have been…

Below are many examples:

내가 가지고 있는 펜 중에 이것은 가장 좋아
= Of all the pens I have, this one is the best

내가 가 본 곳 중에 미국은 가장 무서웠어
= Of all the places I've been, the US was the scariest

내가 한국에서 먹어 본 것 중에 제일 맛있는 것은 떡볶이였어
= Of all the things that I have (tried) eating in in Korea, the most delicious thing was 떡볶이

Often times the choices/options are given in a previous sentence and they are being referred to in a different sentence or clause. When this is the case, you can use "그중에" to mean "among/between those things previously mentioned." For example:

바나나와 사과를 샀어요. 그중에 어떤 것을 먹고 싶어요?
= I bought bananas and apples. Between those two, which one do you want to eat?

In Lesson 22 you learned how to ask questions using 어떤 and 어느. Specifically, you learned that these words are often used when the listener has a list of options to choose from when answering. For example:

어떤 치마를 샀어요? = Which skirt did you buy?
어느 치마를 샀어요? = Which skirt did you buy?

어떤 것을 먹고 싶어요? = Which (thing) do you want to eat?
어느 것을 먹고 싶어요? = Which (thing) do you want to eat?

In the examples above, the options that the listener has would have to be assumed from context. However, we can use 중에 to give the listener options. For example:

이 치마와 저 치마 중에 어떤 치마를 샀어요?
이 치마와 저 치마 중에 어느 치마를 샀어요?
= Between this skirt and that skirt, which one did you buy?

빵과 밥 중에 어떤 것을 먹고 싶어요?
빵과 밥 중에 어느 것을 먹고 싶어요?
= Between bread and rice, which one do you want to eat?
Other examples:

캐나다 국기와 태극기 중에 어떤 국기가 더 예뻐요?
캐나다 국기와 태극기 중에 어느 국기가 더 예뻐요?
= Between the Canadian flag and the Korean flag, which flag is more pretty?
(Which one is prettier? The Canadian or Korean flag?)

지리와 수학 중에 어떤 수업이 더 힘들어요?
지리와 수학 중에 어느 수업이 더 힘들어요?
= Between Geography and Math, which class is more difficult?
(Which is more difficult? Geography or Math class?)

현금과 수표 중에 어떤 것이 나아요?
현금과 수표 중에 어느 것이 나아요?
Between cash and a cheque, which one is better?
(Which is better? Cash or cheque?)

천만 원짜리 차와 천오백만 원짜리 차 중에 어떤 것을 더 좋아했어요?
천만 원짜리 차와 천오백만 원짜리 차 중에 어느 것을 더 좋아했어요?
= Between the 15,000,000 won car and 10,000,000 won cars, which one did you like more?
(Which did you like more? The 15,000,000 won car or the 10,000,000 won car?)

<u>By sometime: 중</u>

중 can also be used to indicate a limit of time for when some action will be done by. This is probably the most advanced usages of 중, but it is still good to know at this point. It is typically placed after an indication of time with "으로" attached to 중. For example:

저는 그것을 내일 중으로 다 할 거예요 = I will do all of it by tomorrow

When used like this, the exact time that the action will be done is ambiguous, so it is common to use the word "sometime" in the translation:

저는 그것을 내일 중으로 다 할 거예요 = I will do all of it by sometime tomorrow

Other examples:

그 장면 촬영을 내일 중으로 끝낼 거예요
= We will finish the filming of that scene by sometime tomorrow

보증 기간은 다음 달 중으로 끝날 거예요
= The warranty period will finish by sometime next month

우리가 편집을 원래 내일 중으로 다 하고 싶었어요
= We originally wanted to do all of the editing by sometime tomorrow

Lessons 26 – 33 Mini-Test

All finished Lessons 26 – 33? Now it is time to test yourself on what you learned in those lessons! Before moving on to our next set of lessons, try to make sure you can understand all the concepts covered here. Good luck!

The answers are at the bottom of the test!

1) In which example is ~는 것 being used incorrectly:

a) 한국에서 사는 것을 좋아해요
b) 아이가 슬프는 것을 보고 있어요
c) 아빠가 사과를 사는 것을 원해요
d) 영화를 보는 것을 좋아해요

2) Which of the following nouns is being described as a noun in the future tense?

a) 먹을 음식
b) 먹은 음식
c) 먹는 음식
d) 먹던 음식

3) Which irregular is being used correctly?

a) 이 집을 짓은 사람은 똑똑해요
b) 어제 팔은 것은 뭐예요?
c) 문을 열을 거예요
d) 이것을 만든 사람은 누구에요?

4) Which of the following describes that you have been living in Korea for 4 months?

a) 한국에서 작년에 사 개월 동안 살았어요
b) 한국에 산 지 네 달 됐어요
c) 한국에 사 개월 후에 갈지 몰라요
d) 한국에 네 달 안에 갈 거예요

101

5) Which of the following would be incorrect:

a) 그것은 옛날에 신었던 신발이에요
b) 그 신발을 신어 보고 싶어요
c) 그 신발을 신는 적이 없어요
d) 지금 신발을 신으려고요

6) Which of the following describes that you went to school yesterday to meet a teacher?

a) 선생님을 만나러 학교에 갔어요
b) 선생님에게 책을 주러 학교에 갔어요
c) 선생님을 만나려고 식당에 갔어요
d) 공부하러 학교에 갔어요

7) Which have you never tried before?

김치를 먹은 적이 없어
떡뽁이를 먹어 본 적이 있어

a) 김치
b) 떡복이
c) 김치랑 떡복이
d) 다 먹은 적이 있다

8) Which of the following has the same meaning of

'공부하러 학교에 가고 있다'

a) 공부를 해 본 적이 있는 것 중에 이것은 가장 어려워요
b) 학교에서 공부하는 중이에요
c) 공부를 학교에서 할 것이다
d) 공부를 하려고 학교에 가는 중이다

The answers are on the next page!

ANSWERS:

1) B
2) A
3) D
4) B
5) C
6) A
7) A
8) D

Lesson 34: Explanations of difficult words

Introduction

This lesson is focused entirely on difficult vocabulary. I will teach you some words that need to be explained before we can move on to more complex grammar. First, let's look at the vocabulary I want you to know:

흔들다 = to shake
흔들거리다 = to be shaking
머뭇거리다 = to hesitate
반짝거리다 = to be shiny
두리번거리다 = to look around
끈적거리다 = to be sticky
출렁거리다 = to be sloshing, to be rocking
자기 = him or her
자신 = oneself
아직 = still, yet
여전히 = still
별로 = not very
전혀 = not at all
훨씬 = much more
관하다 = related to, regarding
관련하다 = related to, regarding
주위 = around the circumference
일단 = once, first, for now
무게 = weight
몸무게 = body weight
살 = flesh, weight
찌다 = to gain weight
빠지다 = to lose weight

Let's look at each word (or groups of words) individually.

~거리다

You will sometimes see "~거리다" at the end of words. For example:

흔들거리다 = to be shaking
머뭇거리다 = to hesitate
반짝거리다 = to be shiny
두리번거리다 = to look around
끈적거리다 = to be sticky
출렁거리다 = to be sloshing/rocking

Some of these words have meaning without ~거리다 attached, or can be used in another form. For example, 흔들다 means "to shake/swing/wave." What meaning could ~거리다 have?

When a word ends in ~거리다, it means that whatever is being done, it is being done repeatedly – in a stopping and starting fashion. For example:

흔들다 = to shake
흔들거리다 = to be repeatedly shaking

Note that you can't just add ~거리다 to every word to give it the meaning of 'being repeated.' Only certain words can use this ending, so I don't recommend adding ~거리다 to random words if you haven't learned that it can specifically be used like that.

In addition, some words only end in ~거리다. That is, other than their ~거리다 form, there is no other way that they can be used. For example:

머뭇거리다 = to repeatedly hesitate
두리번거리다 = to repeatedly look around.

While 머뭇거리다 and 두리번거리다 are words, "머뭇다" and "두리번다" are not words.

The idea of ~거리다 adding the feeling of a "repeated action" doesn't always work in my brain. I feel that it doesn't do the translation or feeling of ~거리다 justice sometimes. I've noticed that ~거리다 is often added to words that indicates one's perception or feeling and where expressing this exact feeling is difficult. For example, if you touched something gooey and it was all gross and "sticky," you could use the word "끈적거리다" to express this feeling. The stickiness is not really repeating – it's more of a weird feeling that I can't describe. Sometimes you will come across words ending in ~거리다 where the translation is more about a strange feeling or perception than an action that repeats itself. In times like these, I like adding the English word "all" to the sentence to express this strange feeling. For example:

"I touched that goo and it was all sticky."

Below are some example sentences with words using ~거리다. Note that there are other words that end in ~거리다 that are not included in the vocabulary list above. Most words using ~거리다 are quite difficult, and the purpose of this lesson is not to introduce you to every word where you can see ~거리다. Rather, the purpose of this lesson is to introduce you to the general meaning/feeling of ~거리다 to allow you to understand its usage when you see it used on words during your studies.

It is also important to note that all words ending in ~거리다 are verbs and therefore must be conjugated as such. Many of these words inherently feel like adjectives, so it is strange at first to consider them verbs. For example, "끈적거리다" is a verb, but it typically translates to the adjective "to be sticky" in English.
Below are some examples:

우리는 흔들거리는 다리를 건넜어요
= We crossed the wobbly bridge (the bridge that keeps shaking, the shaky bridge)

남자가 여자와 얘기하는 것을 머뭇거렸어요
= The man kept hesitating to talk with the girl

사고가 난 후에 차를 다시 운전하는 것을 머뭇거렸어요
= I (continually) hesitated about driving again after the accident

반짝거리는 목걸이를 하고 있었어요
= She was wearing a shiny/sparkly necklace

별이 밤에 하늘에서 반짝거려요
= The stars shine/sparkle in the sky at night

열쇠를 찾으려고 방을 두리번거렸어요
= I looked around the room to find my keys

땀이 나고 나서 몸이 아주 끈적거려요
= After sweating, my body is all sticky

바다에서 물이 출렁거렸어요
= The water rocked back and forth in the ocean

It is common to see words with ~거리다 used in literature where the author wants to describe a certain feeling through language. For example, the sentence immediately above could be translated to "the water rocked back and forth." However, it could also be translated to "the water *sloshed* back and forth in the ocean." The word "slosh" gives me a more descriptive feeling and image of the water. In Korean, these ~거리다 words often give sentences a more descriptive feeling and image.

자기 and 자신

When referring to somebody in the third person, you can use words like "he," "she," or "that person." For example:

그는 한국을 좋아해요 = He likes Korea
그녀는 한국을 좋아해요 = She likes Korea
그 사람은 한국을 좋아해요 = That person likes Korea

자기 is usually used in sentences when a person has already been mentioned, and is being mentioned again. For example, in the sentence:

"He likes his appearance."

You could write that sentence like this:
그는 그의 외모를 좋아해요

However, it could also be written like this:
그는 자기(의) 외모를 좋아해요 = He likes his appearance

Here, you can use 자기 to replace the person you are talking about the *second* time you mention that person. Below are many more examples. I have bolded the word "자기" and its translation to make it clear what "자기" translates to.

우리 아들은 **자기(의)** 일을 항상 혼자 하고 싶어요
= Our son always wants to do **his** work alone

저의 아내는 **자기**가 요리한 것을 보통 안 먹어요
= My wife usually doesn't eat the food **she** cooks

우리 아들은 **자기** 건강에 대해 의사와 상담을 했어요
= Our son consulted with a doctor about **his** health

여자가 변한 **자기** 모습을 보고 실망했어요
= The girl looked at **her** changed appearance and was disappointed

----

In the example sentences above using "자기," some person is being referred to twice in the same sentence. Although this person is mentioned twice, the person is not the subject *and* the object of the sentence. For example:

우리 아들은 **자기(의)** 일을 항상 혼자 하고 싶어요
The subject is "our son." The object is "his work."

저의 아내는 **자기**가 요리한 것을 보통 안 먹어요
The subject is "my wife." The object is "the food (she cooks)."

When one person is both the subject *and* the object of a sentence, the word "자신" is used as the object. The translation of 자신 to English depends on who the person is, but the basic form you will see is "oneself." Depending on the person, the translation would be:

Myself
Yourself
Himself
Herself
Themselves

For example:

저는 자신을 안 믿어요 = I don't trust myself
너는 자신을 안 믿어? = You don't trust yourself?
그는 자신을 안 믿어요 = He doesn't trust himself
그녀는 자신을 안 믿어요 = She doesn't trust herself
그들은 자신을 안 믿어요 = They don't trust themselves

It is common to place the following words before 자신:

나/내/저/제 if the subject is "I"
너/네 if the subject is "you"
그/그녀/자기 if the subject is "him" or "her"
그들 if the subject is "they"

For example:

저는 제 자신을 안 믿어요 = I don't trust myself
너는 네 자신을 안 믿어? = You don't trust yourself?
그는 자기 자신을 안 믿어요 = He doesn't trust himself
그녀는 자기 자신을 안 믿어요 = She doesn't trust herself
그들은 그들 자신을 안 믿어요 = They don't trust themselves

We also see these translations when the person is the subject *and* also placed before ~에 대해 or ~에게 in a sentence. For example:

자신에 대해 = about oneself
자신에게 = to oneself

Below are many examples showing the use of 자신:

청소년들은 그들 자신을 사랑하지 않아요
= Young people don't love themselves

그 학생은 자기 자신에게 자꾸 변명을 해요
= That student always makes excuses to/for himself

저도 제 자신을 몰라요
= Even I don't know myself

저는 제 자신에게 그런 말을 많이 했어요
= I said that (type of thing) to myself many times

그 남자가 수업 시간 동안 자기 자신에게 말을 해요
= That boy talks to himself during class

저는 한국에서 제 자신에 대해 많이 배웠어요
= I learned a lot about myself in Korea

그는 자기 자신에 대해 아무 것도 알고 있지 않아요
= He doesn't know anything about himself

Still - 아직

When used in the present tense, 아직 translates to "still." For example:

저는 아직 기다리고 있어요 = I am still waiting
학생들은 그 선생님을 아직 좋아해요? = Do students still like that teacher?
불이 아직 켜져 있어요 = The light is still on
그 상가가 그 길에 아직 있어요 = That building is still on that street
저는 주름이 아직 많아요 = I still have a lot of wrinkles
저는 한국에 아직 간 적이 없어요 = I still haven't been to Korea

When used in the past tense, it is typically used in negative sentences to indicate that something still hasn't happened. For example:

보증 기간이 아직 안 지났어요 = The warranty period still hasn't passed
수표를 아직 안 받았어요 = I still haven't received the cheque
우리는 그 문제를 아직 해결하지 못했어요 = We still haven't resolved that problem
새로운 휴대폰을 아직 안 샀어요 = I still haven't bought a new phone
우리는 4 번출구를 아직 찾지 못했어요 = We still haven't found exit 4

When used like this, the word "yet" can also be used in the translation. For example:

보증 기간이 아직 안 지났어요 = The warranty period hasn't passed yet
수표를 아직 안 받았어요 = I haven't received the cheque yet
우리는 그 문제를 아직 해결하지 못했어요 = We haven't resolved that problem yet
새로운 휴대폰을 아직 안 샀어요 = I haven't bought a new phone yet
우리는 4번출구를 아직 찾지 못했어요 = We haven't found exit 4 yet

If somebody asks you if you have done something, you can respond with "아직…. 안 했어요." For example:

Person 1: 일을 다 했어요? = Have you done all the work yet?
Person 2: 아직 안 했어요 = I haven't done it yet/I still haven't done it

In these cases, it is common to simplify the sentence and just use "아직" as the answer (~요 can be added in formal situations). For example:

Person 1: 일을 다 했어요? = Have you done all the work yet?
Person 2: 아직요… = Not yet

Above, notice how *only* "아직" is being used (which translates to "yet") and how the English translation includes both "yet" *and* "not." This difference often causes Korean people to make mistakes when saying this type of sentence in English. For example, a conversation with a Korean person (in English) might go like this:
English speaker: Did you do the work yet?
Korean speaker: Yet

Particles ~도 and ~은 can be attached to 아직 to create a more complex meaning of the word "still." The word 여전히 also translates to "still." The following can be very confusing:

아직도 = still
아직은 = still
여전히 = still

I'll explain the subtle nuisances between each one:

<u>아직도</u> is used when you are emphasizing that something is *still* the case – but it shouldn't be. For example:

저는 운동을 아직도 하지 않았어요 = I *still* haven't exercised
(Putting emphasis on "still" meaning that you still haven't exercised – but should have by now)

머리가 아직도 아파요 = My head *still* hurts
(Putting emphasis on "still" meaning that your head *still* hurts, but shouldn't anymore)

아직은 is used when you are saying that something hasn't happened yet, but it will happen soon (or vice-versa). Here, the comparison function of ~은 is used to compare the present (where something has or hasn't happened) with the future (where the opposite will happen). For example:

저는 운동을 아직은 하지 않았어요 = I still haven't exercised
(Indicating that I haven't exercised, but I will exercise shortly)

저는 아직은 공부를 하고 있어요 = I am still studying
(Indicating that I am studying, but I will finish [and therefore won't be studying] shortly)

여전히 is used when the action that is still being done/still hasn't been done will continue into the foreseeable future. For example:

저는 운동을 여전히 하지 않았어요 = I still haven't exercised
(Indicating that you haven't exercised, and you have no plans to exercise soon)

저는 그 여자를 여전히 좋아해요 = I still like that girl
(Indicating that you still like that girl, and will continue to like her)

Honestly, this is more confusing than it needs to be. In most situations, simply using "아직" is sufficient. However, if you ever wanted to be more specific, you could use 아직도, 아직은 or 여전히. It helps if you understand the meanings of ~도 and ~은 on their own to extrapolate how they can be applied to 아직.

Words that need negative endings

In Lesson 25, you learned about using 아무도, 아무 것도, 아무 데도 and 아무 때도. In that lesson, you learned that sentences containing those words should have a negative conjugation. For example, instead of saying:

아무도 나를 좋아해 (incorrect)

You would have to write:
아무도 나를 좋아하**지 않아** or 아무도 나를 **안** 좋아해 = Nobody likes me

There are a handful of other words that require this negative ending. I would like to introduce you to 별로 and 전혀.

별로 and 전혀 both have very similar meanings – but 전혀 is more extreme. 별로 has the meaning of "really" or "that" in these types of sentences:

I'm not **really/that** hungry
I don't **really** want to go
He's not **that** handsome

To say those sentences in Korean, you can use 별로 as an adverb within the sentence, and then finish the sentence with a negative conjugation.

For example:

나는 별로 배고프지 않아 = I'm not really hungry
나는 밖에 별로 나가고 싶지 않아 = I don't really want to go outside
그는 별로 잘생기지 않았다 = He's not that handsome

You should know by now that 이다 usually does not attach to adverbs. 별로 is an exception, as it is very common for Korean people to use this construction to describe their indifference towards something. The most common way you would hear this is in response to a question. For example:

A: 밥은 맛있어? = Is the food delicious?
B: 별로야 = Meh, not really

A: 이 바지는 마음에 들어? = Do you like these pants?
B: 별로야 = Meh, not really

If it is being used in a formal setting, it is more common to just attach "요" to it:

A: 홍콩에 가고 싶어요? = Do you want to go to Hong Kong?
B: 별로요 = Meh, not really

It can also be used in the past tense. In these cases, the past tense conjugation of 이다 is used for both formal and informal situations. For example:

A: 점심을 먹었어요? 어땠어요? = Did you have lunch? How was it?
B: 별로였어요 = Meh, it wasn't that good

A: 그 남자를 만났어? 잘생겼어? = Did you meet that man? Was he handsome?
B: 아니. 별로였어 = Nah, not really.

It can also be used immediately after a noun, almost as if it were an adjective. This allows it to be used by a speaker even if there was not a soliciting question. For example:
우리가 먹었던 피자가 별로였어 = The pizza we ate wasn't that good

This sentence is essentially the same as:
우리가 먹었던 피자가 별로 맛있지 않았어 = The pizza we ate wasn't that delicious

The difference is that using "별로이다" in these cases is colloquial and common in speech.

전혀 has a similar meaning, but it is more extreme. 전혀 has the meaning of "at all" in the following sentences:

I'm not hungry **at all**
I don't want to go outside **at all**
He's not handsome **at all**

For example:

나는 전혀 배고프지 않아 = I'm not hungry at all
나는 밖에 전혀 나가고 싶지 않아 = I don't want to go outside at all
그는 전혀 잘생기지 않았다 = He's not handsome at all

Another way to express a similar meaning to 전혀 is to attach ~도 to 하나. Like 별로 and 전혀, this is commonly used in negative sentences. Technically, this would translate to something like "not even one," for example:

저는 친구가 하나도 없어요 = I don't even have one friend
저는 사진을 하나도 안 찍었어요 = I didn't even take one picture
그 할아버지는 주름이 하나도 없어요 = That grandfather doesn't even have one wrinkle

However, even though the word "하나" is used, it can be used even in situations where nothing is countable. In this case, it is better translated to something like "not at all" like 전혀:

저는 밥을 하나도 안 먹었어요 = I didn't eat at all
학교가 하나도 재미없어요 = School isn't fun at all
그 여자가 하나도 안 웃었어요 = That girl didn't laugh at all

훨씬 = much more

훨씬 can be used in sentences just like 더 (which you learned about in Lesson 19), but the meaning is stronger than 더. For example:

나는 나의 남동생보다 훨씬 똑똑해 = I am way/much smarter than my brother
한국어는 영어보다 훨씬 어렵다 = Korean is much more difficult than English

You can also put 더 in the sentence after 훨씬 with no difference in meaning:

나는 나의 남동생보다 훨씬 더 똑똑해 = I am way/much smarter than my brother
한국어는 영어보다 훨씬 더 어렵다 = Korean is much more difficult than English

관하다 and 관련하다

You learned how to use ~에 대하다 in Lesson 13. The typical translation for ~에 대하다 is "about." For example:

나는 너에 대해 많이 생각했어 = I thought about you a lot
나는 한국역사에 대한 영화를 봤어 = I saw a movie about Korean history

You can use ~에 관하다 instead of ~에 대하다. For example:

나는 한국역사에 대한 영화를 봤어 = I saw a movie about Korean history, and
나는 한국역사에 관한 영화를 봤어 = I saw a movie about Korean history

관하다 indicates some form of "relation." A literal translation would be "to have relation with." Therefore, the sentence above could also be translated to:

나는 한국역사에 대한 영화를 봤어 = I saw a movie about Korean history, and
나는 한국역사에 관한 영화를 봤어 = I saw a movie related to Korean history

Although 관하다 and 대하다 can be used to create a similar meaning in some situations, it is awkward to use 관하다 when "thinking" about something/somebody. For example, the following sentence:

나는 너에 관해 많이 생각했어

Would be better off said as:

나는 너에 대해 많이 생각했어 = I thought about you a lot

A word that is similar in form is ~에 관련하다. It is often used in the same way as ~에 대하다 and ~에 관하다. Notice the difference in meanings:

환경에 대해 = About the environment
환경에 대한 것 = A thing about the environment

환경에 관해 = About/regarding the environment
환경에 관한 것 = A thing about/regarding the environment

환경에 관련해 = About/regarding the environment
환경에 관련한 것 = A thing about/regarding the environment
(관련한 is also often used as 관련돼 and 관련된)

~에 관련해 is usually written/spoken as 관련하여 (or 관련되어). Remember that 해 is actually the shortened form of 하여, and is much more common. In some formal situations, instructions, and signs you might find 하여 used more often than "해," but other than that, "하여" is less commonly used. However, 관련하여 is quite common. Some examples:

환경에 관련된 영화가 많아요
환경에 관련한 영화가 많아요
환경에 관한 영화가 많아요
= There are a lot of movies relating to the environment

이 문제에 관련되어 회의가 있을 것이다
이 문제에 관련하여 회의가 있을 것이다
이 문제에 관해 회의가 있을 것이다
= There will be a meeting relating to this problem

태극기에 관련된 이야기를 했어요
태극기에 관련한 이야기를 했어요
태극기에 관한 이야기를 했어요
= We had a discussion relating to the Korean flag

주위 – Around the circumference

주위 is also a fairly simple word, but a little bit of explanation will probably help you understand it better. In Lesson 2, you learned various words of position, like 'inside,' 'outside,' 'beside,' etc… For example:

학교 앞에 = in-front of the school
학교 뒤에 = behind the school
학교 안에 = inside the school

You can use 주위 in the same way, but to mean "around." For example:

나는 학교 주위를 걷는 것을 좋아해 = I like walking around the school
달은 지구 주위를 돌아요 = The moon spins around the earth
학생들이 넘어진 친구 주위에 서 있었어요 = The students stood around their friend who had fallen

It can also be used to refer to the general surroundings of a place. For example:

그가 주위를 두리번거렸어요 = He looked around at his surroundings
주위가 안전하지 않아요 = This area/surrounding area isn't safe

Finally, you will also see 주위 used to refer to the people who one often comes in contact with. This is often translated to the people "around" a person – but not in a physical sense. Rather, it refers to ones friends, family, coworkers, etc. For example:

그는 주위 사람들을 안 믿어요 = He doesn't trust those around him
주위 사람 중에 그를 좋아하는 사람은 하나도 없어요 = There isn't even one person around him that likes him

일단 = Once

Throughout your studies, you will learn a variety of adverbs that can be placed in sentences that have no real meaning. The purpose they serve is more to add feeling to a sentence rather than to change the meaning in any drastic way. This is hard to describe in English because (to my knowledge) we don't have anything similar. The most common of these words is "만약" which you have yet to learn about at this point (you will learn about it in Lesson 43).

The purpose of these words (or the feeling that they give off) is to allow the listener/reader to expect the type of sentence that is about to be said. For example, when somebody says "일단", one can expect that the speaker will be mentioning that <u>one action will happen before another</u>.

You will usually see the translation of "once" for 일단, although it is hard to correctly decide on a translation for a word whose meaning is more about feeling.

In Lesson 24 you learned about how to use ~ㄴ/은 후에 to say sentences like this:

제가 밥을 먹은 후에 밖에 나갈 거예요 = After I eat, I will go outside

In this sentence, one action (eating) happens before another (going outside). You can use "일단" in sentences like this. For example:

일단 제가 밥을 먹은 후에 밖에 나갈 거예요 = Once I eat, I will go outside

Notice that the two sentences essentially have the same meaning. The only reason I translated them differently is to try to account for the fact that "일단" was used in the second example.

Other examples:

일단 일을 다 한 후에 아빠에게 전화할 거예요
= Once I do all the work, I will call my dad

일단 재료를 산 후에 샐러드를 만들 거예요
= Once I buy the ingredients, I will make a salad

일단 한국어를 배운 후에 중국어를 배우고 싶어요
= Once I learn Korean, I want to learn Chinese

The word "이상" is often used in sentences with 일단 similar to how "후에" is used. You learned about "후에" in Lesson 24. For example:

밥을 먹은 후에 친구를 만났어요 = After I ate I met a friend
밥을 먹은 후에 친구를 만날 거예요 = After I eat, I will meet a friend

이상 is similar to 후에, but when 이상 is used the speaker is specifically indicating that the clause prior to 이상 has already been completed, and that he/she will now complete the clause after 이상. The translation of "now that one has…" is usually appropriate.

For example:

일단 제가 시작한 이상 멈추지 않을 거예요
= Now that I've started, I won't stop

일단 일을 다 한 이상 아빠에게 전화할 거예요
= Now that I'm done all my work, I will call my dad

일단 재료를 산 이상 샐러드를 만들 거예요
= Now that I have bought all the ingredients, I will make a salad

일단 한국어를 배운 이상 중국어를 배우고 싶어요
= Now that I have learned Korean, I want to learn Chinese

In addition to this, you will often see 일단 placed at the beginning of a sentence that has the particle "~부터" attached to the object in the clause that happens first, followed by a verb with ~고 attached. For example:

일단 밥부터 먹고…

You learned about the particle "~부터" in Lesson 12. Although the translation of ~부터 is slightly different, the usage shown above is essentially the same as the usage introduced in that earlier lesson.

When added to a noun like this (as in the example above) preceded by "일단" one is indicating that one action should happen before another action. The construction above (which is not a complete sentence yet) means that the speaker wants to eat first, and then, after finishing eating, another action can take place.

For example:

나는 일단 밥부터 먹고 나갈 거야

Again, this sentence implies that the speaker wants to eat, and then after finishing eating, wants to go out(side). This sentence could translate to many different things in English:

나는 일단 밥부터 먹고 나갈 거야 = I will eat first, and then go outside
나는 일단 밥부터 먹고 나갈 거야 = I will start by (from) eating, and then go outside
나는 일단 밥부터 먹고 나갈 거야 = After I eat, I will go outside
나는 일단 밥부터 먹고 나갈 거야 = Once I am finished eating, I will go outside

Notice that it doesn't matter what you translate the sentence to. In the end, the result is the same in each translation, and the purpose of 일단 is merely there to give feeling to the sentence. More examples:

일단 숙제를 끝내고 친구를 만날 거예요
= Once I finish my homework, I will meet a friend

일단 피자부터 먹고 과자를 먹을 거예요
= Once I finish eating the pizza, I will eat candy/snacks

일단 빵에 땅콩버터부터 바르고 딸기를 놓을 거예요
= Once I spread peanut butter on the bread, I will put strawberries onto it

일단 한국어부터 배우고 중국어를 배우고 싶어요
= Once I learn Korean, I want to learn Chinese

Weight Words

There are a lot of words that relate to weight/body weight that aren't very easy to understand. I want to take some time to explain these words to you.

The word for "weight" is "무게"

You already know that the word for body is "몸." If you are talking about one's body weight, you can say "몸무게."

Korea, like most of the world, uses the metric system. People probably wouldn't understand if you expressed your weight using pounds.

The first way to indicate how much you weigh is like this:
나는 (몸무게가) 70 kg 야 = I weigh 70 kilograms
"kg" is pronounced as "킬로" or "킬로그램" in Korean. You are more likely to see "kg" written instead of "킬로" or "킬로그램."

It is also possible to use "나가다" as the predicating word of the sentence. For example:
나는 (몸무게가) 70 kg 나가 = I weigh 70 kilograms

In both situations, "몸무게" can be omitted from the sentence as the context makes it clear that the speaker is referring to his/her weight. The sentences above could be shortened to:
나는 70 kg 야 = I weigh 70 kilograms
나는 70 kg 나가 = I weigh 70 kilograms

If you want to ask how much somebody weighs, you can turn those two sentences into questions using 몇 (which you learned about in Lesson 22). For example:

(몸무게가) 몇 kg 야? = How much do you weigh?
(몸무게가) 몇 kg(가) 나가? = How much do you weigh?

When talking about weight, it is common to talk about losing or gaining weight. When doing this, the word "살" is typically used instead of "몸무게." 살 literally refers to one's soft tissues (like muscle, fat or flesh) and can also be applied to the meat/flesh of other animals. For example:

그 물고기에 살이 없어요 = There is no meat on that fish

Weight is typically lost and gained in soft tissue, so 살 is used instead of 몸무게. Common verbs you will hear with "살" are:

살이 찌다 = to gain weight
살이 빠지다 = to lose weight (typically used when weight is lost inadvertently)
살을 빼다 = to lose weight (typically used when weight is lost on purpose)

These verbs have other uses than these situations related to weight. For example:

빠지다 is a verb used when something falls, sinks, drops or is deflated
빼다 is a verb used when somebody removes something from somewhere (as in, to remove weight from one's body).
(찌다 doesn't have much use outside of this situation)

찌다 and 빠지다 are passive verbs, so they cannot act on objects. In practice, all this means is that you cannot put ~을/를 in a sentence/clause that ends in 찌다/빠지다. The best way to use these words in situations of gaining and losing weight is:

나는 작년에 살이 많이 쪘어 = I gained a lot of weight last year
나는 살이 많이 빠졌어 = I lost a lot of weight

빼다 is an active verb, and therefore can act on an object. For example:

저는 살을 빼고 싶어요 = I want to lose weight

Lesson 35: To be like, to seem like: ~ㄹ/을 것 같다

Vocabulary

Nouns:
수영장 = swimming pool
보건 = preservation of health
소나무 = pine tree
바닥 = floor
변태 = pervert
홍수 = flood
새우 = shrimp
왕따 = outcast
낚시 = fishing
후배 = one's junior
꿀 = honey
허벅지 = inner thigh
말 = horse
휴가 = holiday, vacation
휴식 = break

Verbs:
넘치다 = to overflow
피하다 = to avoid
펴다 = to unfold, to unroll
답장하다 = to respond to a message
봉사하다 = to volunteer
시도하다 = to try, to attempt
펴지다 = to be unfolded, to be unrolled

Adjectives:
답답하다 = to be stuffy, to be frustrated
평화롭다 = to be peaceful
신기하다 = to be amazing, to be cool
멋있다 = to be stylish

Adverbs and Other Words:
오히려 = on the contrary

Introduction

Over the past 10 lessons, you have been learning a lot about how to use ~는 것 and things related to ~는 것 in Korean. We have just about reached the extent of what you need to know about ~는 것 and how to use it. In this lesson (as well as in Lesson 36), you will learn a variety of grammatical forms that can be used to say "to seem like" or "to look like."

To seem like/to be likely to: ~ㄹ/을 것 같다

In Lesson 15, you learned how to use '같다' in sentences by placing it after a noun connected with ~와/과/랑/이랑/하고. For example:

저 식당은 이 식당과 같아요 = That restaurant is the same as this one
그 나무가 소나무와 같아요 = That tree is like a pine tree

Since then, you have been learning a lot about ~는 것 and how to use it. Here, you will learn about how to use this ~는 것 principle with the word 같다.

If you conjugate a sentence in the future tense (using ~ㄹ/을 것이다), you end up with a sentence like this:

나는 밥을 먹을 것이다 = I will eat rice

Remember again what the ending of this sentence is made up of. The ending is actually made up of '~는 것' in the future tense (~ㄹ 것) followed by 이다.

If we remove the '이다' we are left with "…~ㄹ/을 것. For example:

나는 밥을 먹을 것

This is an incomplete sentence, so it is hard to translate, but it loosely translates to "the thing of me eating rice." Remember again that "것" is a noun (meaning "thing"). If we place 같다 after that noun, it gives the sentence a special meaning:

나는 밥을 먹을 것 같다

Whenever you finish a sentence using ~ㄹ/을 것 같다, the meaning changes to something that *might* happen. This meaning is quite similar to ~ㄹ/을지 모르다, which you learned in Lesson 30. For example:

나는 밥을 먹을 것이다 = I will eat rice
나는 밥을 먹을 것 같다 = I will probably eat rice/I might eat rice
나는 밥을 먹을지 모르겠다 = I don't know if I will eat rice

Here are many more examples:

It is common for Korean people to pronounce 같아(요) as "같애(요)." This is not only true just when using 같다 as it is presented in this lesson, but also in other grammatical forms that you learned about in Lesson 15, and that you will learn about in the next lesson.

저는 친구들이랑 내일 낚시를 할 것 같아요
= I will probably go fishing with my friends tomorrow

우리 아빠는 저것을 싫어할 것 같아
= Dad will probably not like that

선생님이 그 수업을 하지 않을 것 같아요
= The teacher probably won't do (teach) that lesson

남자 친구가 답장하지 않을 것 같아요
= My boyfriend probably won't respond

우리는 휴가를 중국에서 보낼 것 같아요
= We will probably spend our holiday in China

모두는 왕따와 밥을 먹는 것을 피할 것 같아요
= Everybody will probably avoid eating with the outcast

Although the previous examples used a person as the subject, the subject of the sentence can be anything. For example:

비가 올 것 같아 = It will probably rain/it seems like it will rain
문이 열려 있을 것 같아요 = The door will probably be open
내일 홍수가 날 것 같아요 = There will probably be a flood tomorrow

You can also use this same form on adjectives:

우리는 늦을 것 같아 = We will probably be late
새우가 너무 비쌀 것 같아요 = The shrimp will probably be too expensive
그 교실이 아주 답답할 것 같아요 = That classroom will probably be very stuffy

When describing "것 같다" in the future tense these situations are guesses from the speaker. It is possible to change the conjugation of the word before "것 같다" to express that something *may have happened* in past or *might be happening* in the present. When doing this, instead of using the future conjugation of ~ㄹ/을 것, you can use the past (~ㄴ/은 것) or present (~는 것) additions of ~는 것. (If you forget the purpose of these additions, I suggest that you review Lesson 26). For example:

엄마는 기다리고 있는 것 같아요
선생님이 열심히 공부한 것 같아요

When using these past and present conjugations before 것 같다, there is a slight nuance that the speaker has received some information to make him/her express this possibility.

For example, if I am talking with my teacher and he is telling me how difficult it was to get accepted into University back in his day, I could say something like:

선생님이 열심히 공부한 것 같아요
= You (teacher) probably studied hard (when you were younger)

Here, you have heard the evidence of him getting accepted into University, which must have been difficult. Therefore, this evidence leads you to believe that "he studied hard" when he was younger.

In order to describe this nuance, when ~ㄴ/은 or ~는 is used before 것 같다 I prefer the translation of "it seems that" or "it seems as though." Below are examples of this being done in the past tense (using ~ㄴ/은 것 같다):

부장님이 그 일을 이미 다 한 것 같아요 = It seems that the boss already did all that work
In this situation, you could be looking at a pile of papers on your boss's desk that looks like the completed work.

그 사람이 아직 답장을 하지 않은 것 같아요 = It seems that that person still hasn't responded
In this situation, you could be looking at your phone and noticing that you have no new notifications – which would lead you to believe that the person hasn't responded.

옆 집에서 사는 사람은 그 소나무를 자른 것 같아요 = It seems that the person who lives in the house next door cut that pine tree
In this situation, you could be looking outside to your yard and noticing that the tree is missing.

Below are examples that show this being done in the present tense (using ~는 것 같다)

엄마는 기다리고 있는 것 같아요 = It seems as though mom is waiting now
In this situation, your mother may have called you and told you that she would have been finished 10 minutes ago.

그는 휴식을 하는 것 같아요 = It seems as though he is taking a break now
In this situation, the worker may have been very loud a few minutes ago. However, now it seems like he is not making a sound, so he probably taking a break now.

학생들이 요즘에 운동을 하지 않는 것 같아요 = It seems like students don't like exercising these days
In this situation, you could be looking at some students playing on their phones during lunch time instead of playing outside.

후배들이 봉사하는 것을 싫어하는 것 같아요 = It seems like our juniors don't like volunteering
In this situation, you could be looking at your juniors and noticing that they are not enjoying themselves.

When describing 것 같다 in the past tense, it is possible to do so in two ways:

~ㄴ/은 것 같다 (for example: 한 것 같다)
~았/었을 것 같다 (for example: 했을 것 같다)

This next little section is a discussion about the difference in nuance between these two usages. Understanding this nuance is not critical at this point. This nuance is very hard to describe and your understanding of it will develop with your understanding of Korean in general. I never studied this specifically in all of my Korean studies, but my experience with Korean has led me to feel a difference between the two. Simply being aware of this nuance can be helpful for later, but it is not critical to your understanding of this grammatical principle.

Notice the use of ~ㄴ/은 in the sentence below:

아빠가 돈을 이미 낸 것 같아요 = It seems like dad already paid

Here, the speaker probably saw his/her family get up and leave a restaurant (or some similar evidence). This evidence would lead the speaker to believe that the father already paid, and they are ready to leave.

However, by using ~았/었을 것 같다, the speaker is indicating that this sentence is more of a blind guess and hasn't received any evidence that would lead him/her to think this way. For example:

아빠가 돈을 이미 냈을 것 같아요 = Dad probably already paid

Notice the way I translate these sentences to express this nuance.

More examples:
선생님이 살이 찐 것 같아요 = It seems like the teacher gained weight
You would say this if you are looking at the teacher and noticed that (for example) his face looks a little bit fatter than usual. Of course, you can't be sure if the teacher gained weight or not, but the evidence in-front of you leads you to believe that he/she did gain weight.

선생님이 살이 쪘을 것 같아요 = The teacher probably gained weight
You would say this if you are talking about the teacher and how he went on vacation recently. You haven't seen him since he left, but you are guessing that – because he went on vacation, he "probably gained weight."

We see a similar phenomenon with 것 같다 used in the present tense. Even if "것 같다" is being described in the future tense, it doesn't necessarily mean that the meaning of the sentence is based in the future.

For example, look at the following sentence:

후배들이 봉사하는 것을 싫어할 것 같아요

This doesn't necessarily mean that the speaker thinks the juniors "*will* not like" volunteering. It is possible that the juniors are volunteering right now, and the speaker is not with them. Therefore, the speaker has no real way of knowing if the juniors are enjoying themselves or not – and this is merely a guess. However, if the present tense was used:

후배들이 봉사하는 것을 싫어하는 것 같아요

In this situation, the speaker is most likely with the juniors and can directly see (receiving evidence) that the juniors are not enjoying themselves.

후배들이 봉사하는 것을 싫어할 것 같아요
= The juniors probably won't like volunteering, or, depending on the situation:
= The juniors probably don't like volunteering

후배들이 봉사하는 것을 싫어하는 것 같아요
= It seems like the juniors don't like volunteering

Here's an example of how I used this grammatical form in my real life.

A few days ago, I was waiting in line to get into a restaurant. There were a lot of people waiting, and some people were getting fed up with the ridiculous wait time. The wait was so long, that some people just got up and left, which would have bumped us up on the wait list. One couple got up and left, and my girlfriend said:

저 사람들이 그냥 가? = Are those people just leaving?

My response was:

응… 가는 것 같아 = Yes, they are probably leaving/it seems like they are leaving

Notice here that the evidence of the people leaving the restaurant leads me to believe that "they are just leaving."

Remember that the way to describe a noun in the present tense is to use ~ㄴ/은. Therefore, when you want to use an adjective to describe "것 같다," ~ㄴ/은 것 같다 should be used. For example:

친구가 아픈 것 같아요 = It seems like my friend is hurt
엄마는 저랑 얘기하기 싫은 것 같아요 = It seems like mom doesn't want to talk with me
그 음식은 건강에 나쁜 것 같아요 = It seems like this food is unhealthy
시골에서 사는 것이 아주 평화로운 것 같아요 = It seems like living in the country is very peaceful
이 문제는 시민보건에 아주 중요한 것 같아요 = It seems like this problem is very important to the health of the citizens

You can attach ~았/었던 (which you learned in Lesson 27) to an adjective (or verb for that matter) to describe a noun that was (probably) like something in the past, but currently is not like that. For example:

너의 아빠가 너무 행복했던 것 같아 = Your dad was probably very happy

Also remember that 이다 is conjugated as an adjective. Therefore, the ~ㄴ/은 것 같다 form should be added to it. For example:

그 학생이 학교에서 왕따인 것 같아 = It seems like that student is an outcast at school
그 사람은 변태인 것 같아요 = It seems like that person is a pervert
우리가 받은 것은 그 사람의 답장인 것 같아요 = It seems like that thing we received is probably that person's response

그렇다 + ~ㄹ 것 같다

Also, in Lesson 23 you learned a lot about the word 그렇다, and how its meaning is similar to 'like that.' You can treat 그렇다 like a regular verb/adjective, but remember that when conjugating this word you need to remove the ㅎ. So, by adding ~을 것 같다 to 그렇다 you get 그럴 것 같다.

Literally '그럴 것 같다' means "it is probably like that." It is used very often in Korean to indicate that something "might be the case" or "is probably true." For example:

엄마가 어디에 있어요? 병원에 갔어요? = Where is mom? Did she go to the hospital?
그럴 것 같아요 = Probably/I think so/It seems as such

다음 주 목요일은 휴가인가? = Is next Thursday a holiday?
그럴 것 같아 = Probably/I think so/It seems as such

Here as well, you should consider the tense and apply the appropriate conjugation to 그렇다. Also remember that 그렇다 is an adjective, so the present tense conjugation in this case is 그런 것 같다, and *not* 그렇는 것 같다.

For example:

아빠는 낚시하러 갔어요? = Did dad go fishing?
그런 것 같아요 = Probably/I think so/It seems as such

수영장물이 다 넘쳤어요? = Did all the water overflow out of the pool?
그런 것 같아요 = Probably/I think so/It seems as such

그 사람이 말을 잘 타요? = Can that person ride horses (well)?
그런 것 같아요 = Probably/It looks like/It seems as such

Express Possibility with ~겠다

It is also very common to hear ~겠다 (which you learned as a future conjugation way back in Lesson 5) used in a way that is similar to expressing possibility. You'll most commonly hear this used with some simple adjectives; the most common of all being:

맛있겠다!

It is hard to translate that directly into English. People don't usually say this when they're *eating* food – instead, they say it when they're looking at (or hearing about) food and want to express that it "would be delicious" if they ate it. You could argue that this is technically the future tense conjugation, but it's not really about expressing an idea that is occurring in the future.

A better way to describe this is to look at another example.

Imagine you were talking with your friend and he was telling you how he hasn't eaten in 12 hours. In English, you would respond by saying:

"You must be hungry!" or "You are probably hungry!" In Korean, you can say either of these:

배고플 것 같아! = You are probably hungry!
배고프겠다! = You are probably hungry!

Here, you can see that the speaker is not saying "you *will* be hungry", as your friend is definitely hungry in the present. Here, we can see how ~겠다 can take on this function of possibility in the present. I've noticed (and you can see from the examples above) that this form is most commonly used when you see something or hear some fact, and are stating that something "must be the case" based on that evidence you saw or heard.

Other good words that this is commonly used with:

아프겠다! = That must hurt!
배부르겠다! = You must be full!
힘들겠다! = That must be difficult!

Below are some examples along with my explanation of the situation that would cause a Korean person to say such a sentence:

힘들겠다! = That must be difficult!
You would most likely say this if you are looking at somebody do some difficult task.

나는 캐나다에 못 가겠다! = (I guess) I can't go to Canada
You would most likely say this if you just found out (evidence that shows you) how difficult it would be to get to Canada – for example, because the price is too high or because it was too far or something like that.

돈이 부족하겠다! = (I guess) there won't be enough money
You would most likely say this if you were trying to figure out how much money you need, and you just found out (evidence that shows you) that you probably won't have enough money.

허벅지가 아프겠다! = Your inner thigh must hurt!
You would most likely say this if you were looking at your friend do some sort of inner thigh exercise. Like that machine at most gyms where you have to squeeze your legs together against resistance.

Lesson 36: To look like, to look: 보이다, ~아/어 보이다

Vocabulary

Nouns:
소방서 = fire station
무릎 = knee
얼음 = ice
흡연 = smoking
종아리 = calf
관리비 = management fees
치료비 = medical fees
보관료 = storage fees
땅값 = land prices
입장료 = entrance fees
등록금 = tuition/registration fee
교통비 = transportation fees
원룸 = one room (studio) apartment
화장 = makeup
소방 = firefighting
초등학교 = elementary school
첫차 = first bus, first car
가격표 = price tag
여우 = fox
의욕 = drive, motivation
일방적 = one sided   Verbs:
이사하다 = to move to a new house
귀국하다 = to return to one's home country
터지다 = to explode
기대다 = to lean against
얻다 = to gain, to get, to obtain
임신하다 = to get pregnant
보이다 = to be seen
들리다 = to be heard

Adjectives:
짜다 = to be salty

Introduction

In this lesson, you will learn how to use 보이다 to say that something can/cannot be seen and to say that something/somebody looks like something. For example, "You look like a monkey!" The same pattern can be used to say that something smells/tastes like something. For example, "You smell like a monkey!" or "You taste like a monkey!" In addition, you will learn how to use ~아/어 보이다 to say that somebody looks like an adjective – for example "You look happy!"

To Look Like: ~ 같이 보이다

One of the most common words in Korean is 보다 which means "to see." In Lesson 14, you learned the difference between passive and active verbs in Korean (and English). The word 보이다 is the passive form of 보다 and is used to indicate that something can or cannot be seen. For example:

TV가 안 보여 = The TV can't be seen
소방서가 보여요 = The fire station is seen

That being said, the above sentences could also be translated to:

TV가 안 보여 = I can't see the TV
소방서가 보여요 = I can see the fire station

A note for grammar nerds: Notice that the Korean sentences above are predicated by an intransitive verb (보이다), which means they cannot act on an object. The English translations directly above are predicated by a transitive verb (to see), which means they can act on an object. This is a great example that outlines the difficulty of translating sentences from Korean to English (or vice-versa). Literally, the first sentence above would translate "the TV can't be seen," but it is often used to mean "I can't see the TV."

A person is often placed in these sentences to specifically indicate the person who can or cannot see something. These sentences follow the same Subject – Object – Adjective (or Passive Verb) structure that you learned about in Lesson 15. For example:

나는 TV가 안 보여 = I can't see the TV
저는 소방서가 보여요 = I can see the fire station

This same idea can be applied to 듣다 (to hear) and 들리다 (to be heard). For example:

저는 소리가 안 들려요 = I can't hear anything
나는 네 목소리가 안 들려 = I can't hear your voice
목소리가 잘 들려 = I hear you well

Below are many other examples:

입장료가 얼마인지 안 보여요 = I can't see how much the admission cost is
나는 여기서 산이 안 보여 = I can't see the mountains from here
초등학교가 보여요? = Can you see the elementary school?
가격표가 안 보여요 = I can't see the price tags
흡연 구역이 안 보여요 = I can't see the smoking area
첫차가 출발하는 소리가 들렸어요 = I heard the sound of the first car/bus departing
뭔가 터지는 소리가 들렸어요 = I heard something explode

You can also use 보이다 in sentences to indicate that something looks like something. By placing 같이 (which is the adverb form of the word 같다) after a noun and predicating the whole sentence with 보이다, you can create this meaning. For example:

너는 원숭이 같이 보여 = You look like a monkey
저의 남자친구는 교수님 같이 보여요 = My boyfriend looks like the professor
너는 고등학생 같이 보여 = You look like a high school student

The noun before 같이 can also be a more complex noun that is being described by ~는 것.

For example:

네가 새로운 집으로 이사하고 싶은 것 같이 보여
= It looks like you want to move to a new house

그가 공연에 가고 싶지 않는 것 같이 보여
= It looks like he doesn't want to go to the performance

경기를 이긴 것 같이 보여
= It looks like you won the game

그녀가 오늘 화장을 안 한 것 같이 보여요
= It looks like she didn't do her makeup today

The sentences above explain how you can say that one "looks like" something, but in practice, it is often more common to say that something is just "like" something. For example:

You are like a monkey, instead of:
You look like a monkey

Within the meaning of "you are like a monkey" is the inherent meaning that that person (along with other traits like acting like a monkey, smelling like a monkey) would also look like a monkey.

You actually learned how to do this in Lesson 15, where you first learned how to use words like 같다, 다르다, and 비슷하다. In that lesson, you were presented with this sentence:

이 학교는 우리 학교와 같아요 = This school is the same as our school

I mentioned in that lesson that even though the word "같다" means "same", when you want to indicate that something is the *same* as something else in Korean, it is more common to use the word "똑같다" (which typically translates to "exactly the same").

The sentence above is better written as:

이 학교는 우리 학교와 똑같아요 = This school is *the same as* our school

When you want to express that one thing is "like" another thing, it is more natural to use the following form:

너는 여자 같아요 = You're like a girl

Notice that the particle 와/과/(이)랑/하고 is not added in this sentence. Below are many more examples:

그는 여우 같아요 = He is like a fox
그는 원숭이 같아요 = He is like a monkey
캐나다는 미국 같아요 = Canada is like the US
초등학생 같아요 = You're like an elementary school student
진짜 의사 같아 = You're really like a doctor

Next, let's talk about how you can say something *tastes* or *smells* like something.

To Smell/Taste Like: 맛/냄새

The word 맛 is a noun which means "taste." You often see this word as "맛있다," which means "delicious," but literally translates to "to have taste." The word "냄새" is a noun which means "smell." In the previous section you learned how to say:

"___ looks like ___."

In this section, you will learn how to say

"___ tastes like ___." and
"___ smells like ___."

The grammar within these principles is similar to what you were learning previously. What you need to do is place a noun (that has a taste or smell) before 맛 or 냄새, followed by "같다." For example:

____ 맛 같다 = tastes like ____
____ 냄새 같다 = smells like ____

For example:

김치 맛 같아 = Tastes like Kimchi
김치 찌개 냄새 같아 = It smells like Kimchi Jjigae

Throw in a subject and you've got a full sentence:

이 떡은 쓰레기 맛 같아 = This 떡 tastes like garbage
삼겹살은 베이컨 맛 같아요 = 삼겹살 tastes like bacon

Pretty simple, but I thought you should know because I always wanted to know how to say these sentences when I was learning Korean.

To Look (Adjective): ~어/아 보이다

Earlier in this lesson, you learned how to express that something looks like a noun. However, there are many times when you would want to say somebody looks like an *adjective*. For example:

You look happy
You look sad
You look strong

In order to do this, you need to add ~아/어 to an adjective, and then place 보이다 after it.

For example:

행복해 보이다 = to look happy
슬퍼 보이다 = to look sad
강해 보이다 = to look strong

Many more examples:

왜 그렇게 행복해 보여요? = Why do you look so happy?
저의 여자친구는 어제 너무 슬퍼 보였어요 = My girlfriend looked really sad yesterday
그 남자 종아리가 아주 강해 보여요 = That person's calf looks very strong
이 원룸은 깨끗해 보여요 = This (studio) apartment looks clean
화장이 예뻐 보여요 = Your makeup looks pretty
소방 훈련이 힘들어 보여요 = Firefighting training looks difficult
무릎이 아파 보여요 = Your knee looks sore
그 남자가 의욕이 많아 보여요 = It looks like that man has a lot of willpower/drive

Lesson 37: Because, therefore, so: ~아/어서

Vocabulary

Nouns:
도로 = road
고속도로 = highway
스님 = Buddhist monk
당국 = authorities
도시락 = lunch box
여행자 = traveler
피해 = damage
성형 = plastic surgery
연휴 = continuous holidays
최신 = the latest
진심 = sincerity, truth
한편 = on the other hand
반면 = on the other hand

Verbs:
점프하다 = to jump
깜빡하다 = to forget
빨다 = to suck
뜨다 = to open one's eyes
감다 = to close one's eyes
다투다 = to fight verbally
겨루다 = to compete, to fight, to vie for
개설하다 = to establish, to open
설레다 = for one's heart to be beating quickly
떠지다 = to have one's eyes open
감기다 = to have one's eyes closed

Adverbs and Other Words:
왜냐하면 = because
그래서 = therefore

Introduction

Okay, now it is time to get really serious. Up until now, you have not been taught how to say one of the most common words in the English language: because. It's not that I didn't want to teach you this word, but rather that you didn't have the knowledge to fully understand this word up until this point. In Korean, *because* is not generally said as a word. Okay, that is slightly untrue. There is a word in Korean for "because": 왜냐하면. However, "왜냐하면" is not nearly used as much as the grammatical principle that has the meaning of "because" in Korean. For example, Korean people would never say something like this:

나는 밥을 먹는다 왜냐하면 배고팠어

In fact, that sentence makes no sense (I was trying to write it in a way that didn't make any sense).

You *could* technically write something like this:

나는 밥을 먹었어. 왜냐하면 나는 배고팠어 = I ate. Because I was hungry.

However, that wouldn't sound natural at all in Korean. Instead, Korean people use ~아/어서 to connect two clauses to have the meaning of "because." We will look at how this is done in Korean. Let's get started.

<u>Because/Therefore: V/A + 아/어서</u>

~아/어서 is added to the stem of a verb or adjective in a clause to connect it with the upcoming clause. First, let's look at how "because" sentences are formed in English. When saying a sentence with "because," there are two clauses:

I want to eat
I am hungry

Both are independent clauses that can be sentences on their own. However, if we insert "because" between the two, we can create a sentence with two clauses:

I want to eat because I am hungry

The hardest part about saying these sentences in Korean is that the order is <u>reversed</u>. So, instead of saying:

I want to eat because I am hungry
I want to go to the park because I am bored

In Korean, we say:

Because I am hungry, I want to eat
Because I am bored, I want to go to the park

Now let's look at these simple sentences in Korean. We have our two clauses again:

저는 밥을 먹고 싶어요 = I want to eat
저는 배고파요 = I am hungry

Same as in English; both are independent clauses and can be sentences on their own. However, by inserting ~아/어서 between the two, we can create the meaning of "because."

140

For example:

저는 배고프(+~아/어서) 저는 밥을 먹고 싶어요

Remember from Lesson 24 that ~이/가 should be added to the subject of any clause that is not the main clause of a sentence. ~는/은 or ~이/가 can be added to the subject of the main clause of the sentence, depending on the specific meaning you are trying to create (although they both essentially have the same meaning). I encourage you to re-read Lesson 2 and Lesson 24 to remind yourself how changing these particles can slightly change the feeling of a sentence. Therefore, the sentence above could be written as:

제가 배고파서 저는 밥을 먹고 싶어요 = Because I am hungry, I want to eat
제가 배고파서 제가 밥을 먹고 싶어요 = Because I am hungry, I want to eat

However, remember in Korean that when the subject of both (or multiple) clauses in a sentence is the same, you only need to include the subject once. Therefore, the sentences above sound more natural as:

저는 배고파서 밥을 먹고 싶어요 = Because I am hungry, I want to eat

I always found it easier to remember the meaning of "~아/어서" as "Therefore." This way, the order of the clauses is the same in English and Korean. For example:

저는 배고파서 밥을 먹고 싶어요 = I am hungry, therefore I want to eat

Remember that this same addition (~아/어서) can also be added to 가다 and 오다 to express that one does something "after" going/coming from/to a place. This concept was taught in Lesson 17, and examples from that lesson were:

저는 학교에 가서 공부할 거예요 = I will go to school and then study
우리는 집에 와서 바로 잤어요 = We came home and went to sleep immediately

Note that those sentences technically *could* mean "Because I go/went to school, I will study" and "Because I came home, I went to sleep immediately". However, 99.9% of the time the meaning you will want to express using "가서" and "와서" will be the meaning talked about in Lesson 17. Think about how often you would want to say: "The reason I went to sleep immediately is because I came home" or "The reason I will study is because I came to school." I had this same question when I first learned of these two identical looking grammatical principles. At the time, I asked Koreans why these sentences couldn't mean "because…" and they all looked at me with a weird face and said "because nobody would ever say something like that."

Here are many more examples:

그 여자가 너무 예뻐서 저는 그녀를 만나고 싶어요
= That girl is very pretty, therefore, I want to meet her

저는 심심해서 공원에 가고 싶어요
= I am bored, therefore, I want to go to the park

우리 집이 홍수로 피해를 입어서 집에 못 들어가요
= We can't go into our house because it was damaged by the flood

저는 너무 못생겨서 성형수술을 받고 싶어요
= I want to get plastic surgery because I am so ugly

고속도로가 막혀서 일반 길로 갈 거예요
= I will take the normal road because the highway is blocked up

저는 우리 딸을 진심으로 사랑해서 그녀를 위해 모든 것을 할 거예요
= I will do everything for my daughter because I love her from the bottom of my heart

우리가 어제 다퉈서 저는 그랑 얘기하고 싶지 않아요
= I don't want to talk with him because we had an argument (we argued) yesterday

슬기가 임신해서 회사에 오는 것이 힘들겠어요
= It must be difficult for Seulgi to come to the office because she is pregnant

배가 곧 터질 것 같아서 더 못 먹겠어요
= I can't eat anymore because my stomach is (like it is) about to explode

여기에 여행자가 너무 많아서 다른 곳으로 갈 거예요
= I'm going to go to a different place because there are too many travelers here

오늘 너무 피곤해서 눈이 자꾸 감겨요
= My eyes keep shutting because I'm so tired

So far, we have only looked at using ~아/어서 in the present tense. In the next few sections, we will look at how to use it in the past and future tenses:

~아/어서 in the Past Tense

You cannot conjugate a word into the past tense and then use ~아/어서. For example, the following is incorrect:

저는 배고팠아서 밥을 먹었어요

Instead, the tense of the first clause is inferred from the context of the sentence. For example:

저는 배고파서 밥을 먹었어요 = I was hungry, so I ate
Notice that this sentence wouldn't make sense if it were "I am hungry, so I ate."

The final clause of the sentence doesn't necessarily need to be in the past tense in order to suggest that the first clause is in the past. For example, notice how the final clause below is in the present tense, but the first clause is in the past tense:

점심을 안 먹어서 지금 먹고 있어요 = I didn't eat lunch, so I'm eating now
Notice that this sentence wouldn't make sense if it were "I'm not eating lunch so I'm eating now."

Also, it is possible that the final clause of the sentence be in the future tense to suggest that the first clause is in the past tense. For example:

거기에 안 가 봐서 내일 갈 거예요 = I haven't been there yet, so I will go tomorrow
Notice that this sentence wouldn't make sense if it were "I'm not going there yet so I'll go tomorrow."

To somebody who has just learned this, it seems rather confusing and difficult to have to guess whether the first clause is in the past or present tense. As I said – you're not guessing. The context makes this clear. A lot of meaning in Korean is derived from context. As you progress through your studies, this will become easier.

Other examples:

학생들이 너무 시끄러워서 저는 교수님의 말을 못 들었어요
= The students were too loud, so I couldn't hear the professor

저는 공부하지 않아서 시험을 못 봤어요
= I didn't study, therefore, I didn't do well on the exam

제가 눈을 감고 있어서 그것을 못 봤어요
= I didn't see that because my eyes were closed

저는 화장을 하지 않아서 못생겨 보여요
= I look ugly because I didn't do my makeup

도시락을 안 가져와서 점심을 못 먹을 거예요
= I won't be able to eat lunch because I didn't bring my lunch box

공원에 스님이 있어서 우리는 술을 다른 곳에서 마셨어요
= There was a monk in the park, so we drank our alcohol in another place

오늘이 무슨 날인지 깜빡해서 선물을 안 준비했어요
= I forgot what today is (what day it is today) so I didn't prepare a present

애기가 손가락을 계속 빨아서 지금 손가락이 끈적거려요
= The baby kept sucking his fingers, so now they are all sticky

그 남자가 불법 행동을 하는 것을 봐서 저는 당국에 바로 말할 거예요
= I saw that man do something illegal (an illegal act) so I will tell the authorities immediately

일반 도로가 피해를 입어서 고속도로가 막힐 것 같아요
= The regular road was damaged so the highway will probably be blocked up

이상한 소리를 들어서 눈을 뜨고 밖을 보러 일어났어요
= I heard a weird sound, so I opened my eyes and got up to look outside

Before you learn how to add ~아/어서 to verbs/adjectives in the future tense, you need to learn how to add it to 이다.

Adding ~아/어서 to 이다

When adding ~아/어서 to 이다, the same principle applies. Let's look at two clauses:

I want to go to the park = 저는 공원에 가고 싶어요
It is Sunday = 일요일이다

Again, both are independent clauses that can be sentences on their own. However, if we insert "because" between the two clauses, we can make:

I want to go to the park because it is Sunday

Which, in Korean, would be written as:
일요일이다 (+ ~아/어서) 저는 공원에 가고 싶어요

Which is done like this:
일요일이어서 저는 공원에 가고 싶어요 = It is Sunday, so I want to go to the park

~어서 is always added to 이다 and never ~아서 because the last vowel of the stem of 이다 will always be "이." So, for example:

일요일이어서
건물이어서
공원이어서

의사이어서
여자이어서
남자이어서

When the word 이다 is attached to ends in a vowel (like in 의사, 여자 and 남자) 이 and 어 can merge to form 여. For example:

의사**여**서
여자**여**서
남자**여**서

There is a difference simply because of ease of pronunciation. If you were to say "일요일여서" it is hard to pronounce because your tongue has to move from the ㄹ sound to the 여 sound right away.

Adding ~이라(서) or ~라(서) has the exact same meaning of ~이어서 and ~여서 respectively. That is, you can add ~이라(서) to nouns ending in a consonant and 라(서) to nouns ending in a vowel. Both are possible, but I find that ~(이)라(서) is used more often in speech (not to say that it is not used in writing - but when speaking, ~(이)라서 is more common than ~이어서 or ~여서). To me, ~(이)라서 just flows off my tongue better.

Let's look at some examples:
일요일이어서 공원에 가고 싶어요 = It is Sunday, so I want to go to the park
일요일이라서 공원에 가고 싶어요 = It is Sunday, so I want to go to the park

예쁜 여자여서 똑똑하지 않을 것 같아 = She is a pretty girl, so she is probably not smart
예쁜 여자라서 똑똑하지 않을 것 같아 = She is a pretty girl, so she is probably not smart

이번 주말이 연휴라서 우리 엄마 집에 갈 거예요
= This weekend is a long weekend, so I will go to our mom's house

이 방은 원룸이라서 너무 작아요
= This is a studio apartment, so it is too small

이 학교는 초등학교라서 이 동네에 어린이들이 많아요
= This school is an elementary school, so there are a lot of children in this neighborhood

그것이 최신 정보여서 맞는 것 같아요
= That is the latest (most up-to-date) information, so it is probably right

When adding ~아/어서 to 아니다, you can either add ~어서 or ~라(서). For example:

최신 핸드폰이 아니어서 이 앱이 아주 느려요
최신 핸드폰이 아니라서 이 앱이 아주 느려요
= This isn't the latest cell phone, so the app is really slow

Now that you can add ~아/어서 to 이다, you can learn about adding ~아/어서 to clauses in the future tense.

~아/어서 in the Future Tense

When adding ~아/어서 to a verb or adjective in the future tense, it is the same as adding ~아/어서 to 이다. Again, let's look at two clauses:

My friend will come here = 저의 친구는 여기에 올 것이다
I won't leave/I won't go outside = 밖에 안 나갈 것이다

Again, both are independent clauses that can be sentences on their own. However, if we insert "because" between the two clauses, we can make:

저의 친구가 여기에 올 것이다 (~아/어서) 밖에 안 나갈 거예요

Remember that this future tense conjugation is actually just ~ㄹ/을 것 + 이다. Because of this, adding ~아/어서 to clauses in the future tense is done exactly the same as adding ~아/어서 to 이다.

Any of the following would work:

저의 친구가 여기에 올 것이어서...
저의 친구가 여기에 올 거여서...
저의 친구가 여기에 올 것이라서...
저의 친구가 여기에 올 거라서

Remember that 것 can be shortened to 거. So you can choose if you would rather use "것이어서," "거여서," "것이라서" or "거라서."

More examples:
나중에 밥이 없을 거라서 저는 지금 먹고 싶어요
= There will not be any food later, therefore, I want to eat now

친구가 거기에 많을 거라서 그 파티에 가고 싶어요
= Many of my friends will be there, so/therefore I want to go to that party

입장료가 너무 비쌀 거라서 저는 안 갈 거예요
= The price of admission will be so expensive, so I am not going to go

All very confusing, but you really only need to know how to say *one* of the future ~아/어서 conjugations (and then just be aware of the other ones). I personally only ever say ~이라(서) or ~라(서) and never say ~이어서 or ~여서.

그래서

In Lesson 23, you learned that the meaning of the word '그렇다' is close to the meaning of 'like that.' By adding ~아/어서 to 그렇다 you can create "그래서."

When some situation is being talked about, you can use "그래서" to say "Because of (that situation)…". The common translation of 그래서 is simply "therefore" or "that's why." For example:

Person 1: 비가 왔어요? = Did it rain?
Person 2: 응, 그래서 나가기 싫어요 = Yeah, that's why/therefore I don't want to go out

Person 1: 우리 학교가 영어회화 수업이 없어요?
= Our school doesn't have an English Conversation class?
Person 2: 응 없어요. 그래서 제가 다음 학기부터 개설할 거예요
= Right, there isn't any. That's why I'm going to start one beginning next semester

This lesson may have been a little difficult, but everything in this lesson is very important. In the following lesson, you will continue to learn about how to give the meaning of "because" using the word 때문.

Lesson 38: Because, therefore, so: ~기 때문에

Vocabulary

Nouns:
투자자 = investor
주식 = stocks
주식시장 = stock market
교복 = school uniform
여신 = goddess
별명 = nickname
기업 = enterprise
현실 = reality
폼 = posture
제사 = praying to ancestors on a holiday

Verbs:
떨어뜨리다 = to drop
제안하다 = to propose, to suggest
투자하다 = to invest
부정하다 = to deny
되짚다 = to look back (to the past)
망설이다 = to hesitate
세수하다 = to clean one's face
통화하다 = to talk on the phone
북적거리다 = to be crowded, to be packed
떨어지다 = to be dropped

Adjectives:
귀찮다 = to be annoying

Adverbs and Other Words:
고르게 = evenly, flatly

Introduction

In the previous lesson, you learned about how to use ~아/어서 to create the meaning of "because" in Korean sentences. There are actually many ways you can create the meaning of 'because' in Korean – the most common of those being by connecting two clauses with ~아/어서.

In this lesson however, you will learn another very common way to say "because" in Korean, which is pretty much interchangeable with ~아/어서. Let's get started.

Because of: 때문

By placing '때문' after a noun, you can create the meaning of "because of (that noun)." For example:

일 때문에 = Because of work
남자 친구 때문에 = Because of (my) boyfriend

The rest of the clause will indicate some event/action that occurred as a result of the noun preceding 때문에. For example:

일 때문에 나는 너를 못 만날 것 같아
= Because of work, I probably won't be able to meet you

남자 친구 때문에 새로운 남자를 못 만나
= Because of my boyfriend, I can't meet another(/new) man

Notice that this is *not* the same as adding ~아/어서 to 이다, which you learned about in the previous lesson. For example, these constructions:

일이라서… = Because it *is* work
남자 친구라서… Because he *is* my boyfriend

When these constructions are created ~아/어서 is added to 이다. The inclusion of 이다 in these constructions/sentences means that their meanings/translations will have the word am/is/are. When using 때문에 you are simply saying "because of that noun" and are not mentioning the word "to be." For example, notice the difference between these two sentences:

남자 친구 때문에 새로운 남자를 못 만나
= Because of my boyfriend, I can't meet another(/new) man

남자 친구라서 새로운 남자를 못 만나
= Because he is my boyfriend, I can't meet another(/new) man
(I can't think of any situation where this sentence in English or Korean would be appropriate)

That being said, sometimes this difference is irrelevant. Notice how both of these sentences effectively have the same meaning:

우리는 제사 때문에 할아버지 집에 갔어요
= We went to our grandfather's house because of 제사

우리는 제사라서 할아버지 집에 갔어요
= We went to our grandfather's house because it is 제사

Many other examples:

별명 때문에 너의 진짜 이름을 깜빡했어
= I forgot your real name because of your nickname

등록금 때문에 저는 그 대학교에 못 가요
= I won't be able to go to university because of the admission/registration fees

교복 때문에 아주 더워요
= I'm really hot because of my school uniform

주식시장 때문에 요즘에 스트레스를 많이 받아요
= I am very stressed these days because of the stock market

Because/Therefore: ~기 때문에

It is also possible to place an entire clause before 때문에 instead of just a noun to indicate that some event/action occurred as a result of the clause preceding 때문에. The clause before 때문에 must be in the form of a noun, and this is done by adding ~기 to the stem of the word immediately preceding 때문에. For example:

저는 배고프기 때문에 밥을 먹고 싶어요 = I want to eat because I am hungry

Note that this is identical to adding ~아/어서 to the same word (which you learned about in the previous lesson). For example:

저는 배고파서 밥을 먹고 싶어요 = I want to eat because I am hungry

Just like ~아/어서, you can add ~기 때문에 to verbs, adjectives and 이다.

Below are many examples:

저는 행복하기 때문에 죽고 싶지 않아요
= I don't want to die because I am happy

지금 공부를 하고 있기 때문에 너랑 통화하고 싶지 않아
= I don't want to talk with you on the phone because I'm studying now

투자자가 없기 때문에 우리는 다른 방법으로 할 거예요
 = We will do it another way because there are no investors

무릎이 아프기 때문에 저는 걸어가기 싫어요
= I don't want to walk because my knee is sore

이 셔츠에 가격표가 없기 때문에 얼마인지 몰라요
= I don't know how much this shirt costs because there is no price tag

학생들이 교복을 입기 때문에 다 똑같은 옷을 입었어요
= All the students wore exactly the same clothes because they wear uniforms

내가 남자이기 때문에 그런 영화를 좋아해
= I like those kinds of movies because I am a man

입구가 멀기 때문에 다른 곳으로 갈 거예요
= I'm going to go to another place because I can't find the entrance (of this place)

그 여자가 여신 같기 때문에 남자들은 그녀를 다 좋아해요
= She's like a goddess, so all the boys like her

거리가 아주 북적거리기 때문에 우리는 밖에 나가고 싶지 않아요
= We don't want to go out because the streets are very crowded

세수를 하는 것이 귀찮기 때문에 안 했어요
= I didn't wash my face because it is annoying

엄마가 현실을 그냥 부정할 것 같기 때문에 말을 안 할 거예요
= I'm not going to say anything (to mom) because she's probably just going to deny the reality

2월이기 때문에 비행기표 가격이 떨어졌어요
= The prices of flights dropped because it is February

Let's look at how this can be added to clauses conjugated in the past and future tenses.

Past Tense: ~았/었기 때문에

When connecting two clauses with ~아/어서, you should always remember that you do *not* conjugate the verb/adjective that ~아/어서 is being added to in the past tense. For example, you should never do this:

내가 밥을 벌써 먹었어서 지금 먹고 싶지 않아

Instead, you know that you should say this:

내가 밥을 벌써 먹어서 지금 먹고 싶지 않아 = Because I already ate, I don't want to eat now

However, the clause before ~기 때문에 can be conjugated to the past tense. In these cases, ~기 should be added directly to the addition of ~았/었. For example:

내가 밥을 벌써 먹었기 때문에 지금 먹고 싶지 않아
= Because I already ate, I don't want to eat now

Many more examples:

저는 시험을 못 봤기 때문에 대학교에 못 가요
= Because I did bad on the test, I won't be able to go to university

주식을 많이 샀기 때문에 돈이 없어요
= I don't have any money because I bought a lot of stocks

대학교에 갈지 안 갈지 많이 망설였기 때문에 대학교에 갈 기회를 놓쳤어요
= Because I hesitated a lot about going to university or not, I missed the opportunity to go to university

제가 처음부터 그 기업에 투자하지 않았기 때문에 돈을 많이 못 벌어요
= I don't earn that much money because I didn't invest in that company from the beginning

애기들에게 과자를 고르게 안 줬기 때문에 많이 받지 못한 애기들은 울었어요
= I didn't give the candy to the babies evenly, so the babies that didn't get a lot cried

세수를 아직 못 했기 때문에 잠깐 화장실에 갈 거예요
= I haven't washed my face yet, so I'm going to go to the washroom for a second

오늘 공원에 가고 싶지 않았기 때문에 저는 다른 것을 제안했어요
= I didn't want to go to the park today so I suggested something different (a different thing)

핸드폰이 없었기 때문에 연락하지 못했어요
= Because I didn't have my phone, I couldn't contact you

Now let's look at how you can add ~기 때문에 to the future tense.

Future Tense: ~ㄹ 것이기 때문에

As you know, you can conjugate a word into the future by connecting ~ㄹ/을 것이다 to it. For example:

내가 나중에 먹을 것이다 = I will eat later

Adding ~기 때문에 to a word conjugated in the future tense is simply a matter of attaching ~기 때문에 to the 이다 at the end of this future tense conjugation. For example:

내가 나중에 먹을 것이기 때문에 지금 먹고 싶지 않아
= Because I am going to eat later, I don't want to eat now
Notice how there is a noun (것) followed by 이다 followed by ~기 때문에

More examples:

Also notice how 것 can be shortened to 거. In these cases, "이" can merge with "거" and you can see the construction ~ㄹ/을 거기 때문에.

나는 내년에 대학교에 갈 것이기 때문에 지금 열심히 공부하고 있어
= Because I will be going to university next year, I am studying hard now

그녀가 그 셔츠가 거기에 없는 것을 깨닫지 못할 거기 때문에 저는 그냥 가져갈 거예요
= She won't notice that shirt is gone (not here) so I'm just going to take it

우리가 과거를 되짚어 볼 것이기 때문에 사진을 가져왔어요
= We are going to be looking back at old times, so I brought some pictures

<u>Other Uses of 때문에</u>

In Lesson 23, you learned that the meaning of the word '그렇다' is close to the meaning of 'like that.' By adding ~기 때문에 to 그렇다 you can create "그렇기 때문에." The common translation for "그렇기 때문에" is "therefore" or "because of that." For example:

Person 1: 요즘에 사람들은 그 제품을 안 사요 = These days people aren't buying that product
Person 2: 네, 그렇기 때문에 그 회사의 주식이 떨어지고 있어요 = Yes, because of that, that company's stocks are falling

Another good usage of the word 때문 is putting it at the *end* of a sentence as a noun. If I were to write this:

사람들이 너무 많이 있기 때문…

You would think that would mean "because there are too many people…"… but that is an incomplete sentence because you cannot end a sentence with a noun like that.

Instead, you must add 이다 to 때문 to make it a full sentence. For example:

사람들이 너무 많이 있기 때문이야 = Because there are too many people

The best part about that sentence (and this is where this lesson starts to get really hard/confusing) is that "때문" turns into a noun of "[because there are too many people]." I put that "noun" into [brackets] because I'm going to show you what you can do with it. Look at the following example:

내가 방에 들어가지 않은 이유 = translates to "the reason I didn't go in the room"

Because "이유" is a noun (being described by 내가 방에 들어가지 않은) we can make this the subject of our sentence:

내가 방에 들어가지 않은 이유는 = The reason I didn't go into the room…

Now if I wanted to say what the reason *is*, I would need to say:

The reason I didn't go into the room is …:

내가 방에 들어가지 않은 이유는 _____ 이다

What could I put in the place of that blank? I need to put a noun in there. How about the noun we made before: "[because there are too many people]":

The reason I didn't go into the room is [because there are too many people].

In Korean:

내가 방에 들어가지 않은 이유는 [사람들이 너무 많이 있기 때문]이야

Without the brackets:
내가 방에 들어가지 않은 이유는 사람들이 너무 많이 있기 때문이야
= The reason I didn't go into the room is because there are too many people

You could also say that there *were* too many people in the room by adding ~았/었~ before 기. For example:

내가 방에 들어가지 않은 이유는 사람들이 너무 많이 있었기 때문이었어
= The reason I didn't go into the room was because there were too many people

More examples:

내가 한국에 간 이유는 한국어를 배우고 싶기 때문이었어
= The reason I went to Korea was because I wanted to learn Korean

내가 여기서 일하고 싶은 이유는 새로운 경험을 하고 싶기 때문이야
= The reason I want to work here is because I want to have a new experience

All of which are technically the same as these:

사람들이 너무 많이 있어서 나는 방에 들어가지 않았어
= Because there were too many people, I didn't go into the room

한국어를 배우고 싶어서 한국에 갔어
= Because I wanted to learn Korean, I went to Korea

새로운 경험을 하고 싶어서 여기서 일하고 싶어
= Because I want to have a new experience, I want to work here

You might be comfortable using ~기 때문에 in sentences by now, but you are probably still a little bit confused about how to use "~하는 이유는 ____ ~기 때문이다" right now. Don't worry about that. When you become more and more comfortable not only with 때문에 but also with Korean grammar in general, using sentences like that will become more and more natural. In the meantime, keep studying and get ready for our next lesson!

Lesson 39: Honorific ending ~(으)시, Honorific words: 드리다, 계시다, etc

Vocabulary

Nouns:
자네 = you
또래 = age, peer group
세제 = laundry detergent
뒷모습 = one's appearance from behind
봉지 = paper bag, plastic bag
국립 = national
산소 = oxygen
종 = bell
주방 = kitchen

Verbs:
드시다 = to eat (formal)
잡수시다 = to eat (formal)
주무시다 = to sleep (formal)
계시다 = to be in/at a location (formal)
말씀하다 = to speak (formal)
드리다 = to give (formal)
소변을 보다 = to urinate
대답하다 = to answer, to reply
치다 = to tap
망치다 = to spoil, to ruin, to screw up
다가가다 = to approach, to go near
다가오다 = to approach, to come near

Adjectives:
가파르다 = to be steep

Adverbs and Other Words:
그저께 = the day before yesterday

Introduction

In this lesson, you are going to learn something that we haven't specifically looked at in a very long time. Way back in Lesson 6, you learned how to apply Korean honorifics to the endings of verbs and adjectives. In addition to what you learned in that lesson, there is still more that you must know in terms of adding respect to Korean sentences. We will cover more of that here, starting with the use of '~(으)시' in sentences.

Honorific Addition: ~(으)시

This one is hard for English speakers to understand. Before you learn specifically when to add '~(으)시' to your sentences, let's remember when you should use honorifics in the first place. Remember, if you are talking to somebody who deserves a high level of respect, you should use honorifics. These types of people can be: bosses, parents, people older than you, guests, customers, etc… If you are talking to your boss, you should say:

저는 열심히 일했어요/일했습니다 = I worked really hard

But, if you are talking to your friend (for example) you can use the lower form:
나는 열심히 일했어 = I worked really hard

Therefore, the use of those honorifics solely depends on <u>the person you are speaking to</u>. The use of '~(으)시' is a little bit tricky at first. You should add '~(으)시' to verbs/adjectives in which the <u>acting person</u> deserves respect, regardless of who you are speaking to. You can add '~시' to word stems ending in a vowel and '~으시' to stems ending in a consonant.

In Lesson 7, you learned how irregular words change as a result of adding different additions. This is the first time you have been introduced to adding ~(으)시. Let's look at how irregulars change as a result of adding this grammatical principle.

- The ㅅ irregular, ㄷ irregular and ㅂ irregular all follow the same rules that were introduced in Lesson 7. The addition of the vowel causes a change (or elimination) of the last letter of the stem.

- The ㅡ and 르 irregular are not affected by this addition. The final letter in both types of stems is a vowel, so "시" is added instead of "으시."

- Adding ~(으)시 causes a change to stems ending in ㄹ. The ㄹ is removed, and ~시 is added to the remaining portion of the stem.

- Adding ~(으)시 causes a change to ㅎ irregular words. The ㅎ is removed, and ~시 is added to the remaining portion of the stem. For this addition, the ㅎ irregular and ㄹ irregular follow the same rule. Anytime you have the option of adding ~(으) as part of a grammatical addition, the ㅎ will be removed from the stem and the grammatical addition without "으" will be added to the remainder of the stem. For example:
그렇다 + ~(으)시 = 그러시

Below is a table showing the changes that result from adding ~(으)시 to a word.

Irregular	Word	+~(으)시
ㅅ Irregular	짓다 (to build)	지으시
ㄷ Irregular	걷다 (to walk)	걸으시
ㅂ Irregular	돕다 (to help)	도우시
ㅡ Irregular	잠그다 (to lock)	잠그시
르 Irregular	자르다 (to cut)	자르시
ㄹ Irregular	살다 (to live)	사시
ㅎ Irregular	그렇다 (to be like that)	그러시

You will see these same changes to irregulars anytime you add something that begins in

~(으)ㅅ…. For example:
~(으)세요 (Lesson 40)
~(으)십시오 (Lesson 40)

Adding ~(으)시 creates an unconjugated word. You cannot just attach ~(으)시 to a word and use it in a sentence. Rather, a conjugation must be added to it. Once '~(으)시' is added, the verb/adjective gets conjugated as usual as if the stem ended in '~(으)시.'

The following table shows how ~(으)시다 can be added to words, and then how other conjugations can be added on top of it:

Original Word	+~(으)시	+~아/어요	~ㅂ/습니다	~았/었다
짓다	지으시	지으셔요	지으십니다	지으셨다
걷다	걸으시	걸으셔요	걸으십니다	걸으셨다
돕다	도우시	도우셔요	도우십니다	도우셨다
잠그다	잠그시	잠그셔요	잠그십니다	잠그셨다
자르다	자르시	자르셔요	자르십니다	자르셨다
살다	사시	사셔요	사십니다	사셨다
그렇다	그러시	그러셔요	그러십니다	그러셨다

Let's look at an example of when you would use this ~(으)시 addition.

If I am talking to my friend and the person I am talking about is that friend's mother – the mother deserves respect. Therefore, I should not say this:

어머님은 너에게 돈을 줬어? = Did your mother give you money?

Remember, the mother (who deserves respect) is the person *acting* in that sentence. Therefore, ~(으)시 should be added to the verb. This would be more correct:

어머님은 너에게 돈을 주셨어? = Did your mother give you money?

You should always keep the information you learned in Lesson 6 in mind as well – because depending on who you are speaking *to*, the form can change based on what you learned in that Lesson. If I were to say a sentence where I was talking *to* somebody who deserves respect (my boss, for example) *about* somebody who deserves respect, I should say:

어머님은 미용실에 가셨습니까? = Did your mother go to the beauty salon?
Again, notice the situation of this sentence. You are talking to somebody of high respect, about somebody of high respect. Notice all of the situations that can take place:

어머님은 미용실에 가셨어? = Did your mother go to the beauty salon?
Situation: To somebody of low respect, about somebody of high respect

친구는 미용실에 갔어? = Did your friend go to the beauty salon?
Situation: To somebody of low respect, about somebody of low respect

친구는 미용실에 갔습니까? = Did your friend go to the beauty salon?
Situation: To somebody of high respect, about somebody of low respect

어머님은 미용실에 가셨습니까? = Did your mother go to the beauty salon?
Situation: To somebody of high respect, about somebody of high respect

More examples:

선생님은 우리를 너무 잘 가르치셨어
= Our teacher taught us really well

부장님은 그 집을 나무로만 만드시고 싶었어
= Our boss wanted to make that house using only wood

선생님이 대답을 빨리 하셨어요
= The teacher responded quickly

그 선생님은 국립고등학교에서 일하셔요
= That teacher works at a public school

자네 할아버지가 주방에 들어가셨어
= Your grandfather went into the kitchen

종이 칠 때까지 선생님이 수업을 하실 거예요
= The teacher will do the class until the bell rings

할아버지가 아파서 소변을 못 보셔요
= Our grandfather can't urinate because he is sick

교장선생님이 아직 대답하시지 않았어요
= The principal hasn't responded yet

내 부장님은 내 나이 또래 사람들을 좋아하시지 않아
= My boss doesn't like people my age

어떤 할아버지가 저에게 다가오시고 있어요
= Some old man is approaching me

Now that you know all of that, there are certain words that change completely when the acting person in the sentence deserves respect. We will look at those one by one:

To give: 드리다 and ~께
You should use the word 드리다 in place of the word 주다 when one gives something to somebody who deserves high respect. Also, remember the formal version of ~에게/한테 is ~께. Therefore, ~께 should be attached to the person that you are giving something. Let's look at an example:

할아버지께 선물을 드리고 싶어 = I want to give my grandfather a present

If you are also saying this sentence *to* somebody who deserves respect, you can also end the sentence using honorifics as well:

할아버지께 선물을 드리고 싶어요 = I want to give my grandfather a present

Korean people don't say "드리시다." One might think that this would be used when talking *about* somebody of high respect giving something *to* somebody of high respect. However, it appears that 드리다 is formal enough to cover both the person acting and the person receiving in these situations.

More examples:

저는 항상 손님들께 봉지를 드려요 = I always gives bags to the customers
저는 스님께 돈을 드렸어요 = I gave money to the monk
아버지가 매일 쓰실 수건을 드리고 싶어요 = I want to give dad a towel that he will use everyday

To speak: 말씀하다

You should use 말씀하다 in place of 말하다 when the person speaking deserves high respect. The ~하다 portion of the word is usually connected with ~(으)시다 to form 말씀하시다. If 말씀 and ~하다 are separated, 말씀 is the honorific form of the noun "말." For example:

모든 사람들은 교수님이 말씀하시기 시작하는 것을 기다렸다
= Everybody was waiting for the professor to start talking

부장님이 그 일을 망쳐서 부장님이 말씀하시는 것을 듣는 사람이 별로 없어요
= There aren't really that many people who listen to the boss because he ruined that job

선생님이 하시는 말씀을 잘 들었어요?
= Did you listen (well/carefully) to what your teacher said?

회의가 끝나기 전에 교감선생님이 말씀하실 거예요
= Before the meeting finishes, the vice principal will speak

그저께 회의 시간 동안 무슨 말씀을 하셨어요?
= What did you say during the meeting two days ago?

말씀 is also used as the noun when *you* are speaking to a person who deserves high respect. I find this strange because in the examples/explanation above, 말씀 is used when the acting person of the sentence deserves high respect. However, in cases when you are saying something (some words) to a person of high respect (and therefore, *you* are the acting person) 말씀 is used instead of 말. When used like this, the formal word "드리다" is commonly used to indicate that "some words" are given to a person. For example:

제가 드리고 싶은 말씀이 있습니다
= I have something that I want to say
You would say this when you will speaking to a person (or people) who deserves high respect.

To eat: 드시다/잡수시다

When a person who deserves high respect is eating, it is common to use the word 들다 combined with ~(으)시다 to form 드시다. For example:

아버지! 다 드셨어요? = Dad! Have you finished eating?
점심을 드셨어요? = Did you have lunch?
뭐 드시고 싶어요? = What do you want to eat?

Another possible word is 잡수시다. Using 잡수시다 shows a *ridiculous* amount of respect, and saying it to anybody other than people who deserve that amount of respect will most likely just make people laugh. When I first met my girlfriend's parents, I used '잡수시다' and they both thought it was funny. I only reserve that word for the rare times that I have dinner with my girlfriend's grandparents – in which case, after the meal, I ask them:
잘 잡수셨어요? = Did you have a good meal?

To be at/in: 계시다
계시다 is the formal equivalent of the word "있다" when it is used to indicate that a person of high respect is in/at a location, or is staying in a location. For example:

아버지가 집에 계셔요 = Dad is (at) home

계시다 can also replace 있다 in the ~아/어 있다 (Lesson 14) and ~고 있다 (Lesson 18) grammatical forms. For example:

아버지가 아직 서 계셔요 = Dad is still standing
아버지가 아직 드시고 계셔요 = Dad is still eating

However, when 있다 is used to indicate that one "has" a noun, the formal equivalent is 있으시다. For example:

할아버지! 지금 시간이 있으셔요? = Grandpa! Do you have time now?

You will learn more about 계시다 in the following lesson. Until then, let's look at some more example sentences with 계시다:

할아버지가 여기에 계신지 몰랐어요 = I didn't know you were here, grandpa
교장선생님이 학교에 안 계셔요 = The principal isn't in the school
거기에 언제까지 계실 거예요? = Until when will you be there?

사람들이 대통령이 그 건물에 계시는 것을 알아서 그 건물 입구에 다가갔어요
= People knew that the president was in that building, so they approached the entrance

선생님이 안 계셔서 학생들은 다 자고 있어요
= The teacher isn't here, so all the students are sleeping

To sleep: 주무시다
주무시다 is the formal equivalent of the word "자다" (to sleep). For example:

잘 주무셨어요? = Did you sleep well?
아버지가 지금 주무시고 있어요 = Dad is sleeping now

Lesson 40: The imperative mood: ~아/어, ~아/어라, ~(으)세요, ~(으)십시오

Vocabulary

Nouns:
오줌 = urine
권력 = power, authority
수준 = level, standard
학력 = level of education
직원 = employee, staff member
허가 = permission
보안 = security
시선 = one's eyes, one's eye-line
물체 = object

Verbs:
수고하다 = to work hard
말다 = to not do
직진하다 = to go straight
올라가다 = to go up
올라오다 = to come up
올려다보다 = to look up
후들거리다 = to shake, to tremble
남용하다 = to abuse
감시하다 = to monitor, to watch

Adjectives:
부끄러워하다 = to be shy
슬퍼하다 = to be sad
동등하다 = to be equal
유쾌하다 = to be pleasant, to be delightful
온순하다 = to be gentle

Adverbs and Other Words:
먼저 = first, in advance
오른 = right
왼 = left
줄곧 = continuously/constantly/all the time
가만히 = to be still, motionless

Introduction

In this lesson, you will learn how to tell people to do things. If you are a grammar buff, you know this as the *Imperative Mood*. If you're not so into grammar, this "mood" is used when giving people commands/telling people what to do. You will learn how to do this in

Korean, often in conjunction with the word '주다,' which we will talk about in the next lesson.

The Imperative Mood

There are many (many!) ways to end a sentence. Depending on who you are speaking to (and a whole bunch of other factors) the way you end a sentence can vary tremendously. If you just wanted to say "I will eat rice," some of the ways you can say this are:

나는 밥을 먹겠다
나는 밥을 먹겠어
저는 밥을 먹겠어요
저는 밥을 먹겠습니다
나는 밥을 먹을 것이다
나는 밥을 먹을 거다
나는 밥을 먹을 것이야
나는 밥을 먹을 거야
저는 밥을 먹을 것입니다
저는 밥을 먹을 겁니다
저는 밥을 먹을 것이에요
저는 밥을 먹을 거예요

All of those mean exactly the same thing. In the imperative mood as well, there are many different ways you can give a command to somebody. Let's cover these from the least formal, to the most formal.

Imperative mood: Verb stem + ~아/어(요)

The easiest (and least formal) way to give a command in Korean is simply by adding ~아/어 to a verb stem. For example:

밥을 천천히 먹어 = Eat your food slowly
열심히 공부해! = Study hard!

Notice that in both English and Korean, the subject isn't usually used in a sentence when giving a command. This is because the person you are giving the command to is usually the subject, so it is omitted.

You can use this form when you are giving a command to somebody who is younger than you or the same age as you, or somebody who you are close with. Saying something like "빨리 가!" to your superior would most likely warrant a slap in the face.

As you probably guessed, adding "~요" to the ends of the sentences above make them more formal. For example, more polite versions of the sentences above would be:

밥을 천천히 먹어요 = Eat your food slowly
열심히 공부해요! = Study hard!

In that same respect, the formal addition of ~(으)시 could be added to the construction as well. In these cases, ~아/어(요) is added to ~(으)시다. For example:

Original Word	+ ~(으)시다	+ ~(으)시 +~아/어요
가다	가시다	가셔요
공부하다	공부하시다	공부하셔요
알다	아시다	아셔요
찾다	찾으시다	찾으셔요
걷다	걸으시다	걸으셔요
눕다	누우시다	누우셔요

Notice that these imperative conjugations are no different than any regular present tense conjugation. For example, the following two sentences are simply conjugated into the present tense, but the addition to the verb is exactly the same as an imperative conjugation:

저는 월요일마다 운동해요 = I exercise every Monday
저의 할머니가 여기에 자주 안 오셔요 = My grandmother doesn't come here often

In these cases, distinguishing between a regular sentence and an imperative sentence is done through context. When you first learn this, you think it would be impossible to do, but trust me; it is easy to distinguish by considering the situation.

Here are some examples using everything presented so far:

이것을 봐 = Look at this
이것을 봐요 = Look at this
이것을 보셔요 = Look at this

빨리 올라와 = Come up quick
빨리 올라와요 = Come up quick
빨리 올라오셔요 = Come up quick

먼저 올라가 = Go up first (you can go up first)
먼저 올라가요 = Go up first (you can go up first)
먼저 올라가셔요 = Go up first (you can go up first)

이 길에서 직진해 = Go straight on this road
이 길에서 직진해요 = Go straight on this road
이 길에서 직진하셔요 = Go straight on this road

Although they differ in their respective levels of politeness, all of the above are acceptable ways to make a command. That being said, each of the last examples (the one using ~(으)셔요) is less common. Instead, the construction of ~(으)셔요 is often pronounced and written as ~(으)세요, which we will discuss next.

Imperative Mood: Verb stem + ~(으)세요

If you have been studying Korean for a while (and if you are here on Lesson 40 you probably have been), you are probably already quite familiar with the ~(으)세요 form. This is one of the first things people learn when they study Korean, but I waited until Lesson 40 to teach it to you. Trust me, there is a method to my madness.

In the previous section, you learned how to use ~(으)셔요 as a formal way to make a command. These days, especially in speech but also in basically all forms of Korean, it is much more common to pronounce and write ~(으)셔요 as ~(으)세요. This can *only* be done when you see ~(으)셔요 and not with any other form that ~(으)시다 can create. For example, each of the following are the same:

가셔요 = 가세요
공부하셔요 = 공부하세요

However,

가셨어요 can not be said as "가셨으세요"
가셔 cannot be said as "가세"
가시다 can not be said as "가세다"

I will say it again: Only when you see "~(으)셔요" can you use "~(으)세요. As you learned previously, one of the reasons why you would add "~(으)셔요" to a word is if you were making a command. For example:

이것을 보셔요 = Look at this
빨리 올라오셔요 = Come up quick
이 길에서 직진하셔요 = Go straight on this road

This means that ~(으)세요 can replace ~(으)셔요 in each of the examples above.

For example:

이것을 보세요 = Look at this
빨리 올라오세요 = Come up quick
이 길에서 직진하세요 = Go straight on this road

More examples:
수고하세요! = work hard! (A common greeting when people leave a place of business)
열심히 운동하세요! = work out hard!
먼저 가세요! = Go first
칠판을 올려다보세요 = Look up to the board
시선을 돌리세요 = Turn away your eyes
보안을 위해 대통령을 내일까지 감시하세요 = For security, watch/guard the president until tomorrow

Imperative endings are often added to 있다 to command somebody to "stay" in a place or in a state. As you know, 있다 is often an adjective, but there are times when it is considered a verb. When telling somebody to "stay" like this, 있다 is seen as a verb. The fact that it is a verb doesn't really matter. However, it's always good to know what types of words you are dealing with. Below are some examples:

집에 있어! = Stay at home (be at home!)
잠깐 여기 있어 = Stay here for a second
그냥 집에 있어 = Just stay at home

The adverb 가만히 (to stay still or to not move) is often used in sentences like this to tell somebody to "stay" still. For example:

가만히 있어! = Stay still!/Don't move!

As you learned in the previous lesson, 계시다 is the formal equivalent of this usage of 있다. When ~아/어요 is added to 계시다 to create a command, the construction 계셔요 is formed which you now know can be presented as "계세요." This is where the expression "안녕히 계세요" (which translates to "stay in peace") comes from.

The majority of Korean learners don't know that ~(으)셔요 and ~(으)세요 are equivalent ways to end a sentence. To be honest, you don't really need to know this. The use of ~(으)세요 in Korean is much more common when making a command so as an early learner of Korean it isn't immediately important. For now, I would suggest using the ~(으)세요 form when giving a command to a person who deserves respect, but at the same time be aware of the ~(으)셔요 form in case it comes up.

Now… this brings us to another problem.

~(으)셔요 can be added to make a command.
~(으)셔요 is also a regular present tense conjugation. For example, these are acceptable:

나의 엄마는 매일 운동해 = My mother exercises every day
저의 엄마는 매일 운동해요 = My mother exercises every day

But by adding ~(으)시다, the following is also acceptable:

저의 엄마는 매일 운동하셔요 = My mother exercises every day
I will say it again: when you see "~(으)셔요" can you use "~(으)세요."
Therefore, the sentence above could also be used as:

저의 엄마는 매일 운동하세요 = My mother exercises every day

This can be applied to any situation. For example:

네, 가능하셔요 = Yes, that is possible
네, 가능하세요 = Yes, that is possible
(The above sentences are often heard when you ask if you can do something [like use a particular card or combine multiple coupons] at a store/restaurant)

이분은 저의 엄마이셔요 = This person is my mother
이분은 저의 엄마이세요 = This person is my mother

선생님, 어디 가셔요? = Teacher, where are you going?
선생님, 어디 가세요? = Teacher, where are you going?

그 사람이 언제 오셔요? = When is that person coming?
그 사람이 언제 오세요? = When is that person coming?

Adding ~(으)세요 (or ~(으)시다 for that matter) to a stem can create irregulars. If it is added to a word that follows the ㄷ irregular, the following occurs:

걷다 = to walk
걷다 + ~(으)세요 = 걷 + 으 + 세요
걷 + 으 + 세요 = 걸으세요
걸으세요 = walk!

171

If ~(으)세요 is added to a word that follows the ㅅ irregular, the following occurs:

짓다 = to build
짓다 + ~(으)세요 = 짓 + 으 + 세요
짓 + 으 + 세요 = 지으세요
지으세요 = build!

Refer back to Lesson 7 on irregulars to review these concepts.

One weird thing is that people rarely (if ever) say ~(으)세요 connected to 먹다 (to eat). Instead, it is much more natural to add ~(으)세요 to 들다 (which is a more formal way to say "eat"). Another change occurs when adding ~(으)세요 to verbs that follow the ㄹ irregular:

들다 = to eat (formal)
들다 + ~(으)세요 = 들 + 세요
들 + 세요 = 드세요
드세요 = Eat!

I love tables! Let's look at another table that shows how words change when ~(으)세요 is added to them. I specifically chose irregular words.

Irregular Verb	+~아/어	+~(으)세요
짓다 (build)	지어	지으세요
걷다 (walk)	걸어	걸으세요
듣다 (listen)	들어	들으세요
잠그다 (lock)	잠가	잠그세요
고르다 (choose)	골라	고르세요
만들다 (make)	만들어	만드세요
열다 (open)	열어	여세요
팔다 (sell)	팔아	파세요
눕다 (lay down)	누워	누우세요

Let's look at how we can use another form to make a command.

<u>Imperative mood: Verb stem + ~아/어라</u>

Another way to give a command in Korean is by adding ~아/어라 to a verb stem. The formality is similar to the ~아/어 form you learned previously. Some examples:

빨리 가라! = Go fast!
그렇게 해라! = Do it like that

내 말을 들어라 = Listen to what I say
밥을 먼저 먹어라 = Eat (rice) first (you can eat first)

However, the ~아/어라 form is generally used by much older people (parents or grandparents) when they are giving orders to younger people. As I said, the formality is very similar (if not the same) as using ~아/어, but I would much prefer to use ~아/어 over ~아/어라. One time I said something to my girlfriend like "가라" and she just laughed and said "Who are you? My grandfather?"

If you want to give a command to somebody in a formal way, check out the next section.

Imperative Mood: Verb stem + ~(으)십시오

Adding ~(으)십시오 to a verb stem is done in the same manner as when adding ~(으)세요. That is, the same irregulars come in to play. However, adding ~(으)십시오 to a verb stem allows you to give a command *very* formally. You will most likely only use this form in a few circumstances, as it is usually reserved for times when speaking to people who deserve a ridiculous amount of respect. If you were to meet your girlfriend/boyfriend's *grand*parents for the very first time, you might use this ending. You will also see it sometimes in government buildings/stores/restaurants on signs telling you to "come again" or stuff like that. For example:

여기서 내리십시오 = Get off here (I think this is the message that is broadcasted in the Seoul subway at every stop, telling you to "get off")

Now that you know how to say "do this," it is time to learn how to say "*don't* do this"

Negative Imperative Mood: ~지 말다

You can also use the imperative mood to make a negative command. In these sentences, you can tell somebody *not* do something. These sentences require the use of the word "말다." 말다 can be used in other situations as well, but I will present those to you as they become important (for example, you will see 말다 used to eliminate a choice in Lesson 73 and used with ~든지 in Lesson 106).

When used to make a negative command, ~지 말다 should be added to the stem of a word. For example:

공부하지 말다
가지 말다
먹지 말다

In order to make those constructions a command, you should use one of the imperative conjugations that I taught you earlier in the lesson. Let's look at how this is done with a simple word first. If you want to tell somebody to "go," you should add one of the many 'imperative mood' conjugations to the word "가다." For example (in order of formality):

가다 + ~아/어 = 가!
가다 + ~아/어라 = 가라!
가다 + ~아/어요 = 가요!
가다 + ~(으)세요 = 가세요! (가셔요)
가다 + ~(으)십시오 = 가십시오!

The same is done when telling somebody not to do something. If you want to tell somebody to "not go," you should add ~지 말다 and conjugate it using one of the many imperative mood conjugations.

For example:

1) 가지 말다 + ~아/어 = ~~가지 말아~~! 가지 마!
2) 가지 말다 + ~아/어라 = ~~가지 말아라~~! 가지 마라
3) 가지 말다 + ~아/어요 = ~~가지 말요~~! 가지 마요!
4) 가지 말다 + ~(으)세요 = 가지 마세요!
5) 가지 말다 + ~(으)십시오 = 가지 마십시오!

Notice that numbers 1, 2 and 3 go against the normal grammatical rules of Korean. 말다 is an irregular verb in this respect and to my knowledge no other verb follows this pattern. *(These irregular conjugations only apply when specifically attaching the additions shown above. In all other situations,* 말다 *follows the* ㄹ *irregular like a normal verb ending in* ㄹ*.)*

All five of those conjugations are possible. However, the two most common conjugations that you will hear are number 1 and number 4. If you are speaking to somebody informally, you will most likely hear "가지 마." If you are speaking to somebody formally, you will most likely hear "가지 마세요." Some examples of this negative imperative mood being used:

너무 빨리 먹지 마세요 = Don't eat your food too fast!
부끄러워하지 마세요 = Don't be shy!
그렇게 하지 마! = Don't do it like that!
집에 가지 마! = Don't go home!
앉지 마! = Don't sit down!
여기에 오줌을 싸지 마세요 = Don't pee here
권력을 남용하지 마세요 = Don't abuse your power/authority
오늘이 유쾌한 날이라서 슬퍼하지 마세요 = Today is a delightful day, so don't be sad
사람들을 학력 수준으로 평가하지 마세요 = Don't judge people on the basis of education level
그 학생들에게 허가를 해 주지 마세요 = Don't give those students permission

Before we finish, let's talk about specific ways these imperative endings can be used.

~지 말고

In Lesson 17, you learned how to add ~고 to connect two clauses or ideas. For example:

저는 밥을 먹고 갈 거예요 = I will eat then go
저는 자고 한국어를 공부했어요 = I slept then studied Korean

You can also add ~고 to 말다 to connect the negative command with another clause. The clause after ~지 말고 is typically a positive command. This type of sentence is used when you want to tell somebody what *not* to do, and then also tell them what they should do.

For example:

매일 같은 운동을 하지 말고 많이 쉬세요
= Don't do the same exercise every day, and get lots of rest

그렇게 하지 말고 내 말을 들어봐
= Don't do it like that, and listen to what I have to say

한 사람에게 다 주지 말고 사람들과 동등하게 나누세요
= Don't give them all to one person, hand/divide them out evenly

Giving Directions

Now that you know how to give people commands, you are able to give people directions. Check out the following list for commonly used direction-like sentences:

오른 쪽으로 가세요 = Go right
왼 쪽으로 가세요 = Go left
직진하세요 = Go straight
건물을 지나가서 오른 쪽으로 가세요 = Go past the building, then go right
건물을 지나가서 오른 쪽으로 가지 말고 계속 직진하세요 = Go past the building, then don't turn right, but keep going straight

The Imperative Mood with ~아/어 보다

In Lesson 32, you learned how to add ~아/어 보다 to words to create a meaning that is similar to ""attempt/try." For example, you learned these sentences:

엄마가 요리한 음식을 먹어 봤어? = Did you try the food mom cooked?
결혼하기 위해 남자들을 만나 봤어 = In order to get married, I tried meeting a lot of men

Just because of the meaning of "attempt," it is very common to see an imperative ending attached to ~아/어 보다. For example:

그것을 확인해 봐!! = Try checking that
이것을 먹어 봐! = Try eating this!

Although the typical translation of "~아/어 보다" in these cases is "try…" it is often eliminated.

For example, this sentence:
이것을 먹어 봐! Could be translated as: "Try eating this!" or just "Eat this!"

Especially when used in the least formal imperative form (~아/어 봐), it is very common to see this used simply as a command without any meaning of "try/attempt." Nonetheless, the meaning of "try/attempt" is often very subtle and doesn't really change the meaning of much in the sentence.

Here are some more examples:
여기 와 보세요 = Come here (Try coming here)
지금 앉아 봐 = Sit down (Try sitting down)
문을 열어 봐 = Open the door (Try opening the door)
먼저 가 봐 = Go first (Try going first)
이거를 봐 봐 = Look at this (Try looking at this)
이것을 드셔 보세요 = Eat this (Try eating this)
이 차를 마셔 보세요 = Drink this tea (Try drinking this tea)
이 제품 수준을 높여 보세요 = Try to raise the level/standard of this product
그 강아지가 온순해 보여서 한번 만져 보세요 = That dog looks gentle, so try touching it
직원이랑 잠깐 얘기해 봐 = Try talking with a staff member
이 물체가 무엇인지 생각해 보세요 = Try thinking about what this object is

Lesson 41: To do for somebody: ~아/어 주다

Vocabulary

Nouns:
동료 = colleague, peer
사거리 = intersection
어린이집 = day care
유치원 = kindergarten
뿌리 = roots
무역 = trade
턱 = chin
왼발 = left foot
왼손 = left hand
오른발 = right foot
오른손 = right hand
손바닥 = palm
음성 = voice
이마 = forehead
발가락 = toe
발목 = ankle
엉덩이 = butt
신체 = body
감옥 = prison
볼 = cheek
제자리 = in the right place

Verbs:
상대하다 = to deal with people
미치다 = to go crazy

Adverbs and Other Words:
멀리 = far, far away
너무나 = extremely
초 = beginning of a time period
말 = end of a time period
결코 = put with negative sentences to stress
최초 = the first time in history something is done or occurs

Introduction

In the previous lesson, you learned how to give commands using the imperative voice. In this lesson, you will learn how to use 주다 and how it can be used with the imperative voice. Also, you will learn how to use ~아/어 주다 when an action is done for you. Let's get started

주다 = to give

주다 means "to give" and you already know how to use it in a wide variety of sentences when an object is being given. For example:

저는 저의 친구에게 돈을 줬어요 = I gave my friend money
아빠는 나에게 음식을 줬어 = Dad gave me food

When asking/telling/commanding another person to give something to you, you can attach an imperative ending that you learned in the previous lesson. For example, if you want somebody to give you a book, you can attach any imperative form:

그 책을 (나에게) 줘 = Give me that book
그 책을 (나에게) 줘라 = Give me that book (usually pronounced as 주라)
그 책을 (저에게) 주세요 = Give me that book

Other examples:

맥주 한 병을 주세요 = Give me one bottle of beer (please)
저 숟가락을 주세요 = Give me that spoon (please)
밥을 많이 주세요 = Give me lots of rice
왼손만 주세요 = Give me only your left hand
6월 말에 돈을 주세요 = Give me the money at the end of June

The sentences above only involve *objects* being given. It is also possible to use 주다 when an action is being done for a person. Let's talk about this next.

Verb stem + ~아/어 주다

By adding ~아/어 주다 to the stem of a word, you can imply that the action is somehow beneficial to you (or whoever the action is being done for); almost as if it were a favor that another person completed. In these cases, not only is the action completed, but it is completed *for* you (or whoever). For example:

그 선생님은 한국어를 저에게 가르쳤어요 = That teacher taught me Korean
그 선생님은 한국어를 저에게 가르쳐 줬어요 = That teacher taught me Korean

Those sentences essentially have the same meaning, but by adding "~아/어 주다" the speaker is emphasizing that the teacher provided some sort of service/favor by teaching you.

Many more examples:
Notice that ~(으)시 can be added to ~아/어 주다 if the person acting deserves high respect.

엄마가 과자를 내 손바닥에 놓아 주었어
= Mom put some candy into my hands (on my palms) for me

내년 초에 오빠가 돈을 보내 줄 거예요
= My brother will send the money early next year

동료가 그 일을 저에게 설명해 줬어요
= A colleague explained that work to me

할머니가 오늘 멀리에서 와 주셨어요
= Grandma came from far away (for me/us) today

경찰관은 밖에 있는 미친 사람과 상대해 줬어요
= The policeman dealt with the crazy person outside (for me)

제가 외국 사람이라서 이 회사에서 저를 상대해 주고 싶은 사람이 없어요
= Nobody wants to deal with me at this company because I'm a foreigner

선생님은 밤에 우리를 위해 어린이집을 잠깐 열어 줬어요
= The teacher opened the daycare for us at night for a little bit

You learned in the previous lesson how to add imperative endings to words. If you want a person to do something *for* you, you can first add ~아/어 주다 to the stem of the word and add an imperative ending to 주다.

Notice the difference between the following sentences:

빨리 오세요 = Come quick
빨리 와 주세요 = Come quick (for me)

Notice that both sentences essentially have the same meaning. The first sentence is simply a command, but the second sentence (because of the nature of the word "주다") implies that the desired action is beneficial to the speaker. Almost as if the action is a favor that the speaker would like to happen.

Therefore, adding ~아/어 주다 to a stem gives the sentence the meaning of "do __ for me." This often translates more simply to "Please, ….." For example:

점심을 요리해 주세요! = Please, make me lunch
이것을 만들어 주세요 = Please, make this for me

The two sentences above have essentially the same meaning, but a slightly different feel than the following sentences:

점심을 요리하세요 = Make lunch
이것을 만드세요 = Make this

The only difference being that when using '주다' you are specifically asking for some sort of 'service.' When you do not include '주다,' you are just telling somebody to do something. However, by saying 주다, you are indicating that the person is doing something for you.

Many more examples:

그 책을 제자리에 둬 주세요 = Please put that book back in its place
볼에 이 로션을 발라 주세요 = Please put this lotion on my cheeks
이것을 이마에 붙여 주세요 = Please stick this on my forehead
음성 메시지를 남겨 주세요 = Please leave me a voice message
우리 아이를 이 유치원에 받아 주세요 = Please accept our child into this kindergarten
발목이 아파서 잠깐 봐 주세요 = My ankle is sore, so please look at it for a second
이 양말을 오른발에 신겨 주세요 = Please put this sock on my right foot
정답을 모르는 사람은 오른손을 올려 주세요 = The people who don't know the answer, please raise your right hand

In Lesson 36 you learned about the word 보이다 and how it can be used to indicate that one can (or cannot) see something. ~아/어 주다 is often added to 보이다 to ask for something to "be shown" to somebody. 보여주다 and 보여 주다 (with and without the space) are acceptable. For example:

얼굴을 보여주세요 = Please show (me) your face
발가락을 보여 주세요 = Please show me your toe
해외무역건물이 어디 있는지 보여주세요 = Please show me where the international trade building is

----

좀 is an interesting word that is commonly used in Korean – especially in speech. One way that it is used is as a shortened version of "조금." As such, it can replace "조금" in sentences where appropriate, but this is usually reserved for speaking or dialogue in print. For example:

날씨가 좀 추워졌어요 = The weather got a little bit cold
저는 좀 더 올라갈 거예요 = I'm going to go a little bit higher

이마가 좀 아파요 = My forehead is a little bit sore
제가 산 주식은 좀 비쌌어요 = The stocks I bought were a bit expensive

It is also common to find "좀" used in imperative sentences. When asking somebody to do something for you, using "좀" makes the request sound a little bit softer. This is almost impossible to translate to English, as its addition simply adds a feel to the sentence. For example:

밥을 좀 많이 주세요 = Give me lots of rice
이것을 좀 만들어 주세요 = Please, make this for me
그 책을 제자리에 좀 둬 주세요 = Please put that book back in its place (for me)

There are other ways to ask for something in Korean that don't need the imperative mood. For example, you could also say "Can you do this for me?" It would also be appropriate to use "좀" in sentences like this as well. This grammar has not been introduced yet, so I do not want to talk about it here. It will be talked about in Lesson 45.

Using 주다 with Negative Imperative Sentences

Just like you learned in the previous lesson, you can tell a person *not* to do something by adding ~지 말다 to the stem of a word. You can also add ~아/어 주다 after ~지 말다 to have the same effect as described previously. That is, you are asking for somebody to not do something *for* you. For example:

그것을 말하지 마세요 = Don't say that
그것을 말하지 말아 주세요 = Please don't say that

Those sentences essentially have the same meaning, but by adding "주다" the speaker is emphasizing that the listener is providing some sort of service/favor by doing the action. Below are many more examples:

수업 시간 동안 자지 말아 주세요 = Please don't sleep in class
저를 쳐다보지 말아 주세요 = Please don't stare at me
제 엉덩이를 만지지 말아 주세요 = Please don't touch my bum
저를 감옥에 넣지 말아 주세요! = Please don't put me in prison!
자기의 뿌리를 잊지 말아 주세요 = Please don't forget your roots

Thank You For...

This is where everything starts to come together. You can use the concepts you learned in this lesson, the previous lesson, and in Lesson 37 (all together) to say "thank you for...."

If you wanted to say, "thank you for listening," you would have to use multiple concepts.

First off, a word: 들어보다 (to listen)

By adding ~아/어 주다 to 들어보다, we get: 들어봐 주다, which can be used many ways:

그는 제 말을 들어봐 줬어요 = He listened to me
제 말을 들어봐 주세요 = Listen to me, please

If you add ~아/어서 (because) to 들어봐 주다, you get:

들어봐 줘서…

which means something like "because you listen(ed)."

If you add "감사하다" (thank you) after ~아/어서, you get:

들어봐 줘서 감사합니다 = Because you listened, thank you (thank you for listening)

Okay, one more time.

1) Take a verb: 요리하다 (to cook)
2) Add ~아/어 주다: 요리해 주다
3) Add ~아/어서: 요리해 줘서
4) Add 감사하다 = 요리해 줘서 감사합니다 = thanks for cooking

It seems really confusing because there are so many concepts wrapped in one sentence. More examples will help you get the hang of it:

열심히 공부해 줘서 감사합니다 = Thanks for studying hard
이것을 가르쳐 줘서 감사합니다 = Thanks for teaching that to me
문을 열어 줘서 감사합니다 = Thanks for opening the door for me

To make it *even* more confusing, often times ~(으)시 is added to ~아/어 주다 (because, usually when you are thanking somebody, you are trying to be formal). For example:

이것을 가르쳐 주셔서 감사합니다 = Thanks for teaching that to me
(가르치다 + ~아/어 주다 + ~(으)시 + ~아/어서 + 감사합니다)

And *that* is why I waited until Lesson 41 to teach you about this concept. There would have been no way that you would have been able to grasp everything I taught in this lesson if I had taught it earlier. It took us so long to get to the point where I was comfortable teaching concepts like ~아/어서 and '~(으)시,' and now we are using both of those concepts *together* in addition to what you learned in this lesson.

Tough stuff, but hopefully you understood everything correctly.

Lessons 34 – 41 Mini-Test

All finished Lessons 34 – 41? Now it is time to test yourself on what you learned in those lessons! Before moving on to our next set of lessons, try to make sure you can understand all the concepts covered here. Good luck!

The answers are at the bottom of the test!

1) Which of the following is incorrect?:

a) 운동을 하지 않아서 살이 쪘어요
b) 저의 여자 친구는 그 여자보다 훨씬 예뻐요
c) 일단 밥을 먹은 후에 나갈 거예요
d) 저는 한국을 별로 좋아해요

2) Which of the following explains that you will eat dinner tonight, with no doubt implied:

a) 저는 저녁식사를 먹을지 몰라요
b) 저는 저녁식사를 먹을 거예요
c) 저는 저녁식사를 먹었을 것 같아요
d) 저는 저녁식사를 먹을 것 같아요

3) Which of the following describes that you look tired?

a) 피곤해 보인다
b) 피곤할 것 같다
c) 피곤해 같이 보인다
d) 피곤할 보인다

4) Which is the best translation of the following sentence:

제가 많이 먹어서 지금 운동하고 싶지 않아요

a) Because I exercised, I don't want to eat a lot
b) Even though I exercised, I want to eat a lot
c) Even though I ate a lot, I want to exercise
d) Because I ate a lot, I don't want to exercise

5) Which of the following bold areas is conjugated incorrectly:

a) 제가 서울에 곧 **가기 때문에** 지금 너무 기대돼요
b) 제가 서울에 곧 **갈 것이기 때문에** 지금 너무 기대돼요
c) 제가 서울에 곧 **갈 때문에** 지금 너무 기대돼요
d) 제가 서울에 곧 **갈 거라서** 지금 너무 기대돼요

6) Which of the following should you not say to your boss?

a) 부장님! 밥을 드셨어요?
b) 부장님! 잘 주무셨어요?
c) 부장님! 언제 가실 거예요?
d) 부장님! 밥을 먹으시고 싶어요?

7) Choose the incorrect sentence based on honorifics:

a) 아들! 빨리 와!
b) 할아버지! 많이 잡수십시오!
c) 교수님! 다시 한번 설명해라!
d) 오빠! 그것을 주세요!

Answers:
1) d
2) b
3) a
4) d
5) c
6) d
7) c

Lesson 42: When I do, when I did, whenever: ~ㄹ 때, ~했을 때

Vocabulary

Nouns:
레인 = lane
뼈 = bone
뼈마디 = joint
도매 = wholesale
소매 = retail
사인 = autograph
뇌 = brain
집안 = inside a house
배경 = background
복권 = lottery ticket
시간표 = timetable
사막 = desert
곤충 = bug, insect

Verbs:
버티다 = to endure, bear
견디다 = to endure, bear
응원하다 = to cheer on, to root for
응시하다 = to gaze, to look
짐작하다 = to guess
죽이다 = to kill
감다 = to wash one's hair

Adjectives:
예의가 바르다 = to be polite
얕다 = to be shallow

Adverbs and Other Words:
어쨌든 = at any rate, in any case, anyways
깊이 = deeply
겨우 = barely, hardly, narrowly
가짜 = fake

Introduction

In this lesson, you will use the ~는 것 principle to describe a specific time that an action takes place. This can be done using the special noun "때" to makes sentences like:

When I study…
When I meet you…
When I was in Korea…

In addition, we will look at other ways 때 can be used. Let's get started.

Simple Usages of 때

The word "때" typically refers to a "time." In its most simple form, you can see it placed after some event or period to refer to the time during that event/period. For example:

저녁 때 = During dinner/evening time
방학 때 = During the school vacation
회의 때 = During the meeting
휴가 때 = During a vacation
고등학교 때 = During high school
중학교 때 = During middle school
초등학교 때 = During elementary school
대학교 때 = During University

These constructions can be used in sentences where appropriate. For example:

저는 방학 때 집안에서 공부를 할 거예요
= I'm going to study in my house during vacation

휴가 때 어디로 갈 거예요?
= Where are you going to go during vacation?

고등학교 때 저는 친구가 별로 없었어요
= I didn't have many friends during high school

대학교 때 동시에 여자 친구가 두 명 있었어요
= I had two girlfriends at the same time during university

선생님들은 회의 때 시간표에 대해 얘기했어요
= The teachers talked about the schedule during the meeting

Let's look at how 때 can be described by a preceding clause to indicate a more complex time.

When: … ~ㄹ/을 때

때 can be used as the noun being described in the ~는 것 principle. When used like this, it indicates a specific moment in which something happens. The future tense form of ~는 (~ㄹ/을) is usually used to describe 때 in these cases. For example:

내가 밥을 먹을 때

This construction translates to something like "the time that I eat."

The use of ~ㄹ/을 theoretically indicates that this is a time in the future. However, this form could be used to describe a general time (that doesn't necessarily happen in the past, present or future), or to describe a time in the future. Depending on the context and the rest of the sentence, the construction above could be completed as:

내가 밥을 먹을 때 음악을 듣는 것을 좋아해 = When I eat I like to listen to music
내가 밥을 먹을 때 너에게 음식을 조금 줄 거야 = When I eat, I will give you some food

Also notice that (as you should know) when the subject of both clauses is the same, you don't need to write the subject twice.

Below are many other examples:

저는 돈을 받을 때 행복할 거예요 = When I receive (the) money, I will be happy
뼈마디가 아플 때 이 약을 드세요 = When your joints hurt, take this medicine
당신의 눈을 응시할 때 가슴이 설레어요 = When I gaze into your eyes, my heart flutters
머리를 감을 때 비누로 해요 = When I wash my hair, I do it with soap
오랫동안 공부할 때 뇌가 아파요 = When I study for a long time, my brain hurts

대통령을 만날 때 저는 아주 예의가 바를 거예요
= When I meet the president I will be very polite

이 레인에서 운전할 때 앞에 있는 차를 앞지르지 마세요
= When you are driving in this lane, don't pass the car in front of you

선생님이 여기에 계실 때 나는 선생님의 말을 듣기 시작할 거야
= When the teacher is here, I will start listening to him/her

뼈가 아플 때 고통을 버티려고 이 약을 먹어요
= When your bones are sore, in order to endure the pain, take this medicine

사람들이 곤충을 죽일 때 아무 느낌도 없어요
= People don't feel anything when they kill insects

그 그림을 볼 때 배경이 무슨 의미가 있는지 생각해 보세요
= When you look at the painting, try to think about what meaning the background has

----
Notice in the examples above that the main action of the sentence is occurring precisely at the time indicated by the clause describing "때." The main action of the clause is not occurring after the time indicated by "때," or as a result of action. Therefore, be careful of the meaning you create when attaching ~ㄹ/을 때 to 가다 or 오다. For example:

집에 갈 때 아빠를 전화할 거예요

This sentence would not translate to "when I go home, I will call my father." Rather, it is indicating that you will call your father during the "going" part of the sentence. To indicate that you will call your father *after* arriving at home, you should use another grammatical principle like:

집에 가서 아빠를 전화할 거예요 = I will go home and call my father
집에 가면 아빠를 전화할 거예요 = When I go home, I will call my father
The use of ~(으)면 is discussed in the next lesson

In order to indicate that something happened at some time in the past, you can add ~았/었 to the stem of a word followed by ~ㄹ/을 때. For example:

먹었을 때 = When I ate
갔을 때 = When I went
공부했을 때 = When I studied

Just like when used in the future/general tense, the remaining part of the clause can indicate the action that occurred at that time. For example:

내가 밥을 먹었을 때 말하고 싶지 않았어
= When I ate, I didn't want to talk

엄마가 갔을 때 저는 울었어요
= When mom left, I cried

내가 공부했을 때 문법만 공부했어
= When I studied, I only studied grammar

가방을 처음 봤을 때 가짜인 것을 알았어요
= When I first saw the bag, I knew that it was fake

그 연예인의 사인을 받았을 때 너무 설레었어요
= When I got that celebrity's signature, I was really excited

그 사람이 말을 했을 때 그 사람이 경찰관인 것을 짐작했어요
= When that person spoke, I guessed that he is/was a police officer

의사가 뇌에 대한 수업을 가르치셨을 때 아주 깊이 설명하셨어요
= When the doctor taught a class about the brain, he explained it very deeply

이 제품을 소매로 팔았을 때 돈을 많이 못 벌어서 지금부터 도매로 팔 거예요
= When I sold this product through retail, I didn't make any money so from now on I'm going to start selling it through wholesale

Using ~았/었을 때 is the way you can describe what used to happen when you were younger. For example:

제가 어렸을 때 곤충을 먹었어요 = When I was young I used to eat bugs
제가 열 살이었을 때 아주 뚱뚱했어요 = I was really fat when I was ten years old

The particle ~에 can be added to 때 in all of the sentences above. However, when used to refer to a time (which it was in all of the examples above), the ~에 can be omitted. Other particles can be attached to 때 if you want to use "the time in which an action happens" as the subject or object of a sentence. For example:

우리가 지난 번에 만났을 때가 아주 재미있었어요
= The last time we met was really fun

저는 사막에서 살았을 때를 잊어버리고 싶어요
= I want to forget the time I lived in the desert

우리가 처음에 만났을 때를 생각하는 게 좋아요
= I like thinking about the time we first met

More complicated particles can be attached to 때 as well. For example:

키가 클 때까지 얕은 수영장에서만 수영할 거예요
= I'm only going to swim in shallow swimming pools until I am taller

저는 그 팀을 어렸을 때부터 응원했어요
= I've been cheering for that team since I was young

내가 한국에 있을 때마다 한국어로 말하고 싶어
= Every time I am in Korea, I want to speak Korean

제가 저의 여자 친구의 부모님을 만날 때마다 저는 너무 긴장돼요
= Every time I meet my girlfriend's parents, I am very nervous

제가 집에 있을 때는 TV를 봐요
= I watch TV when I'm at home (but not when I'm somewhere else)
(This usage of ~는/은 is discussed more in Lesson 104)

저의 여자 친구는 우리가 같이 있지 않을 때에만 저를 좋아해요
= My girlfriend only likes me when we are not together

~나 is also a particle (which isn't introduced until Lesson 55) that you saw added to 때 in Lesson 25. For example: 아무 때나 좋아요 = Anytime is good

In all of the examples shown so far, the best translation for "때" would be "when," as they indicate the time "when" an action happens. 때 can also be used to indicate that some sort of "time" or "case" has occurred. This usage is usually predicated by a word like "있다" or "없다" to indicate that there is/is not times/cases where some event happens. For example:

그 친구를 죽이고 싶을 때가 있어요 = There are times when I want to kill that friend
밤 늦게 배고플 때가 많아요 = There are many cases/times where I am hungry at night

In this usage, it could be appropriate to attach ~ㄹ/을 때 to 가다 or 오다. For example:

그 학생이 늦게 올 때가 많아요 = There are many times where that student comes late

That's it for this lesson!

Lesson 43: If and when: ~ㄴ/는다면, ~(으)면

Vocabulary

Nouns:
장거리 = long distance
콜라 = Cola
과학자 = scientist
신호 = signal
날개 = wing
가지 = eggplant
고추 = hot pepper
신부 = bride
신랑 = groom
교훈 = moral, lesson
버릇 = habit
햇살 = the rays of the sun
빨래 = laundry
이슬 = dew
비바람 = rainstorm
습도 = humidity

Verbs:
기초하다 = to be based on
보존하다 = to preserve, to conserve
기도하다 = to pray
대접하다 = to serve, to treat
진정하다 = to calm down

Adjectives:
부자연스럽다 = to be unnatural
균등하다 = to be even
어색하다 = to be awkward
낯설다 = to be unfamiliar
수상하다 = to be suspicious

Adverbs and Other Words:
만약 = put in sentences with "if"
양쪽 = both directions

Introduction

In the previous lesson, you learned how to add ~ㄹ/을 때 to words to have the meaning of "when." In this lesson, you will learn about adding ~(으)면 to words to have a similar meaning. Let's get started

When/If… ~(으)면

To create the meaning of "when" or "if," you can add ~(으)면 to the stem of a verb or adjective. If we look at the meaning of ~(으)면 more deeply, it can be separated into three main usages.

Usage 1
To indicate that an action occurs "when/if" another action (that hasn't happened yet) occurs

For example:
집에 도착하면 빨래를 할 거예요 = When I arrive at home, I will do laundry

Notice in this usage that the action in the second clause is a supposition/assumption of what would happen when the first clause occurs. Both actions haven't happened yet and the speaker is merely assuming what will take place. Keep this in mind for later because it will come up again.

Here the event of "arriving at home" hasn't happened yet. Therefore, the speaker is indicating that he/she will "do laundry" when this event occurs. In this example, the event of "arriving at home" seems inevitable and certain. Because it is certain that this action will occur, the translation of "when" is often used.

If there is uncertainty in whether the first event will occur or not, the translation of "if" is often used to express this uncertainty. Notice what happens if you use "if" in the sentence above:

"If I arrive at home, I will do laundry."

In most situations, I can't imagine this being a natural sentence. Of course you are eventually going to arrive at home sometime – so the event isn't really uncertain. Therefore, the translation of "if" is a little bit unnatural. However, if you changed the sentence a little and added a condition that would make the event uncertain, the translation of "if" would be more appropriate. For example:

집에 일찍 도착하면 빨래를 할 거예요 = If I arrive home early, I will do laundry

Either way, I don't want you to get hung up on the English translation of a sentence. I would rather you understand the meaning of the Korean sentence than to worry about whether "when" or "if" is more appropriate. Often times it isn't even clear if the sentence is uncertain or not. For example:

학교에 가면 알려 주세요 = When/if you go to school, let me know

Depending on the situation and context, "When you go to school, let me know" or "If you go to school, let me know" could both be appropriate. In these cases, you need to use the context to distinguish specifically what meaning is being implied.

Below are many examples showing this usage:

신호를 보면 저에게 말을 바로 해 주세요
= When/if you see the signal, let me know immediately please

과학자가 되면 피부에 습도의 영향을 연구하고 싶어요
= When/if I become a scientist, I want to study the effects of humidity on the skin

내일 비바람이 오면 경기가 취소될 거예요
= If it storms tomorrow, the match/game will be cancelled

지금 환경을 보존하지 않으면 미래에 더 큰 문제가 생길 것 같아요
= If we don't preserve the environment, there will probably be bigger problems in the future

오늘 그 사람을 만나면 낯선 사람으로 대할 거예요
= If I meet that person today, I'm going to treat him like a stranger

손님이 오면 맛있는 음식을 대접할 거예요
= When the guests come, I will treat them with delicious food

진정하지 않으면 콜라를 주지 않을 거예요
= If you don't calm down, I won't give you a cola

내일 아침에 이슬이 있으면 고추가 다 죽어 버릴 거예요
= If there is dew tomorrow morning, all of the hot pepper (plants) will die

내일 분위기가 어색하면 이 게임을 한번 해 보세요
= If the atmosphere is awkward tomorrow, try playing this game

신랑이 신부를 보면 그녀가 얼마나 예쁜지 깨달을 거예요
= The groom will realize how pretty the bride is when he sees her

----

In all of the examples so far, the second clause is an assumption of what will happen if/when some action occurs. It is also possible to conjugate the clause attached to ~(으)면 to the past tense to assume/suppose what *would have* happened if something *had* occurred. In order to do this, ~았/었 is added to the stem of the word followed by ~으면. For example:

내가 공부했으면... = If I studied...
내가 먹었으면... = If I ate...
내가 갔으면... = If I went...

Much like the present tense, the action in the second clause is a supposition/assumption of what would have happened if the first clause had occurred.

Usually when the verb/adjective after "if" is conjugated to the past tense, the later clause ends in "would have..." For example:

If I studied, I **would have** passed the test
If I ate, I **would have** not been hungry
If I met my friend, it **would have** been fun

Expressing this meaning of "would have" in Korean is done by adding ~았/었을 것이다 to the final word of the sentence. For example:

내가 공부했으면 시험을 합격했을 것이다 = If I studied, I would have passed the test
내가 밥을 먹었으면 배고프지 않았을 것이다 = If I ate, I wouldn't have been hungry
친구를 만났으면 재미있었을 것이다 = If I met my friend, it would have been fun

Notice that the translation of "if" is more appropriate when using ~(으)면 in the past tense. The use of "when" makes it seem like the action actually did happen – when actually it did not. Many more examples:

돈을 다 쓰지 않았으면 그것을 샀을 거예요
= If I didn't/hadn't spent all of my money, I would have bought that

내가 사과를 다 안 먹었으면 너에게 한 개를 줬을 거야
= If I didn't/hadn't eaten all of my apples, I would have given you one

햇살이 그렇게 강하지 않았으면 밖에 나갔을 거예요
= If the sunlight wasn't so strong, I would have gone outside

음식이 충분했으면 사람들에게 균등하게 줬을 거예요
= If there were enough, I would have given the food out to people evenly

그 남자가 너무 수상하지 않았으면 그를 믿었을 거예요
= If that man weren't so suspicious, I would have believed him

고추를 안 넣었으면 맵지 않았을 거예요
= If you didn't put the hot pepper in it, it wouldn't have been spicy

Using ~(으)면 in the past tense is a common way that you hope or wish for something. Explaining this is beyond the scope of this lesson, but you will continue to learn about this usage in Lesson 61.

In all of the examples above – in both the present and past tenses - the second clause is an assumption of what will happen (or would have happened). When indicating an assumption like this, it is also possible to *conjugate* the verb prior to ~면 first. The words need to be conjugated using the plain/diary form before ~면 can be added on.

Make sure you remember your plain/diary form conjugations, introduced in Lesson 5.

For example:

For verbs in the present tense:
가다 = 간다면
먹다 = 먹는다면

For adjectives in the present tense:
행복하다 = 행복하다면
길다 = 길다면

For verbs in the past tense:
가다 = 갔다면
먹다 = 먹었다면

For adjectives in the past tense:
행복하다 = 행복했다면
길다 = 길었다면

For 이다 and 아니다
이다 = 이라면 (present tense)
이다 = 이었다면 (past tense)
아니라면 (present tense)
아니었다면 (past tense)

I usually refer to this addition as ~ㄴ/는다면 because it shows that the word before ~면 must be conjugated.

All of the examples shown to this point could also be expressed using ~ㄴ/는다면. When used like this, there is a little bit more of an emphasis of the fact that the action is a supposition/assumption than when ~(으)면 is used. Therefore, the translation of "if" is more commonly used with ~ㄴ/는다면. Nonetheless, all of the examples below have the same meaning as their earlier counterparts – just that there is more of an emphasis that the clause before ~ㄴ/는다면 might or might not happen:

집에 도착한다면 빨래를 할 거예요
집에 일찍 도착한다면 빨래를 할 거예요
학교에 간다면 알려 주세요
신호를 본다면 저에게 말을 바로 해 주세요
과학자가 된다면 피부에 습도의 영향을 연구하고 싶어요
내일 비바람이 온다면 경기가 취소될 거예요
지금 환경을 보존하지 않는다면 미래에 더 큰 문제가 생길 것 같아요
오늘 그 사람을 만난다면 낯선 사람으로 대할 거예요
손님이 온다면 맛있는 음식을 대접할 거예요
진정하지 않는다면 콜라를 주지 않을 거예요
내일 아침에 이슬이 있는다면 고추가 다 죽어 버릴 거예요
내일 분위기가 어색하다면 이 게임을 한번 해 보세요
신랑이 신부를 본다면 그녀가 얼마나 예쁜지 깨달을 거예요
내가 공부했다면 시험을 합격했을 것이다
내가 밥을 먹었다면 배고프지 않았을 것이다
친구를 만났다면 재미있었을 것이다
돈을 다 쓰지 않았다면 그것을 샀을 거예요
내가 사과를 다 안 먹었다면 너에게 한 개를 줬을 거야
햇살이 그렇게 강하지 않았다면 밖에 나갔을 거예요
음식이 충분했다면 사람들에게 균등하게 줬을 거예요
그 남자가 너무 수상하지 않았다면 그를 믿었을 거예요
고추를 안 넣었다면 맵지 않았을 거예요

It is also possible to attach ~았/었더라면 to the tenses above in the past tense, for example:

내가 공부했더라면 시험을 합격했을 것이다
내가 밥을 먹었더라면 배고프지 않았을 것이다
친구를 만났더라면 재미있었을 것이다
돈을 다 쓰지 않았더라면 그것을 샀을 거예요
내가 사과를 다 안 먹었더라면 너에게 한 개를 줬을 거야
햇살이 그렇게 강하지 않았더라면 밖에 나갔을 거예요
음식이 충분했더라면 사람들에게 균등하게 줬을 거예요
그 남자가 너무 수상하지 않았더라면 그를 믿었을 거예요
고추를 안 넣었더라면 맵지 않았을 거예요

You can think of ~았/었더라면 as one unit, but it might be helpful for you to see the purpose of adding ~더~ to other constructions. I discuss some of the usages of ~더~ in Lessons 117, 118 and 119.

It is common to end these "assumption" sentences with ~ㄹ/을 텐데, which I discuss in Lesson 100.

I know it is tempting, but I actually hope you didn't look ahead to those future lessons. We still have more to discuss in this lesson. Let's move on and talk about another usage of ~(으)면.

Usage 2
To generally indicate that when one action occurs, another action occurs

In this usage, the first clause indicates the requirement/basis that is needed to make the event in the second clause occur. This cause-and-effect between the first and second clause is typically common knowledge that usually anybody would know. For example:

비가 오면 날씨가 추워져요 = When/if it rains, the weather gets colder

Notice in this usage that the events being described are <u>not assumptions</u> but are general facts.

As these sentences are describing a general cause-and-effect – and not some event that happened in the past or will happen in the future, the final clause is typically conjugated in the present tense.

Again, not that I want you to focus on the English translations, but notice that the usage of "when" or "if" is arbitrary. Both words are appropriate for this situation. Below are many more examples:

잠을 못 자면 다음 날에 몸이 피곤해져요
= When/if you don't sleep well, the next day you will be tired

장거리 운전을 하면 엉덩이가 아파요
= When/if you drive long distances, your bum will be sore

콜라를 매일 마시면 건강이 나빠져요
= When/if you drink cola every day, your health deteriorates/drops

누구나 캐나다에 가면 좋아해요
= When/if anybody goes to Canada, they like it

누구나 자기 전 여자 친구를 만나면 분위기가 어색해요
= When/if anybody meets their ex-girlfriend, the atmosphere is awkward

오후가 되면 햇살이 강해져요
= When/if it becomes (when it gets to be) afternoon, the sun gets stronger

날개가 위로 움직이면 비행기가 떨어져요
= When/if the wings move up, the plane drops.

학생들이 균등한 기회를 받으면 미래가 밝아져요
= When/if students receive an equal opportunity, the future becomes brighter

Let's move on and talk about another usage of ~(으)면.

Usage 3
To indicate that an action occurs whenever another action is repeated

In this usage, every time the first clause occurs, the second clause occurs. For this usage to work, the actions need to be things that are repeated frequently. For example:

피자를 먹으면 저는 콜라를 마셔요 = When/If I eat pizza, I drink cola

Notice in this usage that the events being described are <u>not assumptions</u> but are general facts.

Again, as with the previous usage of ~(으)면, these sentences are not describing some event that happened in the past or will happen in the future. Rather, the actions are events that are repeated frequently. Therefore, the final clause of these sentences is typically conjugated in the present tense.

The typical translation for this usage is "whenever…". This usage of ~(으)면 is almost identical to adding ~마다 to "때," which you learned about in the previous lesson. In any language, there are often many ways to say the same thing. For example, "whenever" and "every time" can both be used to have the same meaning. For example:

피자를 먹으면 저는 콜라를 마셔요 = Whenever I eat pizza, I drink cola
피자를 먹으면 저는 콜라를 마셔요 = Every time I eat pizza, I drink cola

Below are many more examples of this usage:

내가 공부를 하면 엄마는 TV를 끈다 = Whenever I study, my mother turns off the TV
내가 TV를 보면 엄마는 싫어한다 = Whenever I watch TV, my mother doesn't like it
내가 행복하면 숙제를 잘 해 = Whenever I am happy, I do my homework well

그 연예인이 방에 들어가면 양쪽에서 사람들이 그에게 다가가요
= Whenever that celebrity goes into a room, people approach him from both/all directions

아버지가 운전하면 습관으로 담배를 피워요
= Whenever my dad drives, he smokes cigarettes out of habit

제가 경기를 보면 우리 팀이 이기기를 기도해요
= Whenever I watch a game, I pray for my team to win

일요일이면 그 가족이 기도하러 교회에 가요
= Whenever it is Sunday, that family goes to church to pray

만약

There are a handful of Korean adverbs that have no real translation to English because they don't really have any meaning. These words are often used in sentences for feeling and to help the listener expect what the speaker will say. Probably the most common of all of these words is "만약."

만약 is used in sentences when the result of a sentence can't be certain. Due to the nature of sentences where the second clause is a supposition or assumption, it is common to see "만약" used in sentences that follow the first usage of ~(으)면 described in this lesson. For example:

만약 내가 공부했으면 시험을 합격했을 것이다
= If I studied, I would have passed the test

만약 내가 밥을 먹었으면 배고프지 않았을 것이다
= If I ate, I wouldn't have been hungry

만약 내일 비바람이 오면 경기가 취소될 거예요
= If it storms tomorrow, the match will be cancelled

만약 지금 환경을 보존하지 않으면 미래에 더 큰 문제가 생길 것 같아요
= If we don't preserve the environment now, there will probably be bigger problems in the future

----

In Lesson 7, you learned how irregular words change as a result of adding different additions. This is the first time you have been introduced to adding ~(으)면. Let's look at how irregulars change as a result of adding this grammatical principle.

- The ㅅ irregular, ㄷ irregular and ㅂ irregular all follow the same rules that were introduced in Lesson 7. The addition of the vowel causes a change (or elimination) of the last letter of the stem.

- The ㅡ and 르 irregular are not affected by this addition. The final letter in both types of stems is a vowel, so "면" is added instead of "으면."

- Much like how additions starting with ㄹ can be attached directly to the stems of words ending in ㄹ, ~면 can be attached directly to the stems of words ending in ㄹ.

- Adding ~(으)면 causes a change to ㅎ irregular words. The ㅎ is removed, and ~면 is added to the stem. Anytime you have the option of adding ~(으) as part of a grammatical addition, the ㅎ will be removed from the stem and the grammatical addition without "으" will be added to the remainder of the stem. For example: 그렇다 + ~(으)면 = 그러면 (I talk about the meaning of 그러면 in the next section of this lesson)

Below is a table showing the changes that result from adding ~(으)면 to a word.

Irregular	Word	+ ~(으)면
ㅅ Irregular	짓다 (to build)	지으면
ㄷ Irregular	걷다 (to walk)	걸으면
ㅂ Irregular	돕다 (to help)	도우면
ㅡ Irregular	잠그다 (to lock)	잠그면
르 Irregular	자르다 (to cut)	자르면
ㄹ Irregular	살다 (to live)	살면
ㅎ Irregular	그렇다 (to be like that)	그러면

You will see these same changes to irregulars anytime you add something that begins in ~(으)ㅁ…. For example:
~(으)면서 (Lesson 62)
~(으)며 (Lesson 62)
~(으)므로 (Lesson 103)

그러면

In Lesson 23, you learned that the meaning of the word '그렇다' is close to the meaning of 'like that.'

By adding ~(으)면 to 그렇다 you can create "그러면."
By adding ~ㄴ/는다면 to 그렇다 you can create "그렇다면"
(Remember that 그렇다 is an adjective and therefore 그렇는다면 would be incorrect)

When some situation is being talked about, you can use "그러면/그렇다면" to say "If (that situation)…". The common translation of these two is simply "if so." For example:

Person 1: 내일 비가 올 것 같아요 = It will probably rain tomorrow
Person 2: 그러면/그렇다면 공원에 안 갈 거예요 = If so, I'm not going to the park

Person 1: 나는 오늘 집에 안 갈 거야 = I'm not going home today
Person 2: 그러면/그렇다면 나도 안 갈 거야 = If so, I'm not going either

If not: 아니면

In Lesson 8 (and applied in Lesson 9), you learned about 아니다 and how it can be used to mean "to not be." By combining 아니다 with ~면, we get "아니면" which literally means "if not." We can often see 아니면 used at the beginning of a sentence referring to the previous sentence. For example:

저는 밥을 먹고 싶어요. 아니면 죽을 것 같아요 = I want to eat rice. If not, I will probably die
진정하세요! 아니면 제가 교장선생님을 부를 거에요 = Calm down. If not, I will call the principal

It is also possible to see 아니면 used within a clause, often between two nouns. When used like this, 아니면 indicates "if not this (noun), then that (noun)." This is most commonly translated to "or" in English. For example:

저는 밥 아니면 사과를 먹고 싶어요 = I want to eat rice, if not, (I want to eat) apples
(which could be translated as "I want to eat rice or apples.")

아니면 can be used to have this meaning of "or," but another way to create this meaning is to use ~이나 or 거나, which is discussed in Lesson 58.

Lesson 44: Let's, Shall we: ~자, ~ㄹ래(요)

Vocabulary

Nouns:
소망 = hope, desire
숙어 = idiom
장례식 = funeral
연수 = training for work
규정 = rules, regulations
무대 = (a performing) stage
벌 = punishment
쪽지 = a message written on a piece of paper
환불 = refund

Verbs:
외우다 = to memorize
저버리다 = to back out on something
모집하다 = to recruit
복제하다 = to duplicate, to replicate
울리다 = to be ringing, to be vibrating
희망하다 = to hope, to wish
측정하다 = to measure
틀다 = to turn on
작성하다 = to write up, to fill out
연기하다 = to delay
놀리다 = to tease
시행하다 = to enforce, conduct, implement
실시하다 = to enforce, conduct, implement

Adjectives:
공평하다 = to be fair
엄격하다 = to be strict
유창하다 = to be fluent

Adverbs and Other Words:
요새 = these days
알몸 = naked

Introduction

In this lesson, you will learn about ~자 and ~ㅂ/읍시다, which are two common endings that you can use to suggest that you do something with another person. In addition, you will learn how to use ~ㄹ/을래(요) which can sometimes be used in similar situations. Let's get started.

Let's…: ~자 and ~ㅂ/읍시다

By adding ~자 to the stem of a word at the end of a sentence, you can suggest that that action be done together. In English, this typically translates to "Let's..."

This is a very easy ending to learn because (by the nature of the meaning) it is always added to words in the present tense and no irregulars are affected by its usage. Not only that, ~자 gets added to stems ending in consonants and vowels. For example:

밥을 먹자! = Let's eat!
내일 공원에 가자! = Tomorrow, let's go to the park!

If you want to say "Let's **not** do something" you should attach ~자 to ~지 말다, which you learned in Lesson 40. Remember, if you wanted to say "don't' go," you should say:

가지 말다 = Don't go

말다 is usually conjugated with an imperative ending. For example:
가지 마
가지 마라
가지 마세요

However, if you wanted to say "let's **not** go," you can add ~자 to 말다. For example:

내일 공원에 가지 말자 = Let's not go to the park tomorrow
우리 애기를 위해 그것을 사지 말자 = Let's not buy that for our baby

Below are many more examples:
무대에 같이 올라가자 = Let's go onto the stage together
쪽지를 서로 보내자 = Let's send messages to each other
물에 알몸으로 들어가자 = Let's go into the water naked
있던 약속을 그냥 저버리자 = Let's just back out of our plans that we had

요새 벌이 조금 공평하지 않아. 내일 그것을 선생님이랑 얘기하자
= Lately, the punishments have been a little unfair. Let's talk about that with the teacher tomorrow

It is important to note that using ~자 is *informal*, and adding ~요 to ~자 is not done in Korean. Therefore, the sentences above could only be said to people who do not deserve high respect, like your friends or people younger than you.

A slightly more formal way to create this same meaning is to use ~ㅂ/읍시다 instead of ~자. ~읍시다 gets added to stems ending in a consonant, and ~ㅂ시다 gets added directly to stems ending in a vowel. For example:

밥을 먹읍시다! = Let's eat!
내일 공원에 갑시다! = Tomorrow, let's go to the park!

Other examples:
그 규정을 내일부터 시행합시다 = Let's enforce that rule starting tomorrow
연수를 받으러 갑시다 = Let's go to receive the training

This is *slightly* more formal than ~자, but it isn't incredibly formal either. You commonly hear this form being used in offices – when the boss is speaking to a group of his/her subordinates or when coworkers are speaking to each other (of course, there are many other situations where this could be used – "in an office" is just one example). In these cases, some respect should be given to the listeners so ~ㅂ/읍시다 can be appropriate. However, I would advise against using ~ㅂ/읍시다 when speaking to somebody who deserve a high amount of respect – like your boss or your father-in-law. Instead, I recommend simply asking him a question using the information you learned in Lesson 21. For example:

같이 먹고 싶습니까? = Do you want to eat together?

There is another Korean ending that you can use to say something similar to "let's…" that you can add the formal ending ~요 to. We will learn about this next.

~ㄹ래(요)

I will separate my explanation of ~ㄹ/을래(요) into four usages. Each usage has a slightly different feel so I think this separation is helpful. Notice that (unlike ~자 and ~ㅂ/읍시다) ~요 can be added to this ending to make it more formal. Let's discuss these four usages.

<u>Usage 1:</u>
To ask if the listener would like to do an action together

In this usage, the speaker is asking if the listener would like to do an action together. The typical translation for this usage is "Shall we…" For example:

내일 공부하러 독서실에 갈래요? = Shall we go to the library tomorrow to study?
서울에 있는 공연을 보러 갈래요? = Shall we go to see the show in Seoul?

I feel that "Shall we…" is not a very common English expression. Although this is the most common translation for "ㄹ/을래요," the following translation would also be acceptable:

내일 공부하러 독서실에 갈래요? = Would you like to go the library with me tomorrow to study?
서울에 있는 공연을 보러 갈래요? = Would you like to go to see the show with me in Seoul?

More examples:

장례식에 같이 갈래요? = Shall we go to the funeral together?
영화를 볼래요? = Shall we see a movie together?
저녁을 내일 먹을래요? = Shall we eat dinner together tomorrow?
회원을 모집해 볼래요? = Shall we try to recruit some members?
벌을 엄격하게 시행할래요? = Shall we enforce the punishment strictly?
경기를 내일까지 연기할래요? = Shall we delay the match until tomorrow?
영어숙어를 같이 외워 볼래? = Shall we try to memorize English idioms together?

It is also possible for this usage to be applied to a sentence that has a question word in it. The translation of "Shall we…" is usually appropriate in these sentences as well. For example:

언제 할래? = When shall/should we do it?
어디 갈래? = Where shall/should we go?
뭐 먹을래? = What shall/should we eat?

Usage 2
To ask if the listener would like if something happened

In this usage, the speaker typically threatens the listener with some sort of pain. The English equivalent of this would be something like:

"Do you want me to smack you?"

The two most common words that are used in this situation are:

맞을래? = Do you want to be hit? (Do you want me to hit you?)
죽을래? = Do you want to die? (Do you want me to kill you?)

Both of these are (usually) not used literally, and are simply empty threats from the speaker. These are typically used when the speaker becomes annoyed at somebody, and he/she can express her annoyance by threatening the person.

Usage 3
To ask if the listener can do something for the speaker

In this usage, ~ㄹ/을래(요) is typically attached to 주다 (either as a stand alone verb, or as ~아/어 주다 as you learned in Lesson 41). For example:

김치를 더 줄래요? = Can you give me more kimchi?
문을 닫아 줄래요? = Can you close the door?

In Lesson 40, you learned how to use ~(으)세요 (and other imperative endings) to give a command. In effect, using ~ㄹ/을래(요) this way is simply another way you can ask a person to do something for you. Because it is not a direct command, it sounds a little bit softer than telling a person directly to do something – almost like a request instead of a command.

In practice, the honorific ~(으)시 is often added to 주다 to make the request softer and more formal. In English, I would normally translate this to something that conveys this formality – like, "Could you please…". For example:

김치를 더 주실래요? = Could you please give me more kimchi?
문을 닫아 주실래요? = Could you please close the door?

More examples:
환불해 주실래요? = Could you please give me a refund?
에어컨을 틀어 주실래요? = Could you please turn on the air conditioner?
울리는 핸드폰을 받아 주실래요? = Could you please pick up the phone that is ringing?
이것을 다 작성해 주실래요? = Could you please write all of this up for me?

그 파일을 이 컴퓨터로 복제해 주실래요?
= Could you please copy that file to this computer?

소망이 무엇인지 말씀해 주실래요?
= Could you please tell me what your dream/hope is?

이 숙어가 무슨 뜻인지 설명해 주실래요?
= Could you please explain what this idiom means?

<u>Usage 4</u>
To indicate that the speaker wants to do something

In theory, this usage is very similar to ~고 싶다 (which you learned in Lesson 17) or just a simple future tense conjugation. Here, the speaker is indicating that he/she will do something or wants to do something. For example:

나는 집에 갈래 = I'm going home/I want to go home
나는 집에 갈 거야 = I'm going home
나는 집에 가고 싶어 = I want to go home

As you know, a regular future tense conjugation and ~고 싶다 can be applied to very complex sentences. Typically, ~ㄹ/을래(요) is only attached to simple sentences like the one shown above. Other examples:

Also note that ~안 or ~지 않다 can be used to indicate that the speaker doesn't want to do something.

나는 그거를 먹을래 = I'm going to eat that/I want to eat that
나는 안 할래 = I'm not going to do it/I don't want to do it
나는 안 먹을래 = I'm not going to eat/I don't want to eat that
나는 먼저 할래 = I'm going to do it first/I want to do it first

Lesson 45: I can, I can't: ~ㄹ 수 있다, ~ㄹ 수 없다

Vocabulary

Nouns:
정장 = a suit
기한 = time limit, deadline
윤리 = ethics/morals
온몸 = entire body
독 = poison
인권 = human rights
교과 과정 = curriculum
지점 = a "point" when it refers to a place
선거 = election
세탁 = laundry
장기 = a long time period
단기 = a short time period
첫눈 = first sight

Verbs:
자습하다 = to teach oneself
생기다 = to occur, to come up, to arise
미끄러지다 = to slip
비키다 = to step aside, to step away
참고하다 = to refer to, to consult
바르다 = to apply or spread a liquid
고립되다 = to be isolated

Adjectives:
미끄럽다 = to be slippery
시급하다 = to be urgent
동일하다 = to be the same as, to be identical

Adverbs and Other Words:
술술 = smoothly
등 = etc…

Introduction

In this lesson, you will learn about the noun "수" in Korean. With this, you will learn how to say "I can" and "I can't" with the constructions ~ㄹ/을 수 있다 and ~ㄹ/을 수 없다. Let's get started.

One can, cannot… : ~ㄹ/을 수 있다/없다

By adding ~ㄹ/을 수 있다 to the end of a clause/sentence, you can create the meaning of "one can….".

"수" is what I like to call a 'pseudo-noun.' You have already learned a few of these pseudo-nouns in other lessons. For example in Lesson 30 you learned about "지" and how it can be used in sentences like this:

제가 한국에서 산 지 2 년 됐어요 = I have been living in Korea for 2 years

In Lesson 32, you learned about "적" and how it can be used in sentences like this:

김치를 먹은 적이 없어요 = I have never eaten kimchi

In both of the sentences above, the pseudo-noun follows a descriptive word, and thus, must be a noun. However, these 'pseudo-nouns' cannot be placed anywhere but these specific locations, and therefore, are not true nouns. '수' in '~ㄹ 수 있다' is also a pseudo-noun. If you look up "수" in the dictionary, the definition will be something similar to "ability" or "capability" but it is not used as a stand-alone noun. Like "지" and "적," it needs to be described by something.

If we describe "수" with the verb "to study" (공부하다), we can get:

공부할 수: the ability to study

You can now finish the construction by placing "있다" or "없다" after 수 to indicate that one "has" or "does not have" the ability to study. For example:

공부할 수 있다 = I have the ability to study
공부할 수 없다 = I do not have the ability to study

The translations of "one can" and "one cannot" are usually used in these types of sentences.

공부할 수 있다 = I can study
공부할 수 없다 = I can't study

Below are more examples that express that something "can" be done using ~ㄹ/을 수 있다:

저도 그것을 할 수 있어요 = I can do that too
저는 그 지점에서 만날 수 있어요 = I can meet at that point
이 로션을 온몸에 바를 수 있어요 = You can apply this lotion all over your body
저는 세탁을 집에서 할 수 있어요 = I can do laundry at home
저는 이 수학문제를 술술 풀 수 있어요 = I can solve this math question without any issue

저는 몇몇 한국사람들보다 한국어를 더 잘 말할 수 있어요
= I can speak Korean better than some Korean people

선생님이 원하시면 윤리 교과 과정을 바꿀 수 있어요
= If you (the teacher) want, you can change the ethics curriculum

그 문제를 기한 안에 해결한다면 우리는 지금부터 선거를 실시할 수 있어요
= If you solve that problem within the time period, the election can run starting now

이번 선거로 인권 문제를 해결할 수 있어요
= We can solve the problem of human rights through this election

살이 많이 빠져서 지금 정장을 편히 입을 수 있어요
= I can wear a suit comfortably now because I lost a lot of weight

You can also use this form to ask another person if he/she is "able" or "capable" of doing something. For example:

오늘 밤에 만날 수 있어요? = Can you meet tonight?
그것을 빨리 할 수 있어요? = Can you do it quickly?
기한 안에 다 할 수 있어요? = Can you do it all within the time limit?
여기서 자습할 수 있어요? = Are you able to (self-)study here?

Anytime an action is being done for the speaker, it would also be appropriate to attach ~아/어 주다 to the verb before ~ㄹ/을 수 있다. For example:

그것을 빨리 해 줄 수 있어요? = Can you do it faster (for me)?
문을 열어 줄 수 있어요? = Can you open the door (for me)?
TV가 안 보여서 비켜 줄 수 있어요? = Can you move (for me), I can't see the TV

As mentioned in Lesson 41, it would also be acceptable to use the word "좀" in these types of sentences because the speaker is asking for some kind of a favor. For example:

그것을 좀 빨리 해 줄 수 있어요? = Can you do it a little bit faster (for me)?
문을 좀 열어 줄 수 있어요? = Can you open the door (a little bit) (for me)?
TV가 안 보여서 좀 비켜 줄 수 있어요? = Can you move a bit (for me), I can't see the TV

Below are examples that express that something "cannot" be done using ~ㄹ/을 수 없다:

제가 너무 아파서 많이 먹을 수 없어요 = I can't eat much because I am very sick
저 사람은 한국어를 말할 수 없어요 = That person can't speak Korean
이 독을 마시면 치료할 수 없어요 = If you drink this poison, you cannot cure/treat it
그런 시끄러운 방에서 저는 자습할 수 없어요 = I can't (self-)study in such a loud room
시급한 일이 생겨서 지금 나갈 수 없어요 = Something urgent came up, so I can't go out
저는 그 사실을 믿을 수 없어요 = I can't believe that fact

여기가 너무 시끄러워서 저는 집중할 수 없어요
= I can't concentrate here because it is too loud

기한이 이미 지나서 선거를 실시할 수 없어요
= You can't hold an election because the time limit has already passed

그런 일을 하면 장기 휴가를 갈 수 없어요
= If you do that kind of work/job, you can't go on any long/extended holidays

Both ~ㄹ/을 수 있다 and ~ㄹ/을 수 없다 can be expressed in the past and future tenses. When conjugating to the past or future tenses, only 있다 or 없다 should be conjugated. For example:

저는 다음 번에 더 잘 할 수 있을 거예요 = I will be able to do better next time
저는 그 여자를 볼 수 없었어요 = I couldn't see that girl
내년에 캐나다에 갈 수 없을 거예요 = I won't be able to go to Canada next year
어렸을 때 저는 햄버거 다섯 개를 먹을 수 있었어요 = When I was younger, I could eat five hamburgers

One specific phrase that is difficult to translate directly to English is:

I don't understand, or
I can't understand

In English, those two phrases essentially mean the same thing – however, there is a subtle difference. We would use "I can't understand" when you are talking about a general topic – specifically something that you don't get at all and will never understand. For example:

I can't understand Chemistry
I can't understand Korean

To say those in Korean, you can use the ~ㄹ 수 없다 form. For example:

나는 화학을 이해할 수 없어 = I can't understand Chemistry
나는 한국어를 이해할 수 없어 = I can't understand Korean

However, if we say "I don't understand", it could mean that – although you cannot understand something right now – you will probably be able to understand it if somebody (depending on the situation) explains it to you better. This is more likely to be used with specific things that somebody can teach you over a short period of time – or something that you can grasp if somebody explains it to you quickly. In order to create this meaning, you should attach ~지 못하다 to "이해하다." For example:

이 문제를 이해하지 못하겠어요 = I don't understand that question/problem
네가 무슨 말을 하고 있는지 이해하지 못하겠어 = I don't understand what you are trying to say (like, "I don't understand the point you are trying to make")

Notice that the future tense conjugation of ~겠다 is used when talking about something you currently don't understand.

이 문제를 이해하지 못했어요 = I didn't understand this question/problem

They're essentially the same thing (이해할 수 없다 vs. 이해하지 못하겠다), and you don't really need to worry about distinguishing them too much. However, it is something that I learned when I was studying, so it might be something that you should consider as well.

Adding particles to 수

Because 수 is a noun, particles can be attached to it. The three most common particles that are attached to "수" are ~가, ~는 and ~도.

I have discussed the purpose of adding ~가 to "수" with Korean teachers (who teach Korean grammar to Korean people). All of them say that ~가 creates no additional meaning to these types of sentences. For example, each pair of sentences would be the same:

우리는 그것을 정확히 알 수 없어요
우리는 그것을 정확히 알 수가 없어요
= We can't know that for sure

이 사진을 보여줄 수 없어요
이 사진을 보여줄 수가 없어요
= I can't show you that picture

동생의 눈을 볼 수 없어요
동생의 눈을 볼 수가 없어요
= I can't look at my brother's eyes

그거를 어떻게 할 수 있어요?
그거를 어떻게 할 수가 있어요?
= How can you do that?

Even though Korean people say those pairs of sentences are identical, my experience with Korean makes me feel that using ~가 is more likely to happen when the situation is being emphasized. Notice the translations below, which I feel more accurately describe the subtleties of using ~가 with ~ㄹ/을 수 있다:

우리는 그것을 정확히 알 수가 없어요 = There's no way we can even know that for sure
이 사진을 보여줄 수가 없어요 = There's no way I can even show you the picture
동생의 눈을 볼 수가 없어요 = There's no way I can even look at my brother in the eyes
그거를 어떻게 할 수가 있어요? = How can you possibly do that?

Your understanding of this nuance can only really develop with exposure to the language. As you have deeper conversations with Korean people, I hope you might discover this same nuance that I feel.

Explaining the nuance of using ~는 and ~도 with "수" is complex and will be discussed in later lessons. For now, I suggest not going ahead and studying these complex usages. Instead, I suggest sticking to the order of the lessons that I have them presented. If you are dying to see how these particles can be used with "수", you can check out Lesson 104 and Lesson 107.

Lesson 46: I have to, I need to: ~아/어야 되다, ~ㄹ 필요가 있다

Vocabulary

Nouns:
예외 = exception
복사기 = photocopier
신입생 = freshman
운명 = fate
시력 = vision
조개 = clam
캐릭터 = character
영웅 = hero
신화 = myth
왕비 = queen
화면 = screen
울타리 = fence

Verbs:
동의하다 = to agree
검토하다 = to review, to examine
뺏다 = to take something away
뽑다 = to pull out
성공하다 = to succeed
연결하다 = to connect
협조하다 = to cooperate

Adjectives:
생생하다 = to be vivid, graphic
성숙하다 = to be mature

Adverbs and Other Words:
실제 = actual
가까이 = closely
운명적으로 = fatefully
반말 = casual speaking
워낙 = so/very, by nature

Introduction

In this lesson, you will learn how to use ~아/어야 하다 to indicate that something must be done. In addition, you will learn about the word 필요하다 and how it can be used to create a similar meaning as ~아/어야 하다. Let's get started.

To have to: ~아/어야 하다 / 되다 / 지 / 겠다

By adding ~아/어야 하다 to the stem of a word at the end of a sentence, you can create the meaning of "one has to…" or "one must…" For example:

공부하다 = to study
공부해야 한다 = to have to study

먹다 = to eat
먹어야 한다 = to have to eat

가다 = to go
가야 한다 = to have to go

We can see these used in very simple sentences. For example:

저는 밥을 먹어야 해요 = I have to eat
저는 지금 공부해야 해요 = I have to study now
저는 집에 가야 해요 = I have to go home

To English speakers, the words "must/have to" and "should" have different meanings. For example, while the following two sentences feel the same to English speakers:

I must go to the park, and
I have to go to the park

Using "should" creates a slightly different nuance to English speakers. For example:

I should go to the park

However, in Korean, "~아/어야 하다" (and the other similar forms introduced later in the lesson) can be translated to "one must/have to" *or* "one should." Learners of Korean are often confused at how this one grammatical principle can represent two seemingly different meanings in English. In reality, the difference in English between those two words isn't very big. Try to step out of your English brain for a minute and realize that these sentences effectively express the same meaning. Using "must" might feel stronger to an English speaker, but the end result of all these sentences is the same:

I must go to the park
I have to go to the park
I should go to the park

Therefore, sentences like this:

대학교에 가고 싶다면 열심히 공부해야 돼요

Could be translated as:

If you want to go to University, you must study hard
If you want to go to University, you have to study hard
If you want to go to University, you should study hard

Below are many examples of ~아/어야 하다 in use:

친구를 만나러 지금 가야 해요 = I have to go now to meet my friend
제 말에 동의해야 해요 = You need to agree with what I say
먹어야 해서 늦게 왔어요 = I was late because I had to eat

이 일을 끝내고 싶으면 우리는 협조해야 해요
= If you want to finish this work, we need to cooperate

TV를 켜고 싶으면 이거를 TV에 연결해야 해요
= If you want to turn on the TV, you need to connect this thing to the TV

책을 읽은 후에 제자리에 둬야 해요
= After reading the book, you have to put it back in the right place

대학교에 가고 싶다면 열심히 공부해야 해요
= If you want to go to university, you have to study hard

우리 아들이 핸드폰을 많이 쓰고 있어서 핸드폰을 뺏어야 할 것 같아요
= Our son is using his cell-phone a lot, so we'll probably have to take it away from him

Replacing 하다 with 되다 in ~아/어야 하다 can be done with no difference in meaning. I feel that using 되다 instead of 하다 is much more common in speech. For example:

우리는 빨리 가야 돼 = We have to go fast
울타리를 넘어야 돼요 = We need to go over the fence
직장에서 성숙하게 행동해야 돼요 = You need to act maturely at work
시력이 안 좋아서 안경을 써야 돼요 = My eyesight isn't good so I have to wear glasses
실제 나이를 말해야 돼요 = You need to say your real/actual age

성공하고 싶으면 매일 열심히 해야 돼요
= If you want to succeed, you need to work hard every day

모든 사람들이 왕비가 하는 말을 동의해야 돼요
= Everybody has to agree with what the queen says

영어문법을 공부할 때 예외를 그냥 다 외워야 돼요
= When you study English grammar, you just need to memorize all of the exceptions

결과를 발표하기 전에 자료를 검토해야 돼요
= Before announcing the results, we need to examine the data

It is also possible to use "~지" (or the formal equivalent ~죠) instead of 하다 or 되다 in ~아/어 야 하다/되다. Using ~아/어지/죠 like this is mostly done in conversation. You can use 지 to create similar sentences to those above with 하다 and 되다. For example:

우리가 빨리 가야지! = We have to go fast!
우리는 빨리 가야죠! = We have to go fast!
Notice here that there are no spaces between ~아/어야 *and* 지/죠.

Instead of:
우리는 빨리 가야 해요 = We have to go fast!
우리는 빨리 가야 돼요 = We have to go fast!

Below are more examples:
먹어야지! = You have to eat!
신입생들에게 반말을 해야지 = You should speak in 반말 to the freshmen students
운명을 믿어야지 = You need to trust (in) fate
조개를 넣어야지 = You need to put clams in
영웅이 왕비를 살려야지 = The hero should save the queen

Another usage of ~지 (or the formal version ~죠) will be introduced in Lesson 93.

It is possible to conjugate 하다 or 되다 at the end of the clause to reflect that something "had to have" happened or "will have to" happen. For example:

그때 열심히 일해야 되었어요 = At that time I had to work really hard
복사기를 수리해야 되었어요 = We had to repair the photocopier
시력이 워낙 안 좋아서 화면에 가까이 있어야 되었어요 = My eyesight isn't good, so I had to be close to the screen

10분 후에 가야 될 거예요 = We will have to go in 10 minutes
그 이를 뽑아야 될 것 같아요 = We will probably have to pull out that tooth
신입생들을 위해 선물을 준비해야 할 거예요 = We will have to prepare a present for the freshmen

When conjugating these types of sentences to the future, it is possible to attach ~겠다 to the final verb. For example:

밥을 먹어야 하겠다 = I will have to eat (rice)

The construction of "~아/어야 하겠다" is often shortened to ~아/어야겠다 in speech. For example:

밥을 먹어야겠다

When adding ~아/어야겠다 to the end of a sentence like this, the translation of "I will have to…" doesn't perfectly reflect the purpose of this construction. When a speaker uses ~아/어야겠다, he/she has received some sort of information or signal that is causing him/her to say this sentence. For example, if you just looked at the time and realized you had to go, you could say:

나는 지금 가야겠다

It is hard to come up with a perfect translation for this in English. Some translations for the sentence above could be:

I'd better get going now
I guess I better go now
I'll have to go now

Remember that I always suggest to not focus too much on English translations but rather to focus on the meaning that the Korean sentence has. Below are more examples:

남자친구랑 내일 헤어져야겠다 = I'll have to break up with my boyfriend tomorrow
이 사실을 부장님께 알려 줘야겠어요 = I'll have to tell the boss (about) that fact
그녀를 위해 선물을 사야겠어요 = I'll have to buy her a present
결과를 다시 검토해야겠다 = We'll have to examine the results again

To need: 필요하다

You can essentially create the same meaning of "I have to" with "I need to" in Korean by using the word "필요하다." 필요하다 is one of those words like 있다 that feels like a verb, but is considered an adjective in Korean. Like the other adjectives-that-feel-like-verbs, this rarely becomes an issue, except for when conjugating it using the plain (diary) form. Remember, the plain form conjugation for an adjective is the same as the dictionary form. Therefore, the following would be an incorrect conjugation:

필요한다

Instead, the following would be correct:

필요하다

필요하다 can be used to sentences to have the meaning of "to need." Again, because this word acts as an adjective, the use of the object particle (~을/를) would be incorrect:

나는 밥을 필요하다 (*This sentence is incorrect*)

Instead, if you want to say that you "need" something, you should add the particle ~이/가 to the noun that you "need." For example:

나는 밥이 필요하다 = I need food/rice

More examples:

나는 여자 친구가 필요하다 = I need a girlfriend
우리 회사는 새로운 복사기가 필요해요 = Our office needs a new photocopier
그 영화가 영웅 캐릭터가 필요해요 = That movie needs a hero character

You can use the noun "필요" (meaning "necessity") with verbs to create a similar meaning to using ~아/어야 하다. Let's talk about this next.

<u>To need to: ~ㄹ/을 필요가 있다/없다</u>
If you want to say that you "need to" do a verb, as in:

I need to eat
I need to sleep

You can add ~ㄹ/을 필요가 있다 to the stem of a verb/adjective. For example:

나는 밥을 먹을 필요가 있다
나는 잘 필요가 있다

Notice the makeup of this grammatical concept. "필요" acts as a noun that is being described by a verb. For example:

밥을 먹을 필요 = The necessity to eat
잘 필요 = The necessity to sleep

있다 is then used to indicate that the person "has" that necessity. For example:

나는 밥을 먹을 필요가 있다 = I have the necessity to eat
나는 잘 필요가 있다 = I have the necessity to sleep

Those translations are possible, but (especially in speech) I would be much more likely to use "I need to…" For example:

나는 밥을 먹을 필요가 있다 = I need to eat
나는 잘 필요가 있다 = I need to sleep

Below are more examples. Also notice that you have use 없다 instead of 있다 to indicate that one does *not* need to do something:

저는 그 여자랑 결혼할 필요가 있어요 = I need to marry that girl
시험공부를 곧 할 필요가 있어요 = I need to study soon
강한 캐릭터를 만들 필요가 있어요 = We need to make a strong character
예외를 다 설명할 필요가 있어요 = You need to explain all of the exceptions
제자리에 놓을 필요가 없어요 = You don't need to put it back in its place
그렇게 가까이 앉을 필요가 없어요 = There's no need to sit that close
그렇게 할 필요가 없어요 = You don't need to do it like that

Lesson 47: Even though: ~지만

Vocabulary

Nouns:
아파트 = apartment, apartment complex
잔디 = grass
경비 = security
동물 = animal
선 = line
감각 = sense, feeling
한계 = limit
고통 = pain
태양 = sun
상처 = wound

Verbs:
내밀다 = to stick out of, to stretch out of
얼다 = to freeze
소리 지르다 = to shout, to scream
마취하다 = to give someone an anesthetic
로그인하다 = to log in
장난하다 = to joke, to play around
나타내다 = to appear, to come in view
참가하다 = to participate
나타나다 = to appear, come in view

Adverbs and Other Words
혹시 = indicates something is unknown
우선 = to do something first
너머 = beyond, over

Introduction

In this lesson, you will learn how to use ~지만 to connect two clauses. You will also learn about adding this to 그렇다 to make 그렇지만. Let's get started.

Even though: ~지만

One of the most common words in Korean is "하지만," which means "but." This word (in English and Korean) is usually used at the beginning of a sentence. For example:

저는 먹고 싶어요. 하지만 배고프지 않아요 = I want to eat. But, I am not hungry.

Although both of those sentences are correct, there are a lot of syllables that you can eliminate from them. You should be aware by now, that Korean people always want to make their sentences as short as possible. You can create this meaning of "but" by eliminating "하지만" and connecting the two clauses with ~지만. For example:

저는 먹고 싶지만 배고프지 않아요 = I want to eat but I am not hungry.

This often translates to "even though…" in English. Notice how the following two sentences in English are exactly the same:

Even though I want to eat, I am not hungry.
I want to eat, but I am not hungry.

Essentially, by adding ~지만 to the stem of a word, that clause gets negated, and the opposite is usually described in the latter clause. Below are many examples. Notice that it can be added directly to the stems of verbs, adjectives and 이다. Also, because the addition starts with the letter "ㅈ" there are no irregulars that come into play with this addition.

Notice in all of the examples in this lesson that the clauses before ~지만 are true or have already occurred (or are certain to occur in the future). This will become important when I distinguish ~지만 from ~아/어도 in the next lesson.

부산에 가고 싶지만 차가 없어서 못 가요
= Even though I want to go to Busan, I can't go because I don't have a car

물을 마셔야 되지만 물이 아직도 다 얼어 있어요
= I need to drink water, but it is still all frozen

요즘에 한국어를 열심히 공부하고 있지만 아직도 잘 말할 수 없어요
= Even though I am studying Korean hard these days, I still can't speak well

그 연예인이 돈이 많지만 왜 그렇게 행복하지 않아 보여요?
= That celebrity has a lot of money, but why doesn't he look happy

그 아파트가 경비 아저씨가 있지만 안전하지 않아요
= Even though that apartment (complex) has a security guard, it isn't safe

잔디를 깎아야 되지만 밖에 나가기 싫어요
= I have to cut/mow the grass/lawn, but I don't want to go outside

우리 어머니가 강아지를 아주 좋아하지만 다른 동물을 싫어해요
= My mother really likes dogs/puppies, but doesn't like other animals

그 경기에 참가하고 싶지만 네가 안 하면 나도 안 할래
= I want to participate in the match, but if you don't do it, then I won't

모든 사람들이 그를 싫어하지만 그는 파티에 나타났어요
= Even though everybody hates him, he showed up at the party

You can conjugate the clause before ~지만 to the past tense by adding ~았/었 to it. For example:

밥을 먹었지만 배고파요
= Even though I ate, I am hungry

로그인을 이미 했지만 그 화면이 안 보여요
= I already logged in, but I don't see that screen

원래 한국에 여행하러 가고 싶었지만 돈이 없어서 못 갔어요
= Originally I wanted to go to Korea to travel, but because I didn't have any money, I couldn't go

머리를 창문 너머로 내밀었지만 밖에 있는 친구가 저를 보지 않았어요
= I stuck my head out of the window, but my friend outside didn't see me

마취를 했지만 입에 아직 감각이 있어요
= I received freezing/anesthetic, but there is still feeling in my mouth

상처를 치료했지만 아직 고통이 있어요
= I treated the wound, but there is still pain

제가 친구에게 소리를 질렀지만 친구가 제 말을 못 들었어요
= I yelled to my friend, but he didn't hear what I said

그 사람의 얼굴이 기억 안 났지만 갑자기 제 꿈에 나타났어요
= I had forgotten that person's face, but it suddenly appeared to me in my dream

----

You can conjugate the clause before ~지만 to the future tense by adding the ~ㄹ/을 것이다 (or ~ㄹ/을 거다) or ~겠다 forms. In all cases, ~지만 is attached to these constructions after "~다" is removed. For example:

한국에 안 갈 것이지만 여전히 한국어를 배우고 싶어요
= Even though I will not go to Korea, I still want to learn Korean, or:

한국에 안 갈 거지만 여전히 한국어를 배우고 싶어요
= Even though I will not go to Korea, I still want to learn Korean, or:

한국에 안 가겠지만 여전히 한국어를 배우고 싶어요
= Even though I will not go to Korea, I still want to learn Korean

오늘 선생님이 안 올 거지만 우리는 선생님이 준비하신 내용을 공부해야 돼요
= Even though the teacher won't come today, we need to study the material that she prepared

오늘 우리가 달에 대한 것을 배울 거지만 우선 태양에 대한 것을 배워야 돼요
= Today, we'll learn about the moon, but first, we must learn about the sun

그렇다 + 지만

You first learned about the word "그렇다" in Lesson 23. Since then, you have seen other grammatical principles applied to it. For example, in Lesson 37 you saw how it can be used with ~아/어서 to form 그래서. For example:

Person 1: 비가 왔어요? = Is it raining?
Person 2: 응, 그래서 나가기 싫어요 = Yeah, that's why/therefore I don't want to go out

It is also common to attach ~지만 to 그렇다. When some situation is being talked about, you can use "그렇지만" to say "Even though (that situation)…". The common translation of 그렇지만 is simply "however." For example:

Person 1: 주차를 이 선 안에 해야 되지 않아요?
= Don't you have to park between these lines?
Person 2: 그렇지만 차가 너무 커서 그렇게 할 수 없어요
= However, the car is too big so I can't do it like that.

Person 1: 지금 가야 되지 않아요?
= Don't you have to go now?
Person 2: 네, 그렇지만 할 게 많아서 지금 못 가요
= Yes, however I can't go now because I have a lot of things to do

Lesson 48: Regardless of: ~아/어도

Vocabulary

Nouns:
정원 = garden
새끼 = baby animals
어미 = mother for animals
반값 = half price
승패 = the outcome of a game (a win or loss)
개별 = individual/ly
건축 = architecture
건축가 = architect
강가 = area around a river, riverfront, riverside
막내 = youngest person in a family
마법사 = witch
동굴 = cave
보석 = jewel
수레 = cart
태풍 = typhoon
박람회 = fair, exhibition
호수 = lake
호숫가 = area around a lake, lakefront, lakeside
매력 = charm Verbs:
구입하다 = to purchase
교환하다 = to exchange
면담하다 = to talk face to face, to interview
미루다 = to delay
안다 = to hug

Adjectives:
달콤하다 = to be sweet
창피하다 = to be ashamed

Adverbs and Other Words:
미리 = in advance/beforehand
일대일(로) = one on one
정기적으로 = regularly

Introduction

In this lesson, you will learn how to use ~아/어도 to connect two clauses. You will also learn about adding this to 그렇다 to make 그래도 and about the word 아무리. Let's get started.

Regardless of… : ~아/어도

By adding ~아/어도 to the stem of a word at the end of one clause, the second clause is expected to occur regardless of what happens in the first clause. For example:

밥이 있어도 저는 안 먹을 거예요 = Regardless of if there is food/rice, I am not going to eat

Notice here that the clause with ~아/어도 attached is a supposition. That is, it is uncertain if that clause will occur or not. The use of ~아/어도 indicates that the second clause will occur regardless of if the first clause happens or not.

I would like to take a moment to describe how this sentence differs from one that uses ~지만, which you learned in the previous lesson. When ~지만 is added to a clause, that clause is already a fact (or already was a fact, or already will be a fact). The clause that follows ~지만 is a statement that opposes this already accepted/known fact. For example, in the following sentence:

밥이 있지만 저는 안 먹을 거예요 = Even though there is food/rice, I am not going to eat

The common translation for ~아/어도 is "Regardless of if…" Below are many examples:

태풍이 와도 내일 박람회에 가야 돼요
= Regardless of whether there is a typhoon, I have to go to the trade show tomorrow

보석을 그 동굴에 숨겨도 사람들이 찾을 거예요
= Regardless of whether you hide the jewels in that cave, people will find them

네가 건축가가 되어도 손으로 건물을 짓지 않을 거야
= Regardless of if you become an architect, you won't be building buildings with your hands

그랑 일대일로 면담하려고 해 봐도 그는 말을 안 할 거예요
= Regardless of if you try to talk with him (face to face) he won't say anything

그 제품을 반값으로 줘도 저는 안 살 거예요
= Regardless of if you give me that product at half price, I'm not going to buy it

모두 호수에서 수영해도 저는 안 들어가요
= Regardless of if everyone goes swimming in the lake, I am not going in

어미를 찾아도 이미 고양이 새끼가 다 죽었어요
= Regardless of if you find the mother, the baby cats (kittens) all died

달콤한 치킨을 안 좋아해도 이것을 한번 먹어 봐야 돼요
= Regardless of if you don't like sweet chicken, you have to try this

그 정원이 아름다워도 내일 그 장소에서 건물을 지을 거예요
= Regardless of how beautiful that garden is, tomorrow we need to build a building in that place

The fact that the first clause of this sentence is a supposition (i.e. is uncertain to occur) allows question words to be used in these types of sentences. For example:

네가 어디 가도 나는 가고 싶지 않아 = Regardless of where you are going, I don't want to go

Notice the difference in sentences with ~지만 in these cases. Remember, when using ~지만 the first clause is already some accepted/known fact. This means that a question word cannot be used in these types of sentences. Notice how the following is unnatural:

네가 어디 가지만 나는 가고 싶지 않아

Here are other examples of other question words being used with ~아/어도:

우리 엄마가 무엇을 사도 산 다음 날에 항상 교환해요
= Regardless of what my mother buys, she always exchanges it the day after buying it

이 제품을 언제 구입해도 그 가격을 내야 돼요
= Regardless of when you purchase this product, you have to pay that price

공연을 언제 해도 사람들이 안 올 거예요
= Regardless of when you do the performance, people won't come

The word 아무리 usually replaces 얼마나 in these types of sentences that describe "how much" something is done. For example:

네가 나를 아무리 사랑해도 우리는 헤어져야 돼
= Regardless of how much you love me, we need to break up

애기를 안으려고 아무리 노력해도 애기가 나를 안고 싶지 않은 것 같이 보여요
= Regardless of how much I try to hug the baby, it looks like the baby doesn't want to hug me

----

~아/어도 can also be attached to adjectives as well. For example:

여자들이 예뻐도 똑똑하지 않으면 매력이 없어요
= Regardless of how pretty girls are, if they are not smart, they have no charm

강가가 멀어도 우리는 거기 내일 가야 돼요
= Regardless of if the (area around) the river is far, we have to go there tomorrow

그 일이 급해도 저는 오늘 그것을 할 수 없어요
= Regardless of if that task is urgent, I can't do it today

~아/어도 can also be attached to 이다. When added to 이다, it follows the same pattern that we saw when adding ~아/어서 to 이다 in Lesson 37. ~아/어도 can be attached directly to the stem of 이다, for example:

남자이어도
사람이어도

Or, the "~어" can be changed to "~라." For example:

남자이라도
사람이라도

If the noun ends in a vowel, "이" can merge with the addition. For example:

남자여도 (*Notice that* 이 *and* 어 *merge to* 여)
남자라도 (*Notice that* 이 *and* 라 *merge to* 라)

그 남자가 마법사라도 그 문을 열 수 없을 거예요
= Regardless of if that man is a magician, he is not going to be able to open that door

그 사람이 네 엄마여도 나는 그녀와 말을 안 할 거야
= Regardless of if that person is your mother, I'm not going to talk to her

그 일을 하는 사람이 누구라도 창피할 거예요
= Regardless of who does that job, they will be embarrassed

아무리

The word '아무리' has two usages. Earlier in the lesson, you learned that it can replace 얼마나 in sentences with ~아/어도.

It is also a word that is put in sentences to allow the listener to expect what the speaker will say and provide feeling. In Lesson 43, you learned that 만약 is used in sentences where there is a supposition or assumption being made. Where 만약 is often used in sentences with ~(으)면, 아무리 is often used in sentences with ~아/어도. In this usage, 아무리 is used in sentences for feeling to let the listener/reader know that ~아/어도 is coming later in the sentence. For example:

아무리 그 제품을 반값으로 줘도 저는 안 살 거예요
= Regardless of if you give me that product at half price, I'm not going to buy it

그래도

In Lesson 23, you learned that the meaning of the word '그렇다' is close to the meaning of 'like that.' By adding ~아/어도 to 그렇다 you can create "그래도."

When some situation is being talked about, you can use "그래도" to say "Regardless of if (that situation) occurs…". The common translation of 그래도 is simply "regardless" or "it doesn't matter." For example:

Person 1: 같이 가자! 사람이 많을 거야! = Let's go together! There will be so many people
Person 2: 그래도 가기 싫어요 = Regardless. I'm not going.

Person 1: 선생님! 배가 좀 아파요! = Teacher! My stomach is a little sore
Person 2: 그래도 수업에 와야 돼 = Regardless, you have to come to class

Lesson 49: May I, One doesn't need to: ~아/어도 되다, 안 ~아/어도 되다

Vocabulary

Nouns:
감독관 = supervisor, proctor
심장 = heart
수염 = facial hair
명예 = honor
당구 = billiards
얼룩말 = zebra
탁구 = table tennis
시합 = game, match, competition
인문 = humanities, liberal arts
자격 = qualification
자격증 = certificate
기억력 = memory
먹이 = prey, food
교도소 = prison
죄 = crime
죄수 = prisoner

Verbs:
파악하다 = to understand, to grasp
살아나다 = to revive
동반하다 = to accompany
회복하다 = to restore, to recover

Adjectives:
편리하다 = to be convenient, to be handy
불쾌하다 = to be unpleasant, to be nasty
단단하다 = to be hard, to be stiff

Introduction

In this lesson, you will build on your understanding of ~아/어도 to make sentences using 되다. Using these concepts, you will be able to create sentences like "may I go to the bathroom" and "I don't need to go." Let's get started.

Another meaning of 되다

In previous lessons, you learned some uses of the word "되다." For example in Lesson 9 you learned that it can be used as a stand-alone verb which means "to become:"

저는 선생님이 되고 싶었어요 = I wanted to become/be a teacher

In Lesson 14, you learned about its function in passive sentences. For example:

세금은 값에 포함된다 = The tax is included in the price

Another usage of "되다" is to indicate that there is "no problem" with something. Common translations for this can be "for something to be going well" or "for something to be working (well)." You can typically place "되다" after a noun to indicate that there is no problem with that noun. The word "잘" is often included in these sentences as its nature to mean "well:" For example:

사업이 잘 되고 있어요? = Is your business going well?
일이 잘 돼요? = Is your work going well?
여기서 Wi-Fi가 잘 돼요 = The Wi-Fi here works well
심장수술이 잘 됐어요? = Did the heart surgery go well?
문제 해결이 잘 됐어요? = Did the problem get solved okay?

This same usage is often used to say that something has "finished" doing whatever it should be doing, for example

밥이 됐어요? = Is the rice ready?/Has the rice finished cooking?

You can also use 되다 to tell somebody to stop giving you something. For example, if somebody is filling up a glass of water for you, and you want to say "Okay! That's enough!" you can just say "됐어(요)!"

If you wanted to say the opposite – that is – that something is *not* going well, not working or is not finished, you should use the word 안 (even though the usual opposite of "잘" is "못"). "잘" can also be included in these sentences along with "안" (just like how "잘" can be used alongside "못"). For example:

밥이 아직은 안 됐어요 = The rice still isn't ready
여기서 Wi-Fi가 (잘) 안 돼요 = The Wi-Fi doesn't work (well) here
컴퓨터가 안 돼요 = The computer isn't working
로그인이 안 돼요 = The log-in isn't working (I can't log in)

Person 1: 축구 경기를 내일 보러 갈래요? = Shall we go to see a soccer game tomorrow?
Person 2: 저는 가고 싶지만 내일은 안 돼요 = I want to go, but I can't go tomorrow (tomorrow doesn't work for me)

Let's talk about this usage of 되다 and how it can be applied in sentences with ~아/어도.

To be allowed to do: ~아/어도 되다

In this lesson, you will build on your understanding of ~아/어도 to make sentences using 되다. Using these concepts, you will be able to indicate that here is no problem if something is or is not done. Let's get started.

In the previous lesson, you learned how to attach ~아/어도 to the stem of a clause to create the meaning of "regardless of…" For example:

네가 일찍 가도 … = Regardless of if you leave early…

되다 (in the usage described in this lesson) is commonly used after ~아/어도 to indicate that there is no problem with the action being done. For example:

네가 일찍 가도 돼 = Regardless of if you leave early, there is no problem

This typically translates to "one may" or "one is allowed to." For example:

네가 일찍 가도 돼 = "You may go early," or "You are allowed to go early"

Below are many examples:
아무거나 해도 돼요 = You can do whatever you want
지금 문을 열어도 돼요 = You may open the door now
제일 편리한 것을 선택해도 돼요 = You may choose the most convenient one
여기 있어도 돼요 = You are allowed to be here
당구를 여기서 쳐도 돼요 = You are allowed to play pool here
이 직장에서 수염을 길러도 돼요 = You are allowed to have a beard at this job
내일 시합에서 명예를 회복해도 돼요 = You can regain your honor during tomorrow's game
고기에 그 단단한 부분도 먹어도 돼요 = You can/may even eat that hard/stiff part of the meat
문제를 이해하지 못하면 감독관에게 물어봐도 돼요
= You may ask the supervisor/proctor if you don't understand the question

학생들이 들어가도 되지만 부모를 동반해야 돼요
= Students may enter, but they must be accompanied by a parent

These types of sentences can also be used to ask questions. Here, the speaker is asking if there is any "problem" with an action occurring. For example:

제가 일찍 가도 돼요? = Regardless of if I go early, is there any problem?

These types of questions typically translation to "May…?" or "Is it alright if…" For example:

제가 일찍 가도 돼요? = May I go early?

Below are many examples:
밥을 많이 먹어도 돼요? = May I eat a lot?
화장실에 가도 돼요? = May I go to the bathroom?
얼룩말에게 먹이를 줘도 돼요? = May I give feed to the zebras?
우리가 탁구를 해도 돼요? = May we play table tennis?
죄수를 보러 교도소에 들어가도 돼요? = May we go into the prison to see the prisoners?
옆에 있는 사람이 하는 말이 아주 불쾌해서 다른 자리로 가도 돼요?
= What the person beside me is saying is unpleasant, so may I go to another seat?

선생님! 이 문제를 파악할 수 없어요. 나중에 선생님의 교무실에 가도 돼요?
= Teacher! I can't grasp/understand this problem. May I go to your office later?

The final clause of all of these example sentences has been in the present tense. It is possible to conjugate 되다 to the past or future tenses to indicate that there would have been no problem if an action had been done, or will be done in the future. For example:

그때 나가도 되었어요 = It would have been okay if you left at that time
문을 열어도 되었어요 = It would have been okay if you opened the door
그때 나가도 될 거예요 = It will be okay if you leave at that time
문을 열어도 될 거예요 = It will be okay if you open the door

One doesn't have to: 안 ~아/어도 되다

In the previous section, you learned how to indicate that there will be "no problem" if some action was completed. In order to indicate that there will be "no problem" if some action *doesn't* occur, you can conjugate the verb before ~아/어도 negatively using 안 or ~지 않다. For example:

네가 빨리 안 가도 돼 = Regardless of if you don't leave quickly/early, there is no problem

This typically translates to "it is okay if one does not" or "one doesn't have to." For example:

네가 빨리 안 가도 돼 = You don't have to go quickly/early

Below are many examples:

내일까지 다 안 해도 돼요 = You don't need to do it all by tomorrow
저는 밥을 벌써 먹어서 다시 안 먹어도 돼요 = I don't need to eat because I already did
여기에 사인을 안 해도 돼요 = You don't need to sign here
이 음식에 소금을 안 넣어도 돼요 = You don't need to put salt on this food
그런 것을 걱정 안 해도 돼요 = You don't need to worry about that kind of thing

그 시험을 합격하기 위해 공부를 안 해도 돼요
= In order to pass that test, I don't need to study

이 학교가 과학 고등학교라서 인문학을 공부하지 않아도 돼요
= You don't need to study the humanities at this school because it is a science high school

그 나라에서 선생님이 되고 싶으면 특별한 자격이 있지 않아도 돼요
= If you want to become a teacher in that country, you don't need any special qualification

핸드폰에 연락처 기능이 있어서 요즘에 사람들은 기억력이 좋지 않아도 돼요
= Cell phones have contact functions in them so these days people don't need to have a good memory

You could also generally see this form as the opposite of ~아/어야 하다, which you learned in Lesson 46. Notice the opposite meanings that these sentences have:

그 시험을 합격하기 위해 공부를 안 해도 돼요 = In order to pass that test, I don't need to study
그 시험을 합격하기 위해 공부를 해야 돼요 = In order to pass that test, I need to study

This form can be used to ask questions as well. For example:

지금 밥을 안 먹어도 돼요? = You don't need to eat (rice) now?
내일까지 다 안 해도 돼요? = You don't need to do it all by tomorrow?
수염을 안 깎아도 돼요? = You don't need to shave your beard?
자격증을 안 보여줘도 돼요? = I don't need to show you my certification?

<u>Using Words like 좋다 and 괜찮다</u>

In all of the sentences in this lesson using ~아/어도 되다, the common meaning applied to all sentences is "it is okay if…" or "there is no problem if." Instead of using 되다, other words that have a similar meaning can be used as well. The two most common substitutes for 되다 in this usage are 좋다 and 괜찮다. For example:

지금 문을 열어도 돼요 = You may open the door now
지금 문을 열어도 좋아요 = You may open the door now
지금 문을 열어도 괜찮아요 = You may open the door now

밥을 많이 먹어도 돼요? = May I eat a lot?
밥을 많이 먹어도 좋아요? = May I eat a lot?
밥을 많이 먹어도 괜찮아요? = May I eat a lot?

Lesson 50: To have plans to, to be scheduled, to be ready to

Vocabulary

Nouns:
포도 = grape
껍질 = the peel/skin/bark of a fruit/vegetable
복숭아 = peach
참외 = oriental melon
수능 = the Korean SAT
참치 = tuna
통조림 = can
판사 = a judge
변호사 = a lawyer
권리 = a right
채식주의자 = vegetarian
증상 = symptom
섬 = island
규모 = scale, size
소규모 = small scale
대규모 = large scale
눈앞 = in-front of one's eyes

Verbs:
굽다 = to roast, grill
굽히다 = to bend one's body
구부리다 = to bend an object
방어하다 = to defend
그만두다 = to quit a job or task
벗기다 = to undress somebody, to peel a fruit/vegetable
굽다 = to be curved/bent

Adjectives:
불쌍하다 = to be pitiful

Introduction

In the first few lessons of Unit 2, you learned how you can use ~는 것 to describe a noun with a verb. Though we haven't specifically talked about ~는 것 in the past few lessons, there are still a few more related concepts that you should know. In this lesson, you will learn three nouns (예정, 계획 and 준비) that are often described by a preceding verb/clause. Let's get started.

To be scheduled to… :~ㄹ/을 예정

You should remember the function of adding ~는 것 to verb stems from previous lessons. If you forget the purpose of ~는 것, I highly suggest that you review Lesson 26 and the lessons that follow. To review briefly, adding ~는 것 to a verb stem turns the verb into a word that can describe an upcoming noun.

This can be done using ~ㄴ/은 것 to describe the noun in the past tense:
제가 먹은 것 = The thing I ate

Or using ~는 것 to describe the noun in the present tense:
제가 먹는 것 = The thing I eat

Or using ~ㄹ/을 것 to describe the noun in the future tense:
제가 먹을 것 = The thing I will eat

Other nouns can be used instead of "것" in these types of sentences. For example:
제가 먹는 음식 = The food I eat

A common noun that is often described by the ~는 것 principle is "예정" (meaning "schedule"). For example:

제가 할 예정
제가 먹을 예정
Notice that 예정 is being described using the future tense ~ㄹ/을

You should know that "제가 할 예정" and "제가 먹을 예정" are not complete sentences, as they do not have a predicating verb or adjective at the end of the sentence. In order to do this, we should add 이다 to 예정. For example:

제가 할 예정이에요
제가 먹을 예정이에요

By doing this, you create the meaning of "One is scheduled to…" The sentences above would translate to:

제가 할 예정이에요 = I am scheduled to do it
제가 먹을 예정이에요 = I am scheduled to eat

The two sentences above were used to present the grammar structure of these types of sentences. However, they are a little unnatural simply because there isn't really any context or other information that indicates what is "scheduled." The examples below are more natural sounding sentences using this grammatical structure:

우리는 10시에 만날 예정이에요 = We are scheduled to meet at 10:00
수업이 4시쯤에 시작될 예정이에요 = The class is scheduled to start at about 4:00pm
학생들이 수능을 다음 달에 볼 예정이에요 = The students are scheduled to write 수능 next month

비행기가 9시에 출발할 예정이지만 눈이 많이 와서 못 출발할 것 같아요
= The plane is scheduled to depart at 9:00, but it probably won't because it is snowing a lot

그 권리에 대해 얘기하려고 변호사가 판사를 내일 만날 예정이에요
= The lawyer is scheduled to meet the judge tomorrow to talk about that right

To have plans to…: ~ㄹ/을 계획

By using a similar composition that was described in the previous section (~ㄹ/을 예정이다), you can create the meaning of "I have plans to…" or "I am planning to…" By replacing "것" with "계획" in the future tense conjugation of ~는 것, you can create the following meanings::

먹을 계획 = plans to eat
공부할 계획 = plans to study
갈 계획 = plans to go

In English as well as in Korean, we say "I *have* plans to…" Therefore, in order to finish these sentences, we should add "있다" to them. For example:

먹을 계획이 있다 = to have plans to eat
공부할 계획이 있다 = to have plans to study
갈 계획이 있다 = to have plans to go

This form can then be used in more complex sentences:

참치를 잡으러 그 섬에 갈 계획이 있어요 = I have plans to go to that island to catch tuna

제품을 대규모로 안 팔아서 이 일을 그만둘 계획이 있어요
= They don't sell their products on a large scale, so I am planning to quit this job

우리 사업규모를 내년에 늘릴 계획이 있어요
= We have plans to increase the scale of our business next year

공원에 가서 삼겹살을 다 같이 구울 계획이 있어요
= We are planning to all go to the park and grilling 삼겹살 together

제가 친구를 만날 계획이 있었지만 친구는 안 왔어요
= I had plans to meet my friend, but he didn't come

원래 대학교에 갈 계획이 있었지만 수능을 잘 못 봐서 대학교에 갈 수 없었어요
= I had plans to go to university, but I couldn't get in because I did poorly on the SAT test

To be ready… ㄹ/을 준비

Another noun that is commonly placed after the future ~는 것 conjugation is "준비" (preparation, readiness, or the noun form of "to prepare"). The most common ways you will see 준비 used like this are described below.

To be ready to…: ~ㄹ/을 준비(가) 됐다

In the previous lesson, you learned that one meaning of the word "되다" is to indicate that something is "going well" or "working well." For example:

일이 잘 돼요? = Is your work going well?
여기서 Wi-Fi 가 잘 돼요 = The Wi-Fi here works well

By describing "준비" with a preceding clause, you can refer to the *preparation* of that clause. For example:

갈 준비 = the preparation of going
먹을 준비 = the preparation of eating
공부할 준비 = the preparation of studying

By using the word "되다" in these sentences, one can indicate whether this preparation is "going well" or not. For example:

갈 준비가 됐다 = the preparation of going went well
먹을 준비가 됐다 = the preparation of eating went well
공부할 준비가 됐다 = the preparation of studying went well

I like the English translations above because they show how ~ㄹ/을 준비가 되다 takes on this particular meaning. However, the most common translation for these types of sentences is "one is ready to." For example:

갈 준비가 됐다 = to be ready to go
먹을 준비가 됐다 = to be ready to eat
공부할 준비가 됐다 = to be ready to study

Notice that 되다 is conjugated to the past tense to indicate that the "preparation went well" which would also indicate that one "is ready."

In theory you could see 준비가 되다 presented as the passive verb 준비되다, which would mean "to be prepared." The sentences above could be written/spoken as:

갈 준비됐다 = to be ready to go
먹을 준비됐다 = to be ready to eat
공부할 준비됐다 = to be ready to study

I tend to think that this use of "~ㄹ/을 준비되다" is incorrect because ~ㄹ/을 is not describing a noun and instead describing a verb which in theory it cannot do. However, in speech (especially because the use of ~가 on 준비 can be omitted) these two different forms cannot be distinguished from another. Therefore, it is common to also see this form.

We can see this construction used in more complicated sentences. For example:

저는 지금 갈 준비가 됐어요 = I am ready to go now
저는 아무 때나 일을 시작할 준비가 됐어요 = I am ready to start working any time
그 병의 증상을 설명할 준비가 되었어요 = I am ready to explain the symptoms of that disease
우리는 소규모 장소에서 시작할 준비가 됐어요 = We are ready to start in a small (scale) location

You can indicate that one is *not* ready by adding a negative conjugation. For example:

저는 아직 결혼할 준비가 되지 않았어요
= I'm still not ready to get married

저는 5분 후에 갈 예정이었지만 아직 갈 준비가 안 됐다
= I was scheduled to go in 5 minutes, but I'm not ready yet

우리는 아직 대규모 공장에서 할 준비가 안 되었어요
= We aren't ready to do it in a large (scale) factory yet

구부러져 있는 길에서 아직 운전할 준비가 안 됐어요
= I'm not ready to drive on a curved street yet

그런 불쌍한 애기들을 눈앞에서 아직 볼 준비가 안 됐어요
= I'm not ready to see those pitiful/sad babies in-front of my eyes yet

These types of sentences are commonly used in the form of a question to ask if somebody is (or is not) ready. For example:

파티에 갈 준비가 됐어요? = Are you ready to go to the party?
비행기가 아직 출발할 준비가 안 됐습니까? = Is the plane not yet ready to go?
참외껍질을 벗길 준비가 됐어요? = Are you ready to cut the skin off of the melon?
우리 나라를 방어할 준비가 됐습니까? = Are you ready to defend our country?
1년 동안 채식주의자가 될 준비가 되었어요? = Are you ready to be a vegetarian for a year?
몸을 뒤로 굽히고 스트레칭을 할 준비가 되었어요? = Are you ready to bend (your body) over and stretch?

<u>Using the imperative voice to tell somebody to get ready: ~ㄹ/을 준비(를) 하세요</u>
In Lesson 40 you learned how to make commands using the imperative voice. For example:

빨리 올라와 = Come up quick
빨리 올라와요 = Come up quick
빨리 올라오셔요 = Come up quick

You can attach any of these imperative endings to 준비하다 to make a command telling somebody to "get ready." For example:

밥을 준비하세요! = Get the food ready/prepare the food!
모든 것을 준비하세요! = Get everything ready/prepare everything

In order to tell somebody to get ready *to do something*, you should use the ~는 것 principle. To do this, you can describe the noun "준비" with a preceding clause connected to the future ~ㄹ/을 addition. For example:

갈 준비 = the preparation of "going"
먹을 준비 = the preparation of "eating"
공부할 준비 = the preparation of "studying"

After this, the object particle ~를 can be attached to 준비 and 하다 can be used with an imperative conjugation to tell somebody to "do that" preparation. The common translation of this in English is "get ready to…." For example:

갈 준비를 하세요 = Get ready to go!
먹을 준비를 하세요 = Get ready to eat!
공부할 준비를 하세요 = Get ready to study

Just like with the sentences earlier with 준비가 되다, you can also see the sentences above presented as

갈 준비하세요 = Get ready to go!
먹을 준비하세요 = Get ready to eat!
공부할 준비하세요 = Get ready to study

I tend to think that this use of "~ㄹ/을 준비하다" is incorrect because ~ㄹ/을 is not describing a noun and instead describing a verb which in theory it cannot do. However, in speech (especially because the use of ~를 on 준비 can be omitted) these two different forms cannot be distinguished from another. Therefore, it is common to also see this form.

Below are more examples:

몸을 굽힐 준비를 하세요 = Get ready to bend your body
수능을 볼 준비를 하세요 = Get ready to write the 수능 test
일을 곧 그만둘 준비를 하세요 = Get ready to quit your job soon
증상이 계속 나타나면 병원에 올 준비를 하세요 = Get ready to come to the hospital if symptoms persist

---

I have had a few readers contact me to ask why the particle ~를 is used in the sentences above but ~가 is used in the sentences introduced earlier in the lessons (for example, in "저는 지금 갈 준비가 됐어요"). I feel like this is almost too obvious to talk about, but more than one person has asked me, so I want to provide an answer in case other learners have the same problem.

The use of ~를 or ~가 in these cases is due to the nature of the verb that predicates the sentence. In the sentences above, ~를 is used because 하다 is an active verb and can act on objects with ~를/을. However, 되다 is a passive verb and cannot act on objects – and thus a sentence predicated by 되다 cannot have an object with ~를/을 attached. It is the same reason why the following sentences use ~를/을 and ~이/가 respectively:

밥을 준비했어요 = I prepared rice
밥이 준비되었어요 = The rice was prepared

If you are unsure about passive verbs, I suggest that you read Lesson 14.

Lessons 42 – 50 Mini-Test

All finished Lessons 42 – 50? Now it is time to test yourself on what you learned in those lessons! Before moving on to our next set of lessons, try to make sure you can understand all the concepts covered here. Good luck! The answers are at the bottom of the test!

1) Place the correct ending in the blank below:

제가 한국에서 있____ 오랫 동안 만나지 못한 친구를 만났어요

a) 었을 때
b) 을 때
c) 었다면
d) 다면

2) Choose the sentence that has the same meaning as the one below:

제가 그 여자를 만나면 그녀에게 키스를 할 거예요
a) 제가 그 여자를 만나기 때문에 그녀에게 키스를 할 거예요
b) 제가 그 여자를 만나서 그녀에게 키스를 할 거예요
c) 제가 그여자를 만날 때 그녀에게 키스를 할 거예요
d) 제가 그여자를 만나도 그녀에게 키스를 할 거예요

3) Choose the most natural ending to the following sentence:

제가 밥을 먹었더라면…

a) 배고팠기 때문이에요
b) 배고프지 않았을 거예요
c) 배고플 거예요
d) 배고파야 해요

4) Which one best translates to "I cannot read Korean/한글"

a) 저는 한글을 읽어야 해요
b) 저는 한글을 읽을 필요가 없어요
c) 저는 한글을 안 읽어도 돼요
d) 저는 한글을 읽을 수 없어요

255

5) Choose the most natural beginning to this sentence:

…. 아직 집에 안 갈 거예요

a) 제가 공부를 한다면
b) 제가 공부해야 되어서
c) 제가 공부할 때
d) 제가 공부하고

6) Which one would you most likely say to your boss?

a) 밥을 같이 먹을래?
b) 밥을 먹어도 됩니까?
c) 밥을 먹자!
d) 밥을 먹고 싶어?

7) Choose the correct sentence:

a) 만약 그 여자가 예뻐도 저는 안 좋아해요
b) 혹시 그 여자가 예뻐도 저는 안 좋아해요
c) 아무리 그 여자가 예뻐도 저는 안 좋아해요
d) all are incorrect

Answers:
1) a
2) c
3) b
4) d
5) b
6) b
7) c

Unit 2 Test

There are three sections to this test.

1. Comprehension
2. Grammar
3. Listening

Comprehension

1 – 2) Read the Korean sentence and answer the question after it:

1) 제가 한국어를 잘 말할 수 없어서 저의 여자 친구의 아버지랑 어머니를 만나는 것은 조금 불편해요

Why wouldn't you want to go to your girlfriend's house?

a) because you can speak Korean, and it is awkward
b) because you can't speak Korean, and it is uncomfortable
c) because you have never met them before
d) because your girlfriend's parents never invited you

2) 제가 김치를 먹을 때마다 갑자기 아파요

When do/did you get sick?

a) Every time you eat kimchi
b) When you ate kimchi yesterday
c) When you eat kimchi in the morning
d) When you eat kimchi before you sleep

3 – 4) Read the following and answer the next two questions:

제가 내일 고향에 가야 되어서 혹시 이 컴퓨터를 지금 고치실 수 있습니까?

3) Which of the following most accurately describes why you want your computer fixed now:

   a) Because you need to work tomorrow
   b) Because you are going to pick up your cat tomorrow
   c) Because you have to go to your hometown tomorrow
   d) Because you don't have time tomorrow

4) You are you most likely speaking to?

a) your son
b) your student
c) a clerk working at a store
d) your cat

5) Choose the incorrect sentence:

a) 저는 갈 준비를 아직 안 했어요
b) 저의 여자 친구는 내일 자기 가족을 만날 계획이 있어요
c) 저는 사람이 별로 없는 시장이 제일 좋아요
d) 저는 어제 비행기 탈 예정이에요

6) Choose the incorrect sentence:

a) 제가 만나 본 사람들 중에 그 분은 가장 똑똑한 사람이에요
b) 저는 내일 숙제를 한 중이에요
c) 제가 밥을 먹는 중이라서 얘기하기 싫어요
d) 그 사람들 세 명 중에 한 명은 서울 대학교에 갈 거예요

7) 저 사람은 남자 같이 보이지만 여자예요

What does that person look like?

a) a man
b) a woman
c) a doctor
d) a monkey

8) 바나나를 많이 가져와 주셔서 감사합니다

What are you thanking somebody for?

a) buying bananas
b) selling bananas
c) bringing bananas
d) eating bananas

9 – 10) Read the Korean sentence and answer the following two questions:
제가 대학교를 안 다녀서 일자리를 잡기 힘들지만 일을 구하려고 계속 노력하고 있어요

9) What is hard for you to do?

a) meeting people
b) keeping a job
c) finding a job
d) trying to catch

10) What would have made your current situation easier?

a) applying to more positions
b) attending university
c) listening to your boss
d) studying harder

Grammar

11) Which of the following is incorrect:

a) 제가 한국에 산 지 2 년 됐어요
b) 그녀가 언제 올 것을 몰라요
c) 아빠가 어디 가신지 몰라요
d) 거기에 사람이 많을지도 모르겠어요

12) Choose the incorrect usage of honorifics:

a) 나는 부장님께 선물을 드렸어
b) 나는 할아버지를 위해 선물을 샀어
c) 저는 부장님을 위해 선물을 샀어요
d) 저는 저의 할아버지께 선물을 주셨어요

13 – 14) Which particle can replace the underlined portion in the sentence?

13) 저는 한국말을 배우기 위해 한국으로 갔어요

a) 러
b) 고
c) 기 때문에
d) 지만

14) 그녀에게 인사를 했다면 좋았을 거예요

a) 하면
b) 했기 때문에
c) 했더라면
d) 하려고

15 – 16) Fill in the blank of the following sentence with the correct form:

15) 수영을 잘 못 하____ 해변에 가고 싶어요

a) 기 때문에
b) ㄹ래 (할래)
c) ㄹ 때 (할 때)
d) 지만

16) 제가 매일 하____ 똑같은 일은 너무 지루해요

a) 던
b) 는
c) ㄴ (한)
d) ㄹ (할)

17) Choose the incorrect sentence:

a) 저는 가장 여행하고 싶은 곳은 캐나다예요
b) 저는 돈이 있는 여자만 좋아해요
c) 밥이 있는지 없는지 몰라요
d) 영화를 혼자 가김 실어요

18) Choose the correct order of words that can be placed in the blanks:

- 제가 한국말을 배웠기 ___ 한국에 가는 것은 편해요
- 제가 한국에 산 ___ 얼마 안 됐어요
- 제가 한국에 간 ___ 이 없어서 한국에 대해 잘 몰라요

a) 적, 지, 것
b) 사이, 지, 적
c) 때문에, 지, 것
d) 때문에, 지, 적

19) Choose the opposite of the following sentence:

저는 그것이 잘 안 보여요

a) 저는 그것을 볼 것 같아요
b) 저는 그것을 못 봤을 때이에요
c) 저는 그것을 잘 볼 수 있어요
d) 저는 그것을 해야 돼요

20) Which of the following is unnatural:

a) 그 여자를 만났더라면 재미있었을 거예요
b) 아무리 밥을 먹어도 살이 안 쪄요
c) 혹시 안 바쁘면 저를 도와 주세요
d) 만약 병원에 가야 돼었어요

Reading

21) Read the following:

제가 시험을 아직 안 봐서 그 대학교에 갈 수 없어요

Why can't the girl attend university?

a) she hasn't written the exam
b) she did poorly on the exam
c) she isn't smart enough
d) she still doesn't have enough money

22) Read the following:

남: 한국어를 왜 배우고 있어요?
여: 언젠가 한국으로 이사하고 싶어서 우선 한국말을 배워야 돼요

What does the girl hope to do one day?

a) study Korean
b) move to Korea
c) teach Korean
d) move back home from Korea

23) Read the following:

남: 친구는 언제 와요?
여: 언제 올지 모르겠지만 곧 올 것 같아요

When will the friend come?

a) Soon
b) You don't know
c) You don't know, but probably soon
d) he is here now

24) Read the following:

남: 한국에 간 적이 있어요?
여: 한국에 간 적이 없지만 다음 달에 갈 계획이 있어요

Has the girl ever been to Korea before?

a) no, and she doesn't want to go
b) no, but she has plans of going next month
c) yes, she has
d) yes, and she has plans of going next month

25) Read the following:

남: 지금 갈래요?
여: 아니요. 저는 아직 일을 많이 해야 되어서 지금 갈 수 없어요. 먼저 가고 제가 10 분 후에

When will the girl be leaving?

a) immediately
b) right after the man leaves
c) ten minutes from now
d) she has no plans of leaving

Answers

1) b
2) a
3) c
4) c
5) d
6) b
7) a
8) c
9) c
10) b
11) b
12) d
13) a
14) c
15) d
16) b
17) d
18) d
19) c
20) d
21) a
22) b
23) c
24) b
25) c

ABOUT THE AUTHOR

I started learning Korean sometime in 2008, and moved to Korea in 2010 to get more exposure to the language. I never took any formal classes, and taught Korean to myself from piecing it together from whatever information I could find. I would take this information and ask Korean people for more detailed explanations and their opinion, feedback and feelings about anything I learned. Although frustrating and time consuming at the time, in the end this process gave me a very deep understanding of vocabulary, grammatical principles and how they all come together to make Korean sound natural.

I'm very meticulous with everything, and learning Korean was no exception. For more than two years, I kept log-books of every word and grammatical principle that I learned in Korean. At the time, I didn't do this for any purpose other than to organize my learning. After two years, I realized that I unintentionally had written a step-by-step organization of concepts that any English speaker would need in order to begin learning Korean.

These notes ended up being the foundation of this book. However, having gone through the whole process of teaching Korean to myself, I realized I could present these concepts even better than I had originally taught them to myself in the first place. I knew what was difficult; I knew what was easy; I knew what was confusing; I knew what was important; I knew what was not important; and I knew the order in which grammatical concepts should be learned. Each lesson that you see is something that I taught to myself many years ago, but with the benefit of me already having gone through the process before.

Now, here in 2023, I have had many years to reflect on what I learned back when I first started learning Korean. My lessons are a reflection of each concept I learned and explained step-by-step in a way that I would have wanted them to be explained to me as a Korean learner.

I have huge plans to continue to develop the HowtoStudyKorean resource in the future. I am always coming up with new ideas and new things I can add to this website to enhance the learning experience even more.

Printed in Great Britain
by Amazon